The Voyages of the
DISCOVERY

The Voyages of the
DISCOVERY

The Illustrated History of Scott's Ship

Ann Savours

Seaforth
PUBLISHING

Copyright © Ann Savours 2001

This edition first published in Great Britain in 2013 by
Seaforth Publishing,
Pen & Sword Books Ltd,
47 Church Street,
Barnsley S70 2AS

www.seaforthpublishing.com

British Library Cataloguing in Publication Data
A catalogue record for this book is available from the British Library

ISBN 978 1 84832 702 3

Abridged from *The Voyages of the Discovery* (1992) by Margaret Slythe
Maps by Vera Brice
Typeset and designed by Roger Daniels

Printed and bound in China by 1010 Printing International Ltd

FRONTISPIECE:
Under sail in the South Atlantic 1925-27.
(AUTHOR'S COLLECTION)

CONTENTS

PREFACE

IT IS A GREAT PLEASURE to welcome this slimmer, well illustrated edition of the book first published in 1992. Re-reading its pages, I am struck by the aptness of the Duke of Edinburgh's Foreword to the first edition which begins:

'To seafarers, every ship has a personality of its own. Some live out their lives in modest obscurity, others achieve varying degrees of fame and notoriety. Several ships have borne the name *Discovery*... but it is the *Discovery* built in Dundee and launched in 1901, that is probably the best known of all of them.'

She was constructed for the National Antarctic Expedition of 1901-04 and owned during those years by the Royal Geographical Society, whose President, Sir Clements Markham, was her 'managing owner'. It was Captain Robert Falcon Scott who led this very successful exploring and scientific expedition. She spent the next eighteen years as a small cargo ship in the ownership of the Hudson's Bay Company, acting as a supply vessel for their trading posts in northern Canada, carrying munitions from Brest to Archangel during the First World War, coasting the French Atlantic ports and transporting boots, clothes and linen goods to the Russian Black Sea ports during that country's civil war. *Discovery* was refitted as a Royal Research Ship in the 1920s for the expedition of 1925-27 to the South Atlantic which studied the environment and the biology of the great whales. During her third voyage south she explored and charted a great arc of the Antarctic coast with the British Australian and New Zealand Antarctic Research Expedition (BANZARE) of 1929-31, led by the great Australian explorer, Sir Douglas Mawson. Through the generosity of Lady Houston, *Discovery* was afterwards saved from the breaker's yard and used by the Sea Scouts and later the RNVR on the Thames Embankment. As he tells us in his Preface to the first edition, it was during these years that the late Sir Peter Scott's children were christened in her bell. She was owned and partly restored by the Maritime Trust from 1979 to 1986.

Discovery was afloat throughout momentous years of the twentieth century. She played her part in the heroic years of Antarctic exploration and was witness to the two World Wars, narrowly avoiding destruction during the London Blitz. The scientific research which was undertaken in her laboratories and on her decks in the South Atlantic and Southern Oceans during the scientific expeditions of 1925-27 and 1929-31 laid the basis for our understanding of the food chain there and for the conservation of the great whales.

As he lay dying in the tent on the Great Ice Barrier of the Antarctic, Captain Scott wrote of his little son, 'Make the boy interested in natural history – it is better than games.' That little son, the late Sir Peter Scott, played a great part in the conservation movement which has become such a force in the world. Perhaps it was the example of Dr Edward Wilson, a dedicated naturalist, who first went south in *Discovery*, and who died on the return from the South Pole in 1912, which influenced Scott's words. It is that great seabird, the albatross, which needs our help now. Long may the old barque, now in her second century, continue as a symbol of enterprise for the city of Dundee and as an inspiration to her visitors.

I am as grateful as ever to all those acknowledged in the earlier editions of the book. With respect to this one, I thank Margaret Slythe for her skilful abridgement and Julian Mannering, Chatham Publishing's Editorial Director, for his cheerful encouragement.

ANN SAVOURS, Little Bridge Place
March 2001

CHAPTER 1

SOUTH POLAR EXPLORATION

A T THE END OF THE nineteenth century the wilderness which is Antarctica, ice-bound at the bottom of the world, was almost as much *terra incognita* as in Captain Cook's day, over a century earlier. Passing ships had had tantalising glimpses of its coast, and soundings had indicated a continental shelf, but its form and nature remained one of the last great mysteries at the end of a century that had opened up so many once-dark corners of the Earth.

In November 1893 Dr John Murray addressed the Fellows of the Royal Geographical Society (RGS).

'What,' he asked, 'is the nature of the snow and ice-covered land observed at so many points towards the South Pole? Is there a sixth continent within the Antarctic Circle or merely a range of lofty volcanic hills?' Murray had taken part in the *Challenger* deep-sea expedition of 1872-76 and was aware that geographers and sci-

Sir Clements Markham, 1830-1916, who initiated the National Antarctic Expedition, 1901-1904.
(AUTHOR'S COLLECTION)

entists throughout the world sought to determine the scientific problems of the Ice Age, the form and make-up of the Earth and the circulation of the oceans. The investigation of the Antarctic Continent and the acquisition of new knowledge of both land and sea were presented as patriotic challenges.

Murray envisaged the exploration being undertaken by two small ships of the Royal Navy (RN), landing two wintering parties, one near Mount Erebus, the active volcano sighted in the 1840s from the Ross Sea, and the other in Graham Land, discovered by John Biscoe in the 1830s. The ships would

return northwards to the open sea to avoid being frozen in the ice, making observations along the edge of the pack ice during two winter seasons. He called for a 'good workable scheme'. Many eminent Fellows spoke in support of Murray's proposals and the President, Sir Clements Markham, announced the appointment of a committee to renew the discovery of the Antarctic. There was much talk of the spirit of maritime enterprise and the nation's glorious naval traditions.

Almost two years later, in the summer of 1895, Markham chaired the Sixth International Geographical Congress in London, when Dr Georg von Neumayer, director of the Marine Observatory in Hamburg, forcefully advocated the renewal of south polar exploration.

Markham appointed him chairman of a committee which passed a resolution declaring that 'the exploration of the Antarctic regions was the greatest piece of geographical knowledge still to be undertaken' and urged that it should be attempted before the end of the century. Neumayer came to London again in 1898, to hear Dr John Murray speak of the scientific advantages of an Antarctic expedition. It was fifty-five years since Sir James Clark Ross had carried out his great work in the Antarctic, and the assembled scientists showed restless impatience to send an expedition to work in their particular fields.

Markham anticipated that the proposed Antarctic expedition would be an official one, financed by the Government. But his approach in 1895 to the

First Lord of the Admiralty, George Goschen, received a firm refusal to commit the Admiralty to the fitting out of an expedition, however influential the representations. The Admiralty was preoccupied with the growth of the fleet and the changing technology in the last years of the nineteenth century. Other nations would now do the exploring work, once specially our own, Sir Clements replied in disappointment.

The Council of the RGS eventually agreed that the expedition should be a private one, and in 1897 it resolved to subscribe and raise funds. Soon afterwards it was joined by the Royal Society and a joint expedition was organised. In March 1899, when Markham had raised only £14,000, including one donation of £5,000 from Mr Harmsworth, the newspaper magnate, a Mr Llewellyn Longstaff of Wimbledon enquired whether £25,000 would enable the expedition to start. Not only did this enable the societies to equip an efficient expedition with one vessel, but it also financed co-operation in scientific exploration with the Germans while in the Antarctic. Longstaff's contribution changed the attitude of the Government, which offered £45,000 if this sum could be matched. The final £3,000 required

Sir James Clark Ross, c1834. Painted after Ross' attainment of the North Magnetic Pole. The most experienced of all the Arctic officers of the Royal Navy, he commanded the Antarctic expedition of 1839-43 in the *Erebus* and *Terror*, discovering the Ross Sea, the "Great Ice Barrier" and Ross Island. Oil painting by John Wildman,
(NATIONAL MARITIME MUSEUM)

was subscribed by the RGS. The National Antarctic Expedition was duly established, financed from both private and public sources, in 1900. Between 1901 and 1903 not only England and Germany, but also Scotland, Sweden and France joined the great international campaign of geographical and scientific discovery in the Antarctic.

Markham had to convert or build a ship, appoint a leader and staff, and decide on a geographical and scientific programme for the expedition. Committee meetings between the partner societies were noisy and troublesome. The main bone of contention was the respective responsibilities of the leader and the scientific director. Markham had managed to persuade the First Lord of the Admiralty to allow a naval officer to captain the ship, with another as his assistant, plus two or three officers from the Royal Naval Reserve. The Admirals and Markham maintained that the naval commander should be in overall charge of the expedition. Professor J W Gregory, an eminent geologist who had done fieldwork in many parts of the world, had been appointed Scientific Director. After many stormy sessions over his role and the scientific work of the expedition, Gregory resigned. So too did Sir John Murray,

Mt Erebus

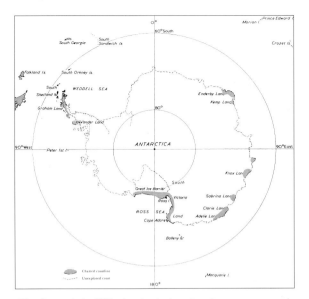

The Antarctic in 1901, showing its largely unknown nature and using contemporary place-names. From Edward Wilson's *Diary of the Discovery Expedition to the Antarctic Regions, 1901-1904.*

who had differences with Markham over the purpose of the expedition. Murray insisted on the scientific work being directed solely by an eminent scientist. Markham could not agree. Markham also maintained that as soon as one ship was prepared it should leave; he was sure the Government would provide a second ship to act as tender to the first. Murray, the greatest British physical geographer, withdrew.

Markham had picked out Robert Falcon Scott as a future leader when the latter was 18, and had won a boat race in the West Indies in 1887. Twelve years later, of the ten men under consideration he still favoured Scott. Markham described his ideal commander as: 'a naval officer in the regular line and not in the surveying branch; young and a good sailor with experience of ships under sail; a navigator with a knowledge of surveying, and with a scientific turn of mind. He must have imagination and enthusiasm, a cool temperament, be calm, yet quick and decisive in action; a man of resource, tact and sympathy.'

The news of the appointment of Scott as leader of the National Antarctic Expedition, and of Royds as his chief assistant, was confirmed on 25 May 1900.

Lieutenant Scott was at the time serving under Captain Egerton, who had Arctic experience and a wide knowledge of the rising generation of naval officers in active service. Egerton considered Scott the ideal choice, describing him as steady, strong, keen and genial, with considerable experience in square-rigged ships. Scott, then aged 30, had expertise in electricity and scientific matters and was expected to gain promotion shortly. If he were given the command of the expedition he would have almost a year to acquaint himself thoroughly with Antarctic questions and superintend all the work. Royds was described as a splendid young fellow. Aged 23, he had spent the past year in charge of a vessel at the mouth of the Thames, within a flotilla in the Channel.

Markham reported Egerton's endorsement of Scott and Royds to the societies' joint committee. The glowing testimonial and the formal certificate of Scott's qualifications are in the archives of the RGS. An equally enthusiastic testimonial was sent to Sir Leopold McClintock, one of the old Arctic officers closely involved with the expedition and the appointment of its leader. 'I feel sure there is nothing in the way of Magnetic or Astronomical observations that Scott would not readily pick up,' wrote Egerton.

In June 1900 Scott was appointed leader of the National Antarctic Expedition, and later that same month he was promoted to the rank of Commander, RN, soon relinquishing his duties as First Lieutenant of the *Majestic*. He could then give his whole attention to the affairs of the expedition.

Mount Erebus and Mount Terror, Ross Island, by Dr E A Wilson, from *Album of Panoramas and sketches*, published in the scientific results on the return of the National Antarctic Expedition 1901-1904.

THE BUILDING
OF THE DISCOVERY

IN THE EARLY DAYS of planning the expedition, probably in 1898, Markham visited Norway to inspect a number of steam vessels built for ice navigation, in the company of Dr Fridtjof Nansen, the great Norwegian explorer who had recently returned from his voyage in the *Fram*. Both agreed that none of them was suitable. Markham also considered buying a Scots wooden whaler, but this was also rejected for the same reason; the building materials would make magnetic observations almost valueless and thus nullify a very important part of the scientific programme. Markham also enquired of the Admiralty about the condition and availability of the former steam whaler *Bloodhound*, which, as HMS *Discovery*, had wintered in the far north with the Nares expedition of 1875-76. The report from the Admiralty left him in no doubt that she was not fit for such rough service as an Antarctic expedition. The Admiralty's advice was to build a new vessel on similar lines. The original drawings of the old *Discovery*

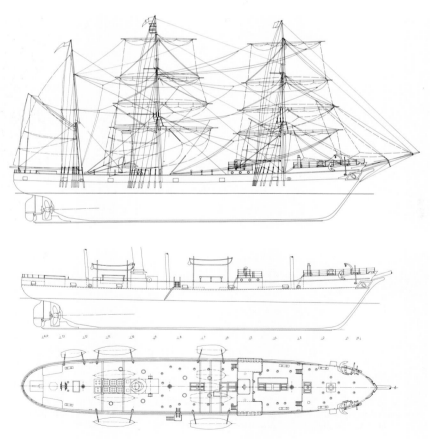

Advertisment for the Dundee Shipbuilders' Company from the *Discovery* exhibition catalogue, Bond Street, 1904. By the turn of the century there were few yards with the skilled men left to build wooden ships on this scale.

LEFT ABOVE: Sail plan of the *Discovery* as built in 1901.

LEFT: Profile and deck plan of the *Discovery*.
(COURTESY NEXUS MEDIA)

were offered for use in the designing of the new.

Longstaff's significant donation had made this possible, but wooden shipbuilding was almost dead and properly seasoned timber of the appropriate curved form would need to be collected from many sources. The Admiralty suggested W E Smith, its own Chief Constructor, who had been brought up as a builder of wooden ships, as technical adviser. Markham had proposed that Colin Archer, builder of Nansen's *Fram* in Norway, who had expertise in designing ships for use in ice, be invited to build the new vessel. The Admiralty response was swift and predictable: 'it would be a matter of great regret that a ship to carry a British Antarctic Expedition should be built outside these Islands. We have only a few wood-ship builders left, but they are quite capable of doing all you want.'

Markham heeded this patriotic advice and the new *Discovery* was constructed in the British Isles. One of the last three-masted wooden ships and the first since Halley's *Paramore* in 1694 to be built solely for scientific research, she was designed by W E Smith. Engineer Commander P Marrack, RN, prepared the plans for the engines, boilers and stern gear.

The new vessel was to be called *Discovery*, the latest in the long line of exploring vessels of that name commanded in the seventeenth and eighteenth centuries by captains such as William Baffin, James Cook and George Vancouver. Admiral Sir Leopold McClintock chaired the Ship Committee. Besides his Arctic experience during the search for Sir John Franklin in the 1850s, when he became noted for his sledge travelling, he was Admiral-Superintendent of Portsmouth Dockyard at the time of the Nares expedition into the Arctic Regions in 1875-76 in the old *Discovery*.

Initially, the lines of the old *Discovery* were to be

Discovery on the stocks. The massive frames, 11in thick, and the first of three tiers of huge beams are clearly visible. These oversize scantlings were intended to resist the enormous strains that would be encountered in the ice. They have also contributed to her survival for 100 years.

copied. Her dimensions, lines and sail area were considered the ultimate development of the nineteenth-century Dundee steam-whalers, with an overhanging stem which enabled her to force a passage more easily through the pack-ice. Special features including strengthening and accommodation were to be improved upon as practicable. On account of the great success of the *Fram*, consideration was given to a midship 'peg-top'-shaped section, as in that vessel, to promote lifting out of danger. A decision was taken finally to have an ordinary ship-shaped section which should allow better behaviour in many thousands of miles of tempestuous seas and trying conditions.

A laboratory and accommodation for forty-three were to be provided, together with stowage for two years' provisions. The new vessel was to be lengthened by 10ft, to allow the commanding officer to be less isolated than in the old *Discovery*. One of the advantages was that the power could be increased to 450ihp. Double topsails, as in modern merchant practice, were required, to facilitate efficient working of the sails by a small complement. A two-bladed lifting screw was to be fitted, which could be readily shipped and unshipped; similarly the rudder was to be easy to install and replace. A thoughtful feature of the design was the provision of two water-ballast tanks, holding 60 tons of water, in the port and starboard bunkers. These tanks strengthened the vessel and could carry coal on the outward voyage. Seven watertight transverse bulkheads and the centreline bulkhead so subdivided the hull as to make

The *Discovery*'s triple expansion engine.
(AUTHOR'S COLLECTION)

The Launch of the *Discovery* in Dundee, on 21 March 1901.
(DUNDEE CENTRAL LIBRARY)

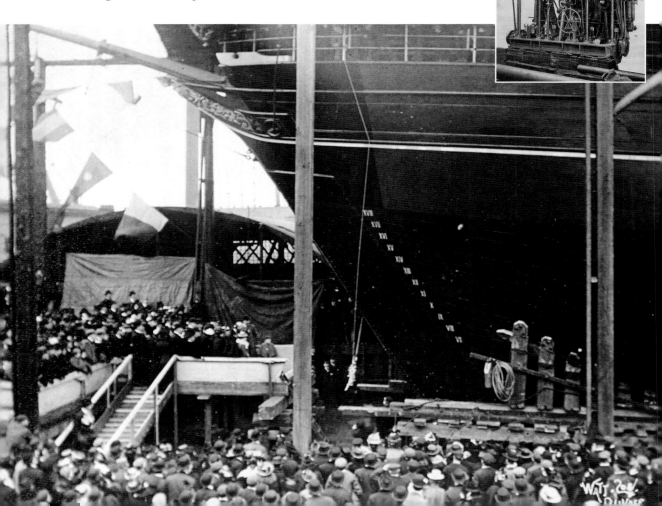

the vessel virtually unsinkable.

The magnetic work of the expedition was also devised. A wholly non-magnetic ship with engines was an impossibility, and the final compromise required the exclusion of iron and steel within a radius of 30ft of the magnetic observatory, which was to be situated on the upper deck. Hemp cordage was used for the main shrouds. The Ship Committee accepted each of the features fully, even though they were aware that smaller vessels had proved to have advantages in previous expeditions. This was the first ship designed for polar exploration; earlier ones had been Whitby colliers, bomb vessels or adaptations of merchant or naval vessels.

Also innovative was the Discovery's rounded overhanging form of stern, which gave better protection to the rudder, rudderpost and screw. The designer reckoned that the new stern would enable the helmsman, of necessity right aft in order to keep his eye on the sails, to keep drier in heavy seas. This proved to be the case, although a disadvantage was the greater noise caused by the falling of the stern on a wave. Bilge keels were rejected. It was recognised that these would decrease the rolling of the vessel but it was thought that they would increase the risk of her becoming entangled in the ice and remaining entangled. Bilge keels were fitted to Discovery during her 1925-27 Antarctic expedition, but her propensity to roll was a constant feature of logs and diaries until then.

On 29 November 1899 Admiral McClintock described the future Discovery concisely:

The Ship will be 172 feet long, 33 feet extreme beam and will be 1,570 tons displacement. She will be built of oak and elm, with an ice casing of green heart. Though somewhat larger, her general lines will be similar to Discovery. Her bows will be sharp and overhanging, like Discovery, and they will be specially strengthened for forcing her way through the ice. The thickness of her sides amidships at the water line, will be 25 inches. The stern and counters will be so shaped as to afford protection to the screw and rudder, both of which will be fitted so as to be raised quickly out of the water.

The consumption of coal is approximately as follows:

Speed (in knots)	6	7	8
Tons per diem	4½	6½	9
Distance for 240 tons of coal	7,700	6,200	5,100

This does not include the amount of coal that will be required for warming, dredging and sounding purposes. It is possible that some 30 tons of coal can be stowed elsewhere in the ship. The full power of the ship will be about 8 knots. In order to fall in with the magnetic requirements, the engine and boilers will be situated aft. The horse power will be 450, and the ship will stow, in bunkers, 240 tons coal. She will be fitted with masts and sails, and barque rigged, so that fuel can be economised while making a voyage, and advantage can be taken of favourable winds, even when navigating in the pack. The Magnetic Observatory, 8ft by 6ft 6in, will be on the bridge before the mainmast, and no ironwork will be permitted within 30 feet of it. [It was in fact fitted on the upper deck.]

For biological work there will be two houses, properly fitted on deck, and a laboratory 10ft by 7ft forward on the lower deck. There will be an auxiliary engine, and special arrangements for sounding to a depth of 4,000 fathoms, and also for dredging-up operations. All other details have been carefully designed for ice navigation, for promoting warmth and dryness below, and for facilitating scientific investigations.

The cabin accommodation includes a sitting and sleeping cabin for the captain, and one for the navigator with places in it for the chronometers and facilities for drawings. Cabins to be provided for the other executive officers, one for the engineer, and three for scientific civilians, of whom one, or more, ought to be surgeons, with one to be in medical charge of the ship. Extra cabin space could be found for two or more scientific civilians, but only by encroaching on the space set apart for the health and comfort of the crew. The total complement of the vessel was not to exceed 48 to 50 souls.

The Ship Committee expressed their indebtedness to the designer and engineer and congratulated themselves on the best-adapted vessel that had ever entered the polar regions.

Tenders were invited for the construction of the vessel but only two were received; the adze and wood

The *Discovery*
alongside at Dundee.
(DUNDEE CENTRAL
LIBRARY)

plane were giving way to the puncher and riveter used in steel shipbuilding. Of the two bids, that of the Dundee Shipbuilders' Company was very much the lower, but it was still higher than the Committee was in a position to accept. In discussion with the company's technical representative, Mr Smith was able to reduce the specification and lower the price to £33,700. At that time there was a great demand for vessels, generated by the Boer War in South Africa, and it was reckoned that this tender could not be bettered. It was accepted on 16 December 1899, on condition that the original beam design of 33ft be retained, and that separate tenders for the auxiliary machinery could be invited. In the end the Dundee Shipbuilders' tender for the engines was also accepted. Marrack's engines were triple expansion, developing 450hp at about 90rpm. Smith was glowing in his praise of Marrack's skill and enthusiasm, declaring the engines and boilers, within the limits of weight and power permissible, 'second to no engines that have ever been built'. Sadly, they were sent for scrap during the Second World War.

The Dundee Shipbuilders' Company was considered to have impressive experience for building or adapting vessels for polar work. It prosecuted the work with vigour and completed it in good time. After the expedition, Scott reported that the 'ship was undermasted; the mainmast from truck to keelson was only 112 feet, extremely short for a vessel with a mainyard of 60 feet in length. She should have carried a much larger sail area, especially in light winds, when she was an extremely sluggish sailer. The barque's sailing qualities were also hindered by the incorrect positioning of the masts, which should have been placed further forward.' These problems were remedied in the vessel's refit of 1924.

The German ship *Gauss* was built on similar lines to the *Fram* at the same time as the *Discovery*, for the German South Polar Expedition of 1900-03. The Ship Committee of the National Antarctic Expedition had chosen to follow the lines of the old Scottish whalers, built to push through the ice rather than remain fast in it. It is interesting to note that while the *Discovery* spent two winters in the ice, albeit in a sheltered bay,

the *Gauss* was beset in the open sea. Ten years later the *Fram* was converted in rig to a topsail schooner and given diesel engines for Amundsen's South Polar expedition of 1910-12 to the Ross Sea.

By February 1900 Mr Smith had decided that it was time to appoint an overseer for the hull of the *Discovery* on behalf of the RGS. Mr E Bate, the retired Inspector of Shipwrights, and formerly of Portsmouth Dockyard, was appointed to the highly complex task.

Captain Scott described the side of the *Discovery* as follows, after pointing out that a modern steel ship was less than an inch in thickness:

> The frames, which were placed very close together, were eleven inches thick and of solid English oak; inside the frames came the inner lining, a solid planking four inches thick; whilst the outside was covered with two layers of planking, respectively six and five inches thick, so that in most places, to bore a hole in the side one would have had to get through twenty-six inches of solid wood. The inner lining was of Riga fir, the frames of English oak, whilst the outer skin was of English elm or greenheart. The massive side structure was stiffened and strengthened by three tiers of beams running from side to side...

Strong as the sides were, the bows were even stronger. The keel at the fore end of the ship rose in an enormous mass of solid wood which constituted the stem. The bow and stem were protected by steel plates 4ft on each side, in preparation for the ice-breaking by her overhanging stem.

The keel was laid on 16 March 1900. The construction was undertaken by the Dundee Shipbuilders for £34,050, plus £10,322 for the engines.

Discovery was launched a year later, on 21 March 1901. Sir Clements Markham's diary recorded the day of the launch. At 3pm Lady Markham was presented with a pair of gold scissors and, at a signal, cut the ribbon. A bottle of wine smashed against the bows and two minutes later the *Discovery* glided into the sea amid tremendous cheers. It was a wonderful sight; the strongest ship ever built, and the first to be built in this country, he believed, specifically for exploring work.

THE FIRST
OUTWARD VOYAGE

WHICH REGION OF THE Antarctic should the expedition explore? Both the hydrographer, Rear Admiral Sir William Wharton, and Sir George Nares wanted the expedition to avoid Victoria Land as a place of operations, one reason being that it had been visited by the private expedition in the *Southern Cross* of 1898-1900. However, Sir Clements Markham opted for the overall advantages of 'McMurdo Bay' (now McMurdo Sound), Victoria Land, as the best place for winter quarters, in full view of the great active volcano, Mount Erebus. A better climate might be found there, and travelling parties could explore inland. A journey due south would enable researches to be made along the edge of the ice-cap, Markham reasoned, while a journey westward into the interior would be of equal importance, and would possibly effect co-operation with the Germans working in from the west. This route, he maintained, offered the best prospect of successfully carrying out the objects of the expedition with the minimum of risk. It was decided that Victoria Land should be Scott's goal.

The *Instructions to the Commander of the Expedition* attained what Sir Clements called their 'final Version' on 20 May 1901. Scott quoted the principal paragraphs of his instructions as:

> The objects of the expedition are, to determine, as far as possible, the nature, condition and extent of that portion of the South Pole lands included in the scope of the expedition; and to make a magnetic survey in the southern regions to the south of the 40th parallel, and to carry on meteorological, oceanographic, geological, biological and physical investigations and researches. Neither of these objects is to be sacrificed to the other.
> ...We, therefore, impress upon you that the greatest

importance is attached to the series of magnetic observations to be taken under your superintendence, and we desire that you will spare no pains to ensure their accuracy and continuity. The base station for your magnetic work will be at Melbourne or Christchurch, New Zealand. A secondary base station is to be established, by you, if possible, in Victoria Land. You should endeavour to carry the magnetic survey from the Cape to your primary base station south of the 40th parallel, and from the same station across the Pacific to the meridian of Greenwich. It is also desired that you should observe along the tracks of the Ross expedition, in order to ascertain the magnetic changes that have taken place in the interval between the two voyages...

...It is desired that the extent of land should be ascertained by following the coastlines; that the depth and nature of the ice-cap should be investigated, as well as the nature of the volcanic region of the mountain ranges, and especially of any fossiliferous rocks...

...You will see that the meteorological observations are regularly taken every two hours ...It is very desirable that there should, if possible, be a series of meteorological observations to the south of the 74th parallel.

As regards magnetic work and meteorological observations generally, you will follow the programme arranged between the German and British Committees, with the terms of which you are acquainted.

Whenever it is possible, while at sea, deep-sea soundings should be taken with serial temperatures, and samples of sea water at various depths are to be obtained for physical and chemical analysis.

Dredging operations are to be carried on as frequently as possible, and all opportunities are to be taken for making biological and geological collections.

...The chief points of geographical interest are as follows: To explore the ice barrier of Sir James Ross to its eastern extremity; to discover the land which was believed by Ross to flank the barrier to the eastward, or to ascertain that it does not exist, and generally to endeavour to solve the very important physical and geographical questions connected with this remarkable ice formation.

Owing to our very imperfect knowledge of the conditions which prevail in the Antarctic seas, we cannot pronounce definitely whether it will be necessary for the ship to make her way out of the ice before winter sets in, or whether she should winter in the Antarctic Regions. It is for you to decide on this important question after a careful examination of the local conditions.

If you should decide to winter in the ice…your efforts as regards geographical exploration should be directed to three objects, namely – an advance to the western mountains, an advance to the south, and an exploration of the volcanic region.

…In an enterprise of this nature, much must be left to the discretion and judgement of the commanding officer, and we fully confide in your combined energy and prudence for the successful issue of a voyage which will command the attention of all persons interested in navigation and science throughout the civilised world. At the same time, we desire you constantly to bear in mind our anxiety for the health, comfort and safety of all entrusted to your care.

Reference was also made to the 'complete details respecting sledge work both by men and dogs' provided by Sir Leopold McClintock and Dr Nansen, as well as to Armitage's previous polar experience in taking scientific observations, sledge travelling and the driving and management of dogs. Records should be deposited during the voyage by pre-arrangement whenever possible.'
The final paragraph read:

The Discovery is the first ship that has ever been built expressly for scientific purposes in these kingdoms. It is an honour to receive the command of her; but we are impressed with the difficulty of the enterprise which has been entrusted to you, and with the serious character of your responsibilities. The Expedition is an undertaking of national importance; and science cannot fail to benefit from the efforts of those engaged in it. You may rely on our support on all occasions, and we feel assured that all

on board the Discovery will do their utmost to further the objects of the Expedition.

The British had played a long and honourable part in polar exploration, beginning with the Cabots, Frobisher and Hudson in the Arctic, and extending to the Antarctic with Captain Cook, Biscoe, Balleny, Ross and Challenger. By 1900, however, the most up-to-date expertise on food and equipment was available in Norway, gained by Nansen's crossing of the Greenland ice-cap and his voyage in the Fram of 1893-96. Captain Scott visited Norway in October 1900 and received practical help from the great Norwegian explorer. He travelled on to Berlin, where he met the leader of the German South Polar Expedition, Professor Erich von Drygalski, who was also planning to leave the following summer, the two expeditions intending to co-operate in the field.

The National Antarctic Expedition was organised from its headquarters in Burlington House in London. The indefatigable secretary, Cyril Longhurst, and the officers, as appointed, took up their duties in London, Kew, Dundee and elsewhere. Scott was kept extremely busy in the office for six days a week, surrounded by sledges, skis, fur clothing and boots. Tables and chairs were littered with correspondence and innumerable samples of tinned foods. His spirits rose and fell, and he often feared that there was no possibility that the expedition could be ready to start on the required date.

Provision lists for three years were drawn up and ordered with care, including tropical and polar clothing, sledges, tents, furs and other equipment. Since the party was to be cut off from the world, tools and stores were required for the boatswain, the carpenter and the engineer, as well as equipment essential for use in the ice, including explosives and rockets for signalling.

There were tobacco, soap, glass, crockery, furniture, mattresses and all requisites for personal comfort; oil lamps and candles for lighting and stoves for heating; medicines and medical comforts; a photographic outfit; a library of hundreds of books; also balloon equipment, canvas boats of various kinds, huts for the shore station, instruments for a wide range of uses and much more besides.

Many commercial firms supplied their goods free. The total sum available of £92,000 was diminished by the cost of the ship, £51,000, while more than £25,000 was reserved for wages and the expenses of the voyage. The remainder was to equip the expedition thoroughly, as befitted a national enterprise.

On 3 June 1901 the *Discovery* berthed in the East India Dock on the Thames and the two busiest months of preparation and loading began, interspersed with numerous dinners and social entertainments during that first hot Edwardian summer, following the death of the old Queen early in the year.

The *Discovery* sailed from London on the last glorious day of July 1901, to be saluted from the training ship *Worcester* and every passing craft as she sailed down river, with flags, hooters and sirens. Crowds were everywhere. The vessel was 'swung' for the adjustment of her compasses at Spithead and then moored in Cowes Harbour during the celebrated yachting week. Here King Edward VII and Queen Alexandra came aboard on 5 August. Edward Wilson, the young second surgeon and zoologist, wrote in his beautifully-kept, illustrated diary of the voyage:

We were fully busy the whole morning, nigh on till 11.30 when the King and Queen came on board, clearing up and tidying and putting our smartest bits of apparatus and our prettiest coloured solutions in prominent positions. Microscopes were set out, water bottles, thermometers, everything arranged and tidied up... The King shook hands with us all round when he came on board, and again when he left. The Queen also. The King gave the Victorian

Order of the Fourth Class to Captain Scott before leaving, having with great difficulty fished it out of his tail-coat pocket, which was a long way round on the wrong side of his stout figure. He gave us a few words of royal encouragement, was shown all over the ship and then left.

Besides Sir Clements Markham, Sir Leopold McClintock and Sir Allen Young, both of Arctic fame, were on board, as were Captain Scott's mother and Dr Hugh Robert Mill of the RGS. The expedition's chief benefactor, Llewellyn Longstaff, was also present. The preceding May he had anonymously donated a fur-

Captain Scott seeing off the Royal party from the *Discovery*, Cowes, 5 August 1901.
(LONGSTAFF COLLECTION)

ther £5,000, which Markham hoped would complete the subscriptions and ensure the despatch of the *Discovery*'s tender, the relief ship. In his letter of thanks Markham told Longstaff that the King had consented to become Patron of the expedition. His Majesty wished the White Ensign to be flown if the Admiralty consented.

The *Discovery* made her departure from Cowes the day after the Royal visit, on 6 August 1901.

Having wished them all God speed, Markham wrote confidently in his diary that night that he believed all of the executives possessed the qualities to make good polar officers, and that they would work well and harmoniously together.

The men who composed the National Antarctic Expedition are named opposite, including those who sailed from Cowes and those who joined or left later. The abbreviation MN after seamen or stoker's names signifies that they were in the Merchant Navy; RMLI stands for Royal Marine Light Infantry. The list is taken from that given by Scott and amended from Erskine's article in the *Naval Review* of 1969.

THE SHIP'S COMPLEMENT

Officers
Robert Falcon Scott,
Captain, RN
Albert B Armitage,
*Lieut RNR, Navigator and
Second-in-Command*
Charles W R Royds,
Lieut RN, First Lieutenant
Michael Barne, *Lieut RN*
Ernest H Shackleton*,
Sub-Lieut RNR
George F A Mulock*, *Lieut RN*
Reginald W Skelton, *Engineer
Lieut RN, Chief Engineer*
Reginald Koettlitz,
surgeon and botanist
Edward A Wilson,
surgeon, zoologist and artist
Thomas V. Hodgson,
marine biologist

Hartley T. Ferrar, *geologist*
Louis C. Bernacchi, *physicist*

Warrant Officers, RN†
Thomas A Feather,
Acting Boatswain
James H. Dellbridge,
Second Engineer
Fred Dailey, *Carpenter*
Charles R Ford,
Ship's Steward

Petty Officers, RN
Jacob Cross
Edgar Evans
William Smythe
David Allan
Thomas Kennar
W MacFarlane*

Marines
Gilbert Scott, *Private, RMLI*
A H Blissett, *L/Cpl RMLI*

Seamen
Arthur Pilbeam, RN
William L Heald, RN
James Dell, RN
Frank Wild, RN
Thomas Williamson, RN
George B Croucher, RN
Ernest E Joyce, RN
Thomas Crean, RN
Jesse Handsley, RN
William J Weller, MN,
dog handler
W Peters*, RN
J Walker*, MN
J Duncan*, MN, *shipwright*
H R Brett*, MN, *cook*

G T Vince, RN.
died March 1902
Charles Bonner, RN.
died December 1901

Stokers
William Lashley, RN
Arthur L Quartley, RN
Thomas Whitfield, RN
Frank Plumley, RN
W Page*, RN
William Hubert*, MN,
donkeyman

Civilians
Charles Clarke, *cook*
Clarence Hare*,
assistant steward
H C Buckridge*,
laboratory attendant

† These were given acting rank in 1901 for the expedition only, but Dailey and Feather attained WO rank during the expedition.   * Wintered for one season only

'Group of officers and men'.
From Robert Scott's *The Voyage of the 'Discovery'*.

TOP ROW: Blissett, Allen, Wild, Croucher, Kennar, Handsley, Lashly, Crean, Dell, Evans, Plumley, Clarke, Weller.

MIDDLE ROW: Pilbeam, Joyce, Williamson, Heald, Cross, Smythe, Scott.

BOTTOM ROW: Ford, Feather, Lt. Armitage, Lt. Mulock, Lt. Shackleton, Dr. Wilson, Lt. Eng. Skelton, Capt. Scott,
Lt. Royds, Dr. Koettlitz, Mr. Bernacchi, Mr. Ferrar, Mr. Hodgson, Dellbridge, Dailey.

THE VOYAGE TO CAPE TOWN

A week after leaving Cowes, *Discovery* anchored off Funchal. Here Captain Scott despatched the first of his official Letters of Proceedings to the presidents of the Royal Society and the RGS. He also wrote more personally to Markham, already concerned by the *Discovery*'s slow speed, which meant there was very little chance to try out the deep-sea sounding and dredging gear on passage to New Zealand before reaching more tempestuous seas. *Discovery* had to arrive in the Antipodes in time to proceed to the Antarctic at the beginning of the southern summer, 1901-02, to have a full season in the Ross Sea after penetrating the pack ice to the north.

Scott's overall satisfaction was evident in his letter to Admiral Markham's wife, written on passage after leaving England. He urged her to tell the Admiral that the scientific people were willing to put their hands to the work of the ship and, although the ship leaked a good bit, this was quite accountable. He was finding that there were advantages in the long journey before the real work began, and reported that all the men were comfortable and happy. He thanked her for offering to keep in touch with the wives of the four married men and for the bunches of white heather for luck distributed among the company. His own sprig was pinned above his desk.

Much has been written since about the man who sat at that desk, and how he came to be appointed leader of the expedition at the age of 33, joining from HMS *Majestic*.

After considerable experience under sail, Scott had learned about surveying, surveying instruments, electricity and magnetism and was what Markham called a 'Torpedo Lieutenant'. He was a fair, well-built man of medium height with true blue eyes. He had a pleasant voice, a ready smile and a crisp and charming manner. His strong sense of justice, truth and right seemed to come from within rather than have religious conviction. He smoked a pipe and was a great reader, as shown in the literary quality of his writing. Perhaps from lack of money to indulge, he was not fond of drinking. He was almost the sole supporter of his widowed mother and four sisters.

Scott could be irritable and impatient, and his occasional moody silences and inactive periods of contemplation contrasted strongly with hard work carried out swiftly and clearly at other times. But he showed considerable solicitude for and sympathy with his men, particularly the naval 'blue jackets'. In his published narrative he praises the loyalty and devotion of his sailor friends. Sensitive and highly strung, he hated driving the sledge dogs to death and killing seals. His deep and reverent attitude towards nature and a most genuine love of science were significant qualities in his appointment as commander of the Antarctic expedition of 1901-04.

As *Discovery* approached the Equator on 30 August, Shackleton, later to become famous as leader of his own Antarctic expeditions in *Nimrod*, *Endurance* and *Quest*, recorded in his diary how a loud voice from forward hailed the ship and bade them back the main yard, as Neptune's messenger was coming on board. In a moment or two an old man was seen on the foc'sle head who demanded the name of the ship. 'The good ship *Discovery*' answered the officer of the watch. At this answer the Triton moved down the ladder towards the bridge and enquired about the candidates for baptism. Next day, at 2pm, Neptune and his consort and court hailed the ship and came on board. After a go of grog they quickly proceeded to a platform about 12ft high amidships, with a stool fastened to it by rope so that when the victim was pushed into the bath below, the stool would not go with him. A large sail filled with sea water served as the bath, and in it the Tritons disported themselves. There stood Neptune and his consort on the platform with the doctor and his greasy soapy pill, and the barber and his foaming tallow lather and huge razor. After being interviewed, the victim was handed over to the tender mercies of the Tritons, and it was generally a gasping, almost breathless creature that emerged from the other end of the bath. Shackleton concluded that the whole affair went off quite well, though the men got a bit rough at the end.

During the voyage south the members of the expedition came to know each other, and some acquired nicknames, including Thomas Vere Hodgson, the marine biologist, who became known as 'Muggins' after claiming to have found something of the sort in the course of a dissection. He later became curator of the Plymouth Museum. Some had sailed together before. Dr Koettlitz, the senior surgeon and botanist, and Armitage, the navigator and second-in-command, had taken part in the Jackson-Harmsworth Expedition to Franz-Josef Land, a group of islands to the north of Russia, in the 1890s. There they had witnessed the excitement of Nansen's arrival after leaving the *Fram*, in an attempt to sledge to the North Pole. Armitage eventually became Commodore of the P & O Steam Navigation Company.

The First Lieutenant, Charles Royds, had charge of the work of the men and the internal economy of the ship. He was also responsible for the meteorological observations, a routine, tedious and time-consuming task. It was largely due to him that *Discovery* was a happy ship. He was regarded with affection and respect by officers and men, whose welfare he had at heart. Michael Barne, the other naval lieutenant, was assistant magnetic observer and also in charge of the sounding apparatus. Scott later described how Barne would disappear from winter quarters for the day with a packed lunch and a sledge rigged with sails named the *Flying Scud*, on which sat a sounding machine for use through holes cut in the ice. The chief engineer, Reginald Skelton, assisted the scientific work in many ways and was also the expedition photographer.

The remaining sea officer was Ernest Shackleton. Educated at Dulwich College in southeast London, he was with the Union Castle Line's *Carisbrooke Castle* when appointed to *Discovery*. Sir Clements Markham got him made a sub-lieutenant in the RNR. Shackleton's one year in *Discovery* was the first step on the ladder of his remarkable twenty-one years of Antarctic exploration. One of the scientists wrote that, just as he had been in his former ships, Shackleton was the life and soul of *Discovery*. His mind was alert, his good humour inexhaustible. Besides being in charge of the holds and stores, he carried out his ordinary duties as an executive officer. A fine, self-reliant seaman, fearless and dominant, with a stern

regard for detail and discipline, he permitted no liberties from those under his command and could be brutally truculent if the occasion arose. But he was singularly sympathetic and understanding, and sentimental to the verge of tears when expressing his own feelings or spouting lines from his favourite poets. In his deep Irish voice he could wheedle and coax. Few could resist him.

The geologist who replaced Professor Gregory was Hartley T Ferrar. A keen oarsman, he had graduated in natural sciences from Cambridge only in the June before the expedition departed. The junior surgeon and naturalist of the expedition was Dr Edward Adrian Wilson. After Cambridge, he trained at St George's Hospital, London, and later worked in the Department of Botany at the British Museum while recovering from a poisoned arm. There he learned how to skin birds and identify the southern birds and seals. He was a fine watercolour painter and loved the birds, trees and flowers of the English countryside. Captain Scott was to develop a great respect and affection for Wilson, and persuaded him to go south again in the *Terra Nova* in 1910, as chief of scientific staff. As they lay dying in the tent on the 'Barrier' in 1912, Scott wrote of him to Mrs Wilson: 'His eyes have a comfortable blue look of hope and his mind is peaceful with the satisfaction of his faith regarding himself as part of the great scheme of the Almighty. I can do no more than to tell you that he died as he lived, a brave, true man – the best of comrades and the staunchest of friends.' Wilson kept a very full diary of the *Discovery* expedition of 1901-04, and his paintings and drawings illustrate Scott's and Armitage's narratives as well as the volumes of scientific results and the expedition's magazine, *The South Polar Times*.

The four warrant officers were important members of the expedition, and Scott was greatly pleased with each of them.

The engines were well tested in the Atlantic. Thirty-three days were spent under steam, at an average daily consumption of just over seven tons of coal, greater than had been hoped. From 24th to 30th August the engines pushed against headwinds in the

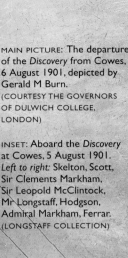

MAIN PICTURE: The departure of the *Discovery* from Cowes, 6 August 1901, depicted by Gerald M Burn.
(COURTESY THE GOVERNORS OF DULWICH COLLEGE, LONDON)

INSET: Aboard the *Discovery* at Cowes, 5 August 1901. *Left to right:* Skelton, Scott, Sir Clements Markham, Sir Leopold McClintock, Mr Longstaff, Hodgson, Admiral Markham, Ferrar.
(LONGSTAFF COLLECTION)

GERALD M BURN

tropics. Being new, they required more than ordinary care and adjustment. Scott praised the engine-room staff, who worked day and night through the tropics to avoid a breakdown, in stokehold temperatures of 140°F.

The *Discovery* called briefly at the uninhabited island of South Trinidad off Brazil, and entered Table Bay on 3 October 1901. Here, at Cape Town, the bunkers were refilled with coal. Then followed a short passage, rolling through an angle of 90°, to the naval station at Simon's Bay, where she was refitted. The ship's magnetic instruments had to be compared carefully with those at the Cape to ensure an accurate survey between South Africa and New Zealand. Armitage wrote to Markham on 14 October 1901, requesting spare magnets and needles for the instruments, especially as the Germans had all the spares they needed. Sir William Wharton, Hydrographer of the Navy, agreed to help if at all possible, but with eight instruments of four different types he could not guarantee that new needles would fit without careful adjustment. The magnetic programme had been arranged by Captain E W Creak, Director of the Admiralty Compass Observatory, who declared the *Discovery* better equipped than any other ship.

Four crew members were discharged at the Cape. They were replaced by volunteers from the fleet, Vince, Plumley and Joyce, the last of whom was later to become well known as one of Shackleton's men. Sinclair, a merchant seaman, also joined, together with Horace Buckridge, domestic and laboratory assistant, who volunteered to come without pay. Scott felt this undesirable, so he was given £5 a month. George Murray of the British Museum also left the ship at Cape Town. Scott had found him excellent as a messmate and director but unpractical in his ideas for working sea tackle. It was Murray who had edited the authoritative *Antarctic Manual* published by the RGS in July 1901 for the National Antarctic Expedition.

CAPE TOWN TO NEW ZEALAND

Discovery suffered a succession of gales after leaving the Cape. On the first day, over a period from 27 October to 3 November 1901, Skelton noted a record run of 217 miles under sail at an average of 9 knots, which he considered to be as much as she could ever do for any time. The amount of fresh water distilled from the sea during the gale was reduced to eight tons, from the ten produced when the ship was steady. Skelton thought it spoke well for her seaworthiness that the tremendous seas running had not even wetted her name. The record was broken again on 21 October, with 223 miles made under sail. Scott recorded his pleasure that she rose easily and lightly to the heaviest seas, and was wonderfully stiff under canvas and surprisingly dry. He had expected the possibility of shipping seas over the stern with some risk of 'broaching to', and attributed the ease with which she rose to heavy following seas entirely to the rounded shape of the stern. The *Discovery* was tossed about like a cork and rolls of 47° were recorded which did not cause discomfort but added difficulties to much of the work, especially the magnetic observations. Armitage was in charge of these, while Royds took on meteorology, Shackleton sea-water sampling and Barne the sounding machines.

Lyttelton, New Zealand, was to be their next port of call after a detour beyond 40°S for a magnetic survey. The 60th parallel was crossed on 15 November, and next day *Discovery* received what Scott called her 'baptism of ice'. Towards nightfall the ship became closely surrounded by the pack, which consisted of small pieces of ice two or three feet thick, much worn at the edges by the constant movement of the swell. The grinding of the floes against the side of the ship mingled with the subdued hush of their rise and fall on the long swell. For the first time they felt something of the solemnity of these great southern solitudes.

By the evening of 17 November the vessel was stopped by heavy ice. It was one solid mass as far as the eye could see. The opportunity was taken while in these latitudes to capture specimens of birds to be found in the pack: the southern fulmar, the Antarctic petrel, the snow petrel and the prions or whale-birds. Wilson's splendid sketches of them were the first accurately to record their colouring, beaks and feet. Four rather unsuccessful attempts to sound were also made between 15 and 21 November. The line kinked and broke repeatedly, causing almost 5,000 fathoms of wire, three or four driver tubes, one thermometer and other sundry equipment to be lost.

The sub-Antarctic island of Macquarie, an isolated speck of land about halfway between Australia and the Antarctic continent, was visited briefly on 22 November 1901. Green, with tussock grass and other plants in summer, unlike South Georgia and the other islands south of the Antarctic Convergence, it has no ice-cap. A haven for thousands of penguins, hundreds of elephant seals and the nesting place of albatrosses, cormorants, petrels, skuas and other sea birds, it has also an interesting flora. The history of the island has been written by Dr J S Cumpston.

Captain Scott's Cabin
(AUTHOR'S COLLECTION).

Discovery anchored off the east coast in Lusitania Bay. The scientists were put ashore through the fringe of thick kelp, a gigantic seaweed, and were soon busy collecting specimens, including eggs and young from the penguin rookeries, which cover a considerable area. Scott recorded that the enthusiasm of the collectors rose to fever heat as they witnessed their first penguins and so many strange sights. His Aberdeen terrier was excited by his run ashore and made short dashes at the penguins, with suppressed growls and hair bristling. Following their visit to the island, penguin was served for dinner and penguin eggs for breakfast. Scott was less than enthusiastic, but rejoiced to see the excellent spirits shown by the crew.

Discovery berthed in Lyttelton Harbour on 29 November 1901. Here Scott received a letter from the presidents of the Royal Society and the RGS, acknowledging their understanding of his heavy responsibilities and confirming their confidence in his ability, skill and judgement in times of hardship and peril. Assuring him they were his 'affectionate friends', they also reminded him that efforts were being made to send a relief ship the following season. The expedition received enormous kindness, both public and private, in New Zealand.

Discovery's rigging was overhauled and refitted with the help of men from HMS Ringarooma. Her stores were restowed and in part replaced, after being damaged by a persistent leak. Here Shackleton, the merchant seaman, came into his own. 'His interest and enthusiasm, combined with shrewd common sense in cargo work has proved invaluable,' wrote Scott. 'No ship ever left on such an expedition with a more accurate knowledge of her resources or the exact position of every comestible she carried.' The coal bunkers were refilled with 285 tons, while 45 tons were later taken on as deck cargo. In an effort to stop the leak the vessel was docked twice. On the second occasion the heavy steels plates protecting her bows were removed and every inch of the bottom examined. It was all in vain and the leak persisted. Captain Scott decided it must be put up with and the water pumped out daily.

A magnetic survey was one of the expedition's main aims. For this a base was needed in the southern hemisphere, such as Hobart had been sixty years earlier for Sir James Clark Ross. The societies' presidents had written to Mr Coleridge Farr, director of the Christchurch Observatory, stating that the necessary absolute and relative magnetic observations should be made with the instruments on board the Discovery and that as complete a base station 'as your resources will permit' should be established. In Chrstchurch, simultaneous observations could be made in accordance with those of the Antarctic expeditions and in international co-operation. The arrival by fast steamer of L C Bernacchi, the physicist, the last officer to join *Discovery*, meant that the base could be set up.

The son of the owner of Maria Island, Tasmania, Louis Bernacchi had been brought up in wild but enchanting surroundings and qualified as astronomer, meteorologist and magnetician during his years at the Melbourne Magnetic Observatory. He joined Borchgrevink's *Southern Cross* expedition as physicist, and his book, *To the South Polar Regions*, was published during the year he joined the National Antarctic Expedition. He was later to write a life of L E G Oates and a 'biography' of *Discovery*.

Such was the appeal of *Discovery* that thousands came to view her or see her off. Some were served lunch on board and departed with a signed photograph of the ship. Despite the hordes of curious visitors, she was at last ready to sail, from Lyttelton, on 21 December 1901. A short farewell service was conducted by the Bishop of Christchurch and vast crowds packed the wharves and quays to give the expedition a magnificent send-off. Two warships and five gaily-dressed steamers escorted her, with bands playing and whistles hooting. In the excitement of departure a young seaman named Bonner had climbed above the crow's nest to the top of the mainmast, from which he hurtled with a wild cry to his death on the corner of an iron deckhouse. The loss of this smart young seaman was felt greatly, and he was buried with naval honours at Port Chalmers. Bonner was replaced by Able Seaman Jesse Handsley, who volunteered from HMS *Ringarooma*, as did AB Thomas Crean. Crean replaced AB Robert Sinclair, who deserted in New Zealand, feeling depressed and in some way responsible for his shipmate's death. Scott took no steps to apprehend him.

Commander A R Ellis, the editor of Lashly's

Last view of *Discovery*, leaving Lyttelton.
(AUTHOR'S COLLECTION)

diaries, commented that this accident brought together the two men, Lashly and Crean, whose names were later to be linked in one of the greatest Antarctic stories during Scott's second and last expedition in the *Terra Nova*.

After taking on the deck coal at Port Chalmers, the port of Dunedin, *Discovery* made her final departure on the morning of Christmas Eve 1901. Below, every hold and stowage space was packed to the gunwales. On deck the scene was more extraordinary, with the after-part occupied by a terrified flock of forty-five sheep, a welcome present from New Zealand farmers. Further forward from the wheel were sacks of food and twenty-three howling dogs in a wild state of excitement. Above the deck, where skid beams carried the boats, were lashed 30 tons of timber for the huts.

By that evening, under steam and sail in the open sea, the blue outline of New Zealand was lost in the northern twilight.

FROM NEW ZEALAND TO THE ANTARCTIC

The Antarctic continent is bounded by the Southern Ocean, one of the stormiest seas in the world. There, in the nineteenth century, the square-rigged fast sailing ships would run their easting down and shorten their voyages to Australia, New Zealand and the Far East, blown by the westerly gales of the forties and fifties on Great Circle courses. Captain Cook's circumnavigation of the globe of 1772-75 in high southern latitude disproved the existence of the theoretical geographers' supposed fertile continent of *Terra Australis*, and showed that if land existed nearer the South Pole it would 'never feel the warmth of the sun's rays and be doomed to everlasting frigidness'. British and American sealers followed, decimating the fur seals, but discovering new lands as well.

Three national expeditions of the early 1840s, French, American and British, charted portions of

Antarctica. The one commanded by Sir James Clark Ross, in HM Ships *Erebus* and *Terror*, penetrated the belt of summer pack ice that surrounds the continent to discover the Ross Sea, the Ross Ice Shelf and the volcanic peaks Mount Erebus and Mount Terror adjoining McMurdo Sound, the area to which Scott was directed to sail in the *Discovery*.

Only one ship had wintered previously in the Antarctic, the *Belgica* of the 1897-99 Belgian expedition led by Adrien de Gerlache, which was beset in the pack of the Bellingshausen Sea to the west of the Antarctic Peninsula for many months. One expedition only had wintered on the continent. Led by C E Borchgrevink, the party landed at Cape Adare from the *Southern Cross* in February 1899. The *Southern Cross* skirted the cliffs of the Ross Ice Shelf, finding it had retreated since Ross's day. A sledging party landed briefly to make a short journey to 78° 50'S. Borchgrevink had been a member of a previous Norwegian whaling voyage in the *Antarctic* in 1894-95, which claimed to have made the first landing on the Antarctic at Cape Adare and to have first discovered plant life there.

Fine weather enabled *Discovery* to traverse the stormy seas south of New Zealand largely under sail, without losing any deck cargo. New Year's Day saw the first twenty-four hours of daylight. The first iceberg was sighted on 2 January 1902, when approaching the Antarctic Circle. Seventeen of these flat-topped bergs were sighted, none more than 100ft high. Calved from the ice shelf, these were small in comparison with some recorded with a length of 50 miles or more. Wilson wrote that they passed close to several and enjoyed the blue depths and pure whiteness of the flat tops, and the caves and grottoes, into which the spray dashed and rose some 80 or 90ft.

The Antarctic Circle was crossed on 3 January, and soon *Discovery* felt 'slight shocks as her ironclad prow forced a way through the honeycombed floes, the outriders of the pack'. Navigator and second-in-command Lieut Armitage, chosen for his Arctic experience, found the southern sea ice much more level than that in the north. Known as the 'Pilot', he observed from the snug crow's nest that ahead and all around was a 'vast, illimitable field of ice', which in the distance appeared to be absolutely impervious to attack. Somewhat closer were thin black-looking streaks of water, indicating the weak places in the line of least resistance, where one could guide the ship. From the crow's nest Armitage was able to estimate the respective mass of each ice floe and assess which to avoid and which could be passed over. Long, cruel-looking spurs extended far under water from some of them, while others were quite smooth-sided. Whether the ship would glide safely past a dangerous mass of ice or be brought up against it, quivering in every timber, depended upon the speed of the officers at the engine-room telegraph, in the engine-room and at the wheel in obeying orders from the crow's nest. At times, the only way to get from one 'lead' or channel of open water to another was to charge the obstruction and break down the neck of ice.

The crow's nest.
Pencil drawing by Edward Wilson.
(SCOTT POLAR RESEARCH INSTITUTE)

Under sail and steam, *Discovery* made an easy passage through the 270-mile belt of pack ice in five days, emerging on 8 January 1902. The crew had spent time celebrating both a belated Christmas and their entry into the Antarctic regions, many trying skis for the first time. The ship was watered from the ice and seals captured for specimens and food. Once again, Scott owned to some squeamishness but found seal steaks and joints much more palatable than penguin.

Tow-netting was carried out to collect the microscopic flora and fauna from the surface of the sea. The sheep were slaughtered and the joints of mutton hung in the rigging as a special treat later on Sundays. All around, the birdlife of the pack was abundant: the southern fulmars, the Antarctic petrels, the skuas, the giant petrels, the dainty snow petrels and the penguins which squawked constantly and followed the ship with great curiosity.

A sounding of 1,480 fathoms was made at the southern edge of the pack, and sea-water temperatures were obtained at various depths. Land was seen on entering open water, and at midnight the sun shone on Mount Sabine, one of the high peaks of Victoria Land. *Discovery* anchored in Robertson Bay, and parties landed at the site of Borchgrevink's winter quarters near Cape Adare. Bernacchi and Armitage took magnetic instruments ashore to determine dip and total force, while others examined the hut and the large rookery of Adélie penguins, despite its pungent odour. The naturalists sought specimens, and in the evening Bernacchi led a pilgrimage to visit the high and lonely grave of his former shipmate in the *Southern Cross*, Nikolai Hanson.

Scott described their first smiling glimpse of Antarctica after they had returned for their late evening meal:

The scene…was very beautiful; the surface was calm and placid, beyond it the sunlight fell on the bold peaks and splendid glaciers of the Admiralty Range, the sharp summits of Mounts Minto and Adam were well defined… The placid deep-shadowed sea was dotted with streams of brilliantly white pack-ice, whilst here and there a table-topped iceberg showed the sharpest contrast of light and shadow… The tide was making out of the bay with considerable strength, and now and again it bore past us a floe alive with busy, chattering penguins.

The hut, a well-constructed log cabin rather superior to the one they were carrying, and some of the stores, were found in good condition. Despatches and letters were left in the hut, later to be picked up by the relief ship *Morning*.

Discovery then stood to the south, against adverse winds, along the mountainous and mainly ice-bound coast of Victoria Land. Armitage recorded that the auxiliary barque had her first real test in ice while steaming away from Robertson Bay, when heavy ice was being brought in on the tide. She

emerged from the ordeal triumphant. Armitage had been woken by Captain Scott to con the ship from the main top, at a time when she seemed likely to be swept against one of the huge grounded bergs or on the shore. She rode out a storm in the lee of Coulman Island, where winds of 90mph made her almost unmanageable. They left a written record of the proceedings, protected by a cylinder and attached to a tall red-painted pole, conspicuous from the sea.

Hodgson was delighted with the best haul of marine life so far. Thirty-one seals were killed for use during the winter months as fresh meat, and the skins thought worth preserving as specimens were flensed of their layer of blubber and slated in barrels containing brine. While accepting that man must live, Scott deplored the terrible massacre of innocent inhabitants and the staining of white snow with blood.

The ship gradually worked her way from Lady Newnes Bay to Wood Bay. Armitage observed that the atmosphere was exceedingly clear, and that both Coulman Island and Mount Erebus could be seen at the same time, although 240 miles apart. This clarity could prove very deceptive, as Scott found when approaching Coulman Island. Distant objects, later seen on sledging journeys, could assume extraordinary false appearances, and many errors made by earlier explorers could be ascribed to this phenomenon. Heavy ice blocked Wood Bay, making it impossible to leave a record there. The magnificent solitary volcanic cone of Mount Melbourne could be admired from this point. They were by then south of the magnetic pole, towards which the south-seeking end of the compass still pointed, so that although they were still travelling south, they appeared to be heading north.

It was time to begin a search for secure winter quarters. A possible site was found in an inlet later named Granite Harbour, where a large party bounded ashore, leaping from floe to floe. McMurdo Sound proved too full of ice, with floes 12ft thick, to penetrate far beyond lat. 77° 30' S. Scott noted that a plain seemed to stretch directly south, but there was no sign of the Parry Mountains charted by Ross. A cone-shaped hill was named Mount Discovery and the western mountains were dubbed the Royal Society Range. On 21 January *Discovery* turned east to follow Ross's 'Great Ice Barrier'.

ALONG THE ICE SHELF: CAPE CROZIER TO EDWARD VII LAND

The expedition was later to ascertain that Mount Erebus and Mount Terror form Ross Island, a triangle whose extremities are Cape Armitage to the south, Cape Bird to the north and Cape Crozier to the southeast. The existence of the active volcano Mount Erebus in these icy regions was one of the more remarkable discoveries made by Sir James Clark Ross. Its white slopes, rising to nearly 14,000ft and crowned by a plume of smoke or an orange glow in winter, have become familiar to those interested in the Antarctic from the splendid photographs taken by H G Ponting during Scott's *Terra Nova* expedition and from Edward Wilson's watercolours. *Discovery* rounded the northern corner at Cape Bird, between it and off-lying Beaufort Island. A whaleboat managed to land through the surf at Cape Crozier, where Bernacchi and Barne made magnetic observations and another post and record cylinder was set up on the mountainside, in the midst of an extensive penguin rookery.

From the summit of a nearby volcanic cone Scott, Royds and Wilson were able to look down on Ross's other remarkable discovery, the 'Great Ice Barrier'. For the first time this extraordinary ice formation was seen from above. Scott described the clear blue sea to the north, dotted by snowy-white bergs; the barrier edge in shadow, like a long black ribbon as it ran to the eastern horizon; and, to the southeast, a vast plain extending indefinitely, with faint shadows on its blue-grey surface.

On 23 January *Discovery* began to steam eastward along the Barrier. The officers surveyed the undulating heights of the sheer ice cliffs, recording that they ranged from 50 to 240ft. The ship was stopped three times in every 24 hours to make a sounding. The use of steam gave *Discovery* a great advantage over *Erebus* and *Terror*, which had relied on sail alone and could not approach too near to the ice front. It was found that the ice had receded since the 1840s, and that *Discovery*'s course was south of the Barrier as charted by Ross. By 29 January she was not only south but east of Ross's farthest venture of 1842, from which he had seen a strong appearance of land to the southeast. The

On board *Discovery*: Dr Wilson and P O Cross skinning birds.
(AUTHOR'S COLLECTION)

character of the ice shelf soon changed. Behind an ice front of some 10 to 20ft above the sea, the snow surface rose in long undulating slopes to rounded ridges. A sounding of 100 fathoms confirmed that this was indeed land. Fog hindered exploration on the next day, but in the evening it cleared sufficiently to reveal, at a height of some 2,000ft, patches of 'real live rock', the actual substance of their newly discovered land, which Scott named King Edward VII Land. *Discovery* reached her southernmost point of 78° 36'S on 26 January 1902, the fourth day along the Barrier.

By 31 January shallow soundings alone indicated the nearness of the land. The fog lifted to reveal numerous grounded icebergs, round which lay heavy pack of great extent. Emperor penguins were seen and three were killed as specimens. In the evening, from the crow's nest, Edward Wilson saw thousands of them in groups of a hundred or more through the big telescope, while smaller groups were dotted everywhere on the ice floes. New ice was forming on the sea where the ship lay, so that a visit to discover the Emperors' rookeries five miles inland was out of the question.

On 1 February Scott decided it was time to return westward to establish winter quarters. Wilson's sketches, made in between skinning birds in an empty coal bunker, show the new land that had been discovered. The highest part of the Barrier had been found to be 280ft. It was noted that at least in some places it was afloat. On the return voyage to McMurdo Sound a bight about three miles long in the ice shelf was investigated. The ship was able to lie alongside the ice front, and balloon ascents were made by Scott and Shackleton to 700ft, from which height no land, only ice, could be seen. Armitage, Bernacchi and four men sledged south to examine the undulating surface of the Barrier. They spent a cramped night in their tent ashore, and the southernmost point they reached was lat. 79° 03'.5S. in long. 194° 55'.25E. Borchgrevink had landed and reached lat. 78° 34'S on 16 February 1900 from the same or a similar natural harbour in the Barrier, probably that named 'Bay of Whales' by Shackleton in 1908. What Scott called 'Balloon Bight' seems to have been renamed Discovery Inlet, and it probably merged later into the Bay of Whales through changes in the Ross Ice Shelf. The return along the Barrier was made as quickly as possible. By 8 February 1902 *Discovery* was once more in McMurdo Sound, which was by then clear of ice.

'An inlet in the Barrier, January 28, '02'. A watercolour by Edward Wilson.
(SCOTT POLAR RESEARCH INSTITUTE)

WINTER QUARTERS,
McMurdo Sound, 1902

A LIKELY SITE for winter quarters was found in a small ice-filled bay, later known as Winter Harbour, at the head of McMurdo Sound, near the southern tip of Ross Island. It was protected to the west by a small rocky promontory which became known as Hut Point, and on the other side by Cape Armitage, named after *Discovery*'s navigator. It appeared to be sheltered from the ice pressure, and shallow enough for there to be no danger from icebergs. Scott wrote at the time that to the south-south-east, as far as the eye could see, all was smooth and even, and seemed to be a continuation of the Great Barrier, within easy distance for the exploration of the mainland and within land communication of their post office at Cape Crozier.

Although *Discovery* was secured by ice anchors, sudden squalls would cause the ship to uproot these from time to time, and it was necessary to keep the fires alight so that steam could be got up at short notice. She was also carried by tide and swell into awkward positions in relation to the ice foot or shallow bank, sometimes parting her cables. Wilson wrote of disturbed nights, when the ship bumped and groaned, squeaked and grunted close in to the ice foot. Scott used gun cotton to blow up some of the ice ahead to edge her further in. The vessel was eventually frozen into the most perfect natural harbour by 8 February 1902. She had shelter from all ice pressure from the north, south and west, and there was a low shore and ice foot on the east where the huts could be built on rocks. Within sight of Erebus and Terror, she was also sheltered from the southeast prevailing winds, not only by a range of

A general view of the *Discovery* in winter quarters, McMurdo Sound, with the huts in the foreground
(ROYAL GEOGRAPHICAL SOCIETY)

The track of the *Discovery* in the southern hemisphere during the National Antarctic Expedition 1901-04.

its sledge parties and will go up by Cape Adare and Cape North to see if anything can be made out of Wilkes Land, and when the season comes to an end, run straight up to Lyttelton, arriving there about the end of March 1903. Here we spend the winter months refitting, and then in December '03 we start south again to get further information about this east end of the Barrier where we found our new land. We go straight for this part and spend the whole summer working it out and then run up in March, out of the ice, and home round Cape Horn without going again to New Zealand at all.

In the event, Scott's plans were modified. Having found a sheltered harbour, free from danger for the ship, Scott decided to winter *Discovery* there and use her for the expedition's living quarters. The prefabricated hut, designed and made in Australia, was described by Armitage as more suitable for a colonial shooting lodge than for a polar dwelling-place. Several pickaxes were broken in excavating holes for the corner posts in the iron-hard frozen ground, but the outer building was completed with considerable difficulty and with the temperature at zero, between 15 and 26 February. The two observation huts were erected with less trouble. The magnetic hut was completed on 27 February 1902, when Duncan recorded that the instrument for registering magnetic elements was one of only three in existence. The earthquake register was fitted on to a large stovepipe let into the earth to receive any shock, and another instrument registered the amount of electricity in the air.

Penguins and seals were butchered to provide fresh food for the winter, and supplement the tinned and other provisions. Kennels were made for the dogs, though they preferred to sleep curled up in the snow outside.

The young geologist Hartley Ferrar was the first to climb one of the nearby hills – Observation Hill – and to realise they were on an island: Ross Island. He built a cairn to mark the event. Gradually the area surrounding winter quarters was explored on foot or on skis and the local landmarks given names which have become familiar over the years: Arrival Bay, Crater Heights, Pram Point, Castle Rock and the Gap. By

hills, but by an immense range of mountains, hitherto unknown, which caught and reflected the pink glow of the sun. Away to the south a new island, high on a plain of ice, revealed their field of sledging work for the next year. A further advantage was the abundance of Weddell seals, which Wilson thought a wholesome sight, because fresh meat put scurvy out of the question. Nothing was wanting and their hopes ran high.

Scott had earlier outlined the three-year programme of work, summarised by Wilson as:

Make straight for McMurdo Bay; find good winter quarters and get settled into them as far south as possible. Spend the winter there. Give up next summer chiefly to sledging in three directions. One party to go due south from winter quarters. The ship to wait for its return. Other smaller parties and excursions to make out in the immediate neighbourhood of McMurdo Bay and Erebus and Terror, and to come back to the ship. By this time our letters at Cape Crozier will have been found by the relief ship, which will come to us in McMurdo Bay. The relief ship will now take Armitage and a party to Wood Bay to go inland, for the Magnetic Pole, and await their return, when they and the relief ship will return to Lyttelton. Meanwhile the Discovery will have collected mid-February 1902 the long Antarctic summer was coming to an end, with the sun very near dipping at midnight and with the effects of both sunsets and sunrise in the evening and morning. Wonderful violet light tinged the snow slopes and ice foot, fading into the purple outline of the distant mountains. Wilson painted many of these glorious scenes.

The 'blue jackets' made a football pitch on the fast ice and challenged the officers to a match. Skiing proved popular, but was not without accidents. Skis were unknown to the old British Arctic expeditions and were a novelty on this one. Scott greatly enjoyed the exercise, but considered at first that they would be of little use when dragging sledges.

As they settled down to life and work beneath the great smoking volcano, the Antarctic took its toll. On 11 March Seaman Vince slid down an icy slope in murky weather and drowned in the sea. Miraculously, another shipmate, young Hare, found his way back to the ship after getting lost and falling asleep for 36 hours. Both had been members of a sledge party sent to deposit a record at Cape Crozier for the relief ship, directing her to her winter quarters. Shackleton led a boat party to search for the missing men, and the ship's siren sounded. Everyone was overjoyed at Hare's return. In a final search for Vince, *Discovery* rounded

Hut Point to leave no shadow of doubt. A number of lessons were learned from this tragedy. Scott considered Hare's survival a great tribute to the clothing the expedition members wore, and during this emergency Seaman Wild's powers of leadership were shown in bringing his shipmates back to the ship and safety.

Discovery was still not completely frozen in by the end of March. Young ice kept forming and then dispersing, making it difficult for the boats to maintain communication with the shore and posing a dilemma for Scott. He was anxious about the ship's vulnerability to gales until she was well frozen in, as they had extinguished the boilers to save coal. He was also unwilling to commit a large party ashore because the men would be needed if the ship were driven from the ice. On the other hand, there was a great deal to do before winter really set in.

However, the ship gradually became frozen in from astern, and by 28 March the sea ice appeared to have come to stay. On 30 March, Easter Sunday, perfectly formed ice flowers sprang up on the surface of the frozen sea, their delicate petals waxen white in the shadow and radiant with prismatic colours when touched by the sun. Meanwhile, preparations for the winter progressed. The meteorological screen was erected ashore about 60 yards astern

LEFT: Midwinter 'Christmas' dinner on the lower deck of the *Discovery*, June 1902. (AUTHOR'S COLLECTION)

BELOW: Midwinter 'Christmas' Dinner menu 1902. (AUTHOR'S COLLECTION)

of the ship and an anemometer, to measure the wind speed, was set on the mizzen cross trees. Tide poles were set up and a windmill was briefly operated on board to generate electric light. *Discovery* was covered with an awning of wagon cloth, as were the Arctic ships wintering in years gone by. Scott had gone to some trouble to acquire this material, but thought in fact that ordinary canvas would have been stronger and better. The boats had been earlier landed on the ice to make room for the awning to be spread.

THE DARK WINTER

Shackleton provides a good picture of the routine of a winter's day and the long winter nights on board the *Discovery* during April to August, the months of darkness.

At six o'clock the quartermaster whose night watch it is calls the cook. He immediately gets up and lights the fire. Then, at seven o'clock, the men and officers turn out, and a working party of men proceed with their sledge to a small glacier, about a hundred yards from the ship, and there with pick and shovel, break up the ice, put it into a big box on the sledge and cart it back to the ship. Another party on board puts the ice into the melter over a galley stove, and the first party comes back for a fresh supply. In two journeys we could get enough ice to supply the whole ship for the day.

Then the wardroom servants and other men pick out of the ice-box whatever they want for themselves or for the officers, and melt down their ice in other receptacles. At eight o'clock all hands go to breakfast, which consists of porridge, seal meat, bread, butter, jam and tea and coffee or cocoa. At nine o'clock the Captain reads prayers on the mess deck, and after that the men are told off to their various jobs. Some are employed making sleeping bags for sledging, others repairing the weather cloth that

covers the whole ship, which occasionally gets holes in it owing to the blizzards and the weight of snow which settles on it. Another party starts shovelling the thick snow off the vessel, for tons of drift accumulate on and around the ship. We never minded the vessel's sides being piled up with snow, for this kept us warm inside...

Other men assisted the officers, continued Shackleton, helping to skin and stuff birds and seals, which would be used as specimens in museums when the ship returned, or went out with the officers who had charge of the soundings to get the depth of water within three or four miles. A couple more men would help Hodgson, the biologist, whose work it was to collect as many marine specimens as possible. Working right through the long winter in the dark, he managed to obtain more than 500 new kinds of marine animals, spiders, shrimps, star- and shellfish and various other things that live and swim in the sea. Hodgson also took charge of cleaning the skulls of seals, putting them down the hole where he drew his fish nets in a pillow case with holes in, and in about two days the millions of shrimps completely cleaned all flesh away from the bones. Another party of men helped the officer in charge of stores to get up the necessary rations for the day, and a couple more helped the geologist, who roamed around collecting such rock specimens as could be found on volcanic land.

At one o'clock comes dinner for the men, the officers' dinner not coming on until six. The men prefer a good meal

Discovery in winter quarters in McMurdo Sound from a watercolour by Edward Wilson. The painting was a prize awarded to James Duncan, shipwright, for winning a ski race during the Antarctic sports day, November 1902.
(DUNCAN COLLECTION, DUNDEE ART GALLERIES AND MUSEUMS)

in the middle of the day, and then they take an afternoon sleep. At eight o'clock at night the officer for the day makes an inspection of the ship and reports to the Captain. Then the time for play begins. Our hut, which was not used, as nothing happened to the ship, was converted into the "Royal Terror Theatre" and there all sorts of plays and concerts and minstrel shows were given. Lieutenant Barne was manager, as he had a great gift for writing and localising plays…Cards were in great demand, and not only the officers, but the warrant officers and blue-jackets became adept at bridge. Some of the blue-jackets could remember every card that was playing in a "no trump" hand.

Edited by Shackleton, the expedition magazine The South Polar Times was published each month during the winter. The officers grew their own 'garden' in the wardroom, consisting of two crocuses and mustard and cress, sufficient for a small mouthful for half-a-dozen returning sledgers. There were two-hourly meteorological readings to take and special midnight suppers were cooked by the observers after ten minutes freezing in a blizzard on deck. Almost all members of the expedition kept some kind of diary and collected souvenirs to take home.

Shackleton, with his love of poetry, expressed their world for many of them:

All was brightness and light within the ship and the noise of the howling wind outside could hardly be heard, but what a change it was to open the door and go on deck. The swirling snow got into your eyes and every crevice of your clothes and the cold air quite took one's breath away. But the weather was not always like this.

Sometimes, a full moon rode high in the sky and the whole country was bathed in glorious light, and on those clear nights we sometimes saw a gleam of light away in the Northward, which was a sign that still there was a Sun…I cannot imagine anything more wonderful and awe-inspiring than this great white plain, the huge mountains rising away in the distance beyond; and that great volcano with its heavy pall of smoke hanging over our little camp day and night. There we were, forty-eight men, with a Continent to ourselves.

Shackleton's diary entry of Thursday 19 June 1902 records a typical day in winter:

Went up Crater Hill with Wilson. It was snowing, misty and blowing with heavy drifts and as black as Hades. The temperature at the time was minus forty-six F. Wilson got his nose frost-bitten. We killed a couple of seals later on, which curiously enough came out on the floe though they do not usually in this sort of weather. I find I can handle ropes and even pull up the fishing line without having to put my gloves on for at least two minutes. Hodgson went in tonight to the mess deck with a bottle of his spiders and shrimps, to explain to the men the anatomy of the beasts, their method of getting food, and their general habits.

We are making a point of taking turns once a week to give the men a general idea of our scientific work, and they are very keen on it. We have just taught the warrant officers bridge. The temperature in the ward-room was allowed to get above sixty-something tonight, with the result that the ice in my cabin has melted, and half my socks have to be dried as the water ran into one of the drawers containing my clothes.

Bread and cakes were fresh baked continually, seal meat was eaten three times weekly, tinned meat also three times, mostly in pies, and the New Zealand mutton was saved for Sundays. There was ample butter, milk, cheese, jam and bottled fruits. Wilson examined every tin as it was opened each morning and officers and men ate the same food. Once the fires were let out, the wardroom and officers' cabins became very cold, there being no insulation between them and the icy bunker below. Scott records having to sit in his cabin with his feet in a box of hay to keep them warm. Each week had its routine, and the captain made sure that every member of the ship's company had sufficient exercise and fresh air. There was ample tobacco for the smokers.

Bernacchi was the only one who had already spent a winter in the Antarctic, and he draws an interesting comparison between life in *Discovery* and that in the hut at Cape Adare, where ten officers and men lived together in so restricted a space that tempers wore thin long before the winter ended. In contrast, in *Discovery* each officer had his own sanctum and the men in their quarters could enjoy their leisure in their own way. He also found that the comparative formality of meals helped to preserve an atmosphere of civilised tolerance, seldom found in polar exploration, and that the traditions of the naval service were of infinite benefit.

The diary kept by James Duncan provides a continuous record of the first winter as experienced on the lower deck, where the sailors slept in hammocks. On 20 April 1902 he wrote that the morning was fine, looking just like a winter morning at home. He took plenty of exercise on foot or skis by the light of the aurora, the stars and the moon, sometimes going for a run before breakfast. He had charge of a dog named Maggie. 'A very disiloute look around never the less we are Happy,' he wrote. One of his only three complaints was about the 'heartbreaking' French salamander stoves, which smoked out their sleeping quarters, filling the place with sulphur. Only one worked, the other being covered in frost. Duncan began a scrap album of magazine cuttings and a half-model of *Discovery*. A draughts tournament was won by Wild. A second complaint was that the officers were slack in

providing amusement or any instruction classes, and that the men were not informed about the scientific work going on. Scott at first thought that regular organisation of lectures and entertainments would disturb the mess deck rather than add to the comfort of the community, but, as Shackleton recorded, Hodgson did give a lecture on his marine catches, giving the mess deck, in Duncan's words, great satisfaction. He had to make a blackboard for the lectures. Ferrar, the geologist, gave the next lecture about his work, and Armitage gave a lantern lecture on his experiences during the *Windward* Arctic expedition. The last lecture of the winter was given by the captain, who spoke about sledging, sledging gear and its care. A play and a minstrel show were staged in the hut on shore, icy cold as it was, and afterwards the audience walked home to the ship through drifting snow.

Christmas was celebrated at midwinter, some of the hands having turned out the hold to retrieve the Christmas puddings and cakes. Coloured paper was issued to decorate each mess. Bloaters were served for breakfast on 23 June, which, Duncan wrote, was 'Christmas morning with us'.

The captain and officers walked around the mess deck at 12.30 and admired the decorations. Each of the men received small presents, which Mrs Royds and Mrs Wilson had sent. They were given three hearty cheers. Dinner served at one for the mess, with a small bottle of Bass, consisted, in Duncan's words, of 'Real Turtle Soup, Boiled Ham, Kidney Beans and Potatoes, Plum Pudding and Brandy Sauce'. This feast was followed by a sleep and afterwards by tea, cakes and sweets. Grog was served at night, which ended with a concert.

As the sun began to return, with only a little twilight at first, preparations were started for the spring and summer sledging journeys. This involved furs, sleeping bags, tents, provision bags, boxes for the stores, handles for the ice-axes and runners for the sledges. In addition, Duncan began to make a cross of English oak in memory of George Vince. The boats were found to have almost sunk through the ice, and the sailors spent much time over several weeks trying to dig them out.

SLEDGING SOUTH, 1902-03

IN HIS NARRATIVE of the expedition, Scott goes into some detail concerning the early sledging journeys made soon after *Discovery*'s arrival in Winter Harbour, partly to show how they learned by their failures, but also because he felt it necessary to point out that sledging is not such an easy matter as might be imagined. Everything at first was wrong; the food, the clothing, the whole system. At least their experience was put to good use, and the general sledging work of the second summer was vastly superior to that of the first. He also described the charm and fascination of sledging, as well as its hardships and trials, distinguishing between the chilly spring journeys and the warmer summer ones.

'Sledging,' he wrote, 'draws men into a closer companionship than can any other mode of life exposing the fraud, but where the true man stands out in all his natural strength. A sure test of a man's character and it daily calls for the highest qualities of which he is possessed. Throughout my sledging experience it has been my lot to observe innumerable instances of self-sacrifice, of devotion to duty and of cheerfulness under adversity.'

On 11 September 1902 Armitage left with Ferrar and four men with a sledge, all on skis, to cross the sea ice to the west to find a way through the mountain range and on to the inland ice. The party's object is occasionally given as the South Magnetic Pole, the aim 60 years earlier of Sir James Clark Ross. Geographical considerations must have caused the modification of this earlier proposal. Royds was to travel southwest to search, unsuccessfully, for another route inland.

Scott, Barne and Shackleton began an abortive southern reconnaissance with two dog teams on 17 September. A fresh departure had to be made on 24 September, with the boatswain, Feather, replacing Barne, whose fingers had been badly frostbitten. A depot marked with a black flag was laid near the end of the Bluff, which Scott described as a long peninsula thrust out into the great ice sheet and which was later named Minna Bluff after Lady Markham. Beyond the Bluff, new country curved sharply westwards. The dogs brought them swiftly home to the comfort of the ship on 3 October 1902, where it was possible to bath, change and creep into bed with-

Dog team on the march with Nigger leading.
The dogs came from Siberia. Nigger was ruler of the pack.
From Scott's *The Voyage of the 'Discovery'*.
(AUTHOR'S COLLECTION)

out the usual accompaniment of ice, and to address their sledging hunger in the midst of plenty.

However, all was not well aboard *Discovery*. Armitage's western reconnaissance party had returned with scurvy, the dreaded deficiency disease of long sea voyages caused by lack of vitamin C. There were also signs of scurvy in other members of the expedition, and Scott was puzzled as to how this had come about. Precautions had been taken but, even so, the evil had come and now had to be banished. Armitage, in consultation with the doctors, took immediate steps by serving out fresh meat regularly and by increasing the allowance of bottled fruits. The cause of the outbreak remained in doubt, but it appeared to Scott and his advisers to have been due to the tinned food. It was known that fresh food would keep the disease at bay, so more sealing parties went out. This enabled Scott to ban tinned food altogether and pronounce

the end of the outbreak of scurvy by 20 October 1902. Wilson noted his own recovery, without recourse to lime juice, which disagreed with him. Fine crops of mustard and cress were grown by Koettlitz in boxes of Antarctic soil.

One of the priorities of the sledging season was to place a record of the expedition's whereabouts in the cylinder at Cape Crozier. Royds, Skelton and their party left to do this on 4 October 1902, the doctors having pronounced them to be in good shape. They returned safe and well on 24 October, having successfully sledged across the ice skirting the southern slopes of Mounts Erebus and Terror on Ross Island to reach the record pole among the Adélie penguins to the north. However, this was not all they had accomplished. They bore the joyful news of a remarkable discovery in the realm of natural history, the breeding place of the Emperor penguin, first seen by Skelton from the tall cliffs at Cape Crozier. Skelton's diary of 12 October 1902 relates how he, Quartley and Wild, equipped with lunch, a half-plate camera, alpine rope, crampons, etc, were trying to find a way down the cliffs to the sea ice, below the slopes of Mount Terror. From the bare rocky cliff they looked down into a bay formed between the junction of the Barrier and the land where the sea ice appeared to have remained fast all winter. In the corner of the bay a large number of Emperor penguins were huddled together in a space not more than 100 yards square. Skelton took photographs of the 250 to 300 birds in sight.

On 18 October the party moved camp to a lower level after being confined for five days during a very fierce blizzard. With the aid of crampons, ice-axes and a climbing rope, Skelton, Quartley and Evans set off to cross the hard hummocky ice ridges and crevasses which lay for some miles between their camp and the ice front. Arriving at the edge of the Barrier, they looked directly down on what they realised immediately was an Emperor penguin rookery, as several dead young birds could be seen. At this spot the ice cliff was only some 25ft high and they were able to find an easy route down to the sea ice, arriving at the rookery in time to stay for most of the afternoon. Skelton

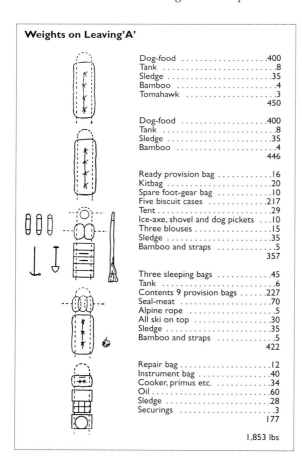

Weights on Leaving 'A'

Dog-food	400
Tank	8
Sledge	35
Bamboo	4
Tomahawk	3
	450
Dog-food	400
Tank	8
Sledge	35
Bamboo	4
	446
Ready provision bag	16
Kitbag	20
Spare foot-gear bag	10
Five biscuit cases	217
Tent	29
Ice-axe, shovel and dog pickets	10
Three blouses	15
Sledge	35
Bamboo and straps	5
	357
Three sleeping bags	45
Tank	6
Contents 9 provision bags	227
Seal-meat	70
Alpine rope	5
All ski on top	30
Sledge	35
Bamboo and straps	5
	422
Repair bag	12
Instrument bag	40
Cooker, primus etc.	34
Oil	60
Sledge	28
Securings	3
	177
	1,853 lbs

Able Seaman James Dell and his team of six dogs born during the first winter in the Antarctic, 1902. From the *Canterbury Times*, 1904.

noted the behaviour of the penguins in some detail and justified Markham's prediction that he would prove an invaluable member of the expedition.

THE SOUTHERN JOURNEY, SUMMER 1902-03

Scott chose Dr Wilson and Lieutenant Shackleton to accompany him on this sledge journey across the Great Ice Barrier, now more prosaically known as the Ross Ice Shelf. They set off on Sunday 2 November 1902, an overcast, cold and windy day, with twenty-three dogs, five sledges and many eager helpers. Wilson wrote in his diary beforehand that it was beyond anyone's experience to leave the ship, which had become a home, and all one's companions except two, for three months in this desolate region, and to walk with a few possessions on a small sledge down into the absolutely unknown south, where, as far as one could see, nothing awaited but an icy desert, all the comforts and home associations of one's cabin, that small sanctuary for happy recollections, being left behind.

Scott used a soft-covered sketchbook as his diary of the southern journey. Its pages confirm his talent for vivid and descriptive writing, although the published narrative has been extended and polished. The weights pulled on leaving the first depot, together with the equipment of the sledges, are shown left.

It was believed that the ice shelf would continue southwards, so snowshoes, crampons and other items useful in rough climbing were omitted. The

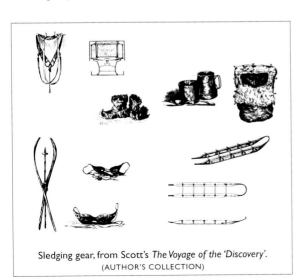

Sledging gear, from Scott's *The Voyage of the 'Discovery'*.

bamboo was to mark depots, and the seal meat was to ensure the party's good health. Despite Scott's earlier prediction, skis were used.

A sledge meter, like a bicycle wheel, made by *Discovery's* engine-room staff, recorded the distances pulled. A prismatic compass was taken but Scott, as navigator, depended upon the compass attached to their small theodolite, which possessed a simple light needle and seemed to give greater accuracy.

The expedition's Siberian sledge dogs, twenty dogs and three bitches, were of three different types and had come to the Antarctic via Archangel, the London Zoo and Lyttelton. By the beginning of the southern journey each could answer to its own new English name. The king dog, named Nigger, was bought in Russia and had worked in a pack of 400 dogs on a previous expedition. A black dog with tawny markings, he had a magnificent head and powerful chest. Gentle and dignified in peace, he could be swift and terrible in war. He chose his place as leader quite naturally, and if placed farther back would behave so unpleasantly to his neighbours that he was quickly moved to the front. It was a delight to see him work. He seemed to know the meaning of every move, and a slow wagging of his tail showed approval. At the evening halt after a long day, Nigger would remain perfectly still, knowing that the tent had to be put up first, while the others clamoured for food. However, when the dog food was distributed it was best to serve Nigger first.

Scott also characterised the other dogs, some of which come alive in his accounts. Lewis, a big, thick-coated brindled dog, was a very powerful but inconsistent puller, noisily affectionate and hopelessly clumsy. Jim was a sleek, lazy, greedy villain, up to all the tricks of the trade. He could pull splendidly when he chose, but preferred often to pretend to pull. Kid and Bismarck were the only two dogs of the team who bore a superficial likeness, both being short-legged with long, fleecy, black-and-white coats. But Bismarck was counted among the lazy 'eye-servers', whereas Kid was indefatigable and stopped only when he died of exhaustion. Wolf was the most hopelessly ill-tempered animal, with no redeeming virtue. Only the whip could control him.

The high land discovered on the southern journey, lying between the Ross Ice Shelf and the high inland ice sheet, was called the Western Mountains. They form part of what are now called the Transantarctic Mountains, linking the Ross and Weddell seas on either side of the continent.

Shackleton later wrote up the trip for a popular magazine. The journey lasted ninety-four days, and for a great part of the time 15 miles a day were covered. A fortnight out from the ship the dogs began to die, so half the sledges had to be hauled five miles, then the three men walked back for the other sledges. Thus only five miles were covered each day. This went on for a month, until they reached as near to the high land as possible, where it was safer to leave a depot of provisions for later retrieval. With the remaining dogs they pushed straight south.

With their dogs dying, they shortened their own food ration to a cold lunch on the march of seven lumps of sugar, a small piece of dry seal meat and a biscuit and a half. To economise on oil, the stove was lit only twice a day. The poor dogs were always looking for a dropped crumb, as their food had gone bad and had to be thrown away. At the end of the day one of the dogs had often to be killed to feed the others.

The aluminium pannikins had to be warmed over the stove to avoid damaging the men's lips. It proved a great trial even to get such small amounts of food as they had into their mouths. They became seriously hungry, and so tired that they had to lift their legs with their hands to get into the tent. They began to dream of food. Shackleton dreamt that jam tarts were flying around him, and Wilson used to dream he was cutting up sandwiches for a school treat. So they went on, all through November, all through December, and on 31 December they reached their farthest south, where they hoisted the British flag.

Besides being leader of the party, Scott was navigator and surveyor, taking sights and rounds of angles to ascertain their own position, also checked by the dead-reckoning of the sledge meter, and that of the mountains and headlands seen to the west. On 25 November he described the joy of passing lat. 80°S, aware that none of their charts showed any details other than a plain white space beyond that parallel. The published version of his diary for 27 November records the sickening work of driving southwards the weary, miserable, ill-nourished dogs.

Two days later they observed a display of mock suns, the most striking atmospheric phenomenon they had yet seen. Shortly after four o'clock they were enveloped in a light, thin stratus cloud of small ice crystals. Above these drifting crystals the sun's rays were reflected in such an extraordinary manner that the whole arch of the heavens was traced with circles and lines of brilliant prismatic or white light. The coloured circles of a double halo were parallel to the horizon, while away from the sun was a white fog bow with two bright mock suns.

On 4 December Scott described beauty in miniature; snow crystals falling on a calm, cool night. Exquisite, shimmering six-pointed feathery stars, quite flat and smooth on either side, floated gently down, resting in all positions, receiving the sun's rays at all angles.

Despite troubles with the dogs, constant gnawing hunger and symptoms of scurvy, the party experienced the excitement of discovering and recording new land each day, as the great chain of the Western Mountains unfolded. Scott had made the course slightly to the east of south rather than due south, to be nearer to the new land at the edge of the ice shelf. One of the most impressive features of this strange and lifeless landscape was the coastline to their right. The coast itself was indented, with its many bays bordered by white snow slopes, glaciers and broken ice-cascades, contrasting with conspicuous black rocky headlands and precipitous uncovered cliffs.

At the end of a fine day Dr Wilson sketched with

Three men in pyramid tent.
A pencil drawing by Edward Wilson.
(SCOTT POLAR RESEARCH INSTITUTE)

astonishing accuracy the great line of the Western Mountains. This caused him to be snowblind at times, making his eyes very painful. One day, after a particularly bad attack, he went blindfold on skis, after which he recounted that he had the strangest daydreams, all suggested by the intense heat of the sun.

Entries in Scott's manuscript diary conclude that their ration of dried fish, advised by the great Norwegian explorer Nansen, which might have putrefied in the tropics, was poisoning the dogs. They also suffered from the heat of the sun, struggling in the soft snow. By 10 December, when Snatcher died from inflammation of the bowel, the party had to face the possibility of losing all of them and failing to attain a high latitude. The animals improved when fed on the remains of their dead comrade, raising Scott's hopes. He thought that many of the difficulties and delays might have been avoided if they had taken seal meat and biscuit. On 14 December they covered a mere two miles, despite strenuous exertions. However, the unfolding of the chain of Western Mountains buoyed up the party's spirits, despite the realisation that land was farther away than had appeared, having been thrown up by a mirage.

Christmas Day saw them coming up to 82°S. Wilson read Holy Communion in his sleeping bag, and his diary that day records the naming of a snow peak abreast of their camp as 'Christmas Height'. Scott described the advance towards the inlet, later named after Shackleton, which was to be their turning point and their furthest south. He began to think that their discovery of 'so much new land and so much new matter for discussion' might earn their trip a corner in polar history, and if so their hard work and harsh experiences would be repaid. His diary entry for 27 December is filled with dramatic descriptions of the highest and most glorious mountain peaks and ridges they had yet seen. At last they had found something fit to honour the 'father of the expedition' in the incredible twin-peaked mountain of some 12,000ft, and Mount Markham it became.

The next day they pitched their farthest camp in glorious weather, which allowed them to take angles and to sketch a breathtaking view of the landscape. To the south they made out a striking cape, beyond which rose a mountain of some 10,000ft, named Mount Longstaff after the expedition's greatest benefactor. Scott concluded that the mountainous country must continue beyond Mount Longstaff for some 50 miles, and that the direction of the coastline for at least a degree of latitude must be S 17°E. A blizzard followed by fog prevented their seeing farther south, and they turned for home between lat. 82° 16'S and 82° 17'S, the dogs being too exhausted to notice the change. Unfortunately, a great chasm in the ice prevented the party from actually reaching the land from the ice shelf, and no specimens of its rock were brought back.

Scott had hoped to reach a more southerly latitude, but the failure of the dogs, who 'left their bones on the great southern plains', made this impossible. He had realised that a number of the weaker dogs would be sacrificed to the stronger, but the Norwegian dried stock-fish contained no vitamins or preservatives. By New Year's Day 1903 the state of the dog team had become pitiable, with only a few able to pull. A sail improvised from the floorcloth of the tent helped the remaining two sledges along when the wind blew from the south. By 7 January the surviving dogs merely walked beside the sledges, and Scott admitted to his moral cowardice in allowing Wilson and Shackleton to do his share in the hateful task of killing all but the last two animals.

On 13 January they picked up depot B and were able to have a really filling and nourishing hooch. A medical examination the following day revealed more symptoms of scurvy, especially in Shackleton, whose throat seemed congested, causing him to cough and occasionally spit blood. Everything now had to be sacrificed, including a closer look at the northern coast, in the efforts to reach the next depot and keep Shackleton on his feet. He was to do little pulling and no camp duties. He wrote afterwards that he broke down and haemorrhaged at depot B. Everything they did not absolutely need was thrown away as the weight of pulling devolved on his two companions. Their care and kindness enabled him to struggle just ahead of the sledges. Scott and Dr Wilson were pulling 270lb each at the start, and were themselves in a weakened state, with signs of scurvy and lack of food. Shackleton declared that no man ever had the good fortune to have better, stronger and more self-denying friends.

Scott decided to retain the heavy instruments but, with great sadness, to sacrifice the last two dogs to lighten the sledges of animal food. Nigger and Jim were taken a short distance from the camp and killed. This was the most heartbreaking scene of all. Through even their most troubled days they had looked forward to getting some of the animals home.

An increase in the ration of seal meat helped slightly to lessen the party's symptoms of scurvy. Over changing snow surfaces they made their way northwards, greeting familiar landmarks such as the plume of Mount Erebus with joy. They reached depot A on 28 January, so ending short rations. Shackleton kept going on skis, but he and his companions were far from well, with scurvy still advancing in rapid strides. The southern journey ended with the home-

Cape Goldie   Mᵗ Longstaff   Cape Lyttleton

Southern sledge party on departure, November 1902;
from left to right are Shackleton, Scott and Wilson. Scott's
broad-brimmed hat was to protect him from the sun.
(ROYAL GEOGRAPHICAL SOCIETY)

'A sledging experience' by Edward Wilson, from *The
South Polar Times* of April 1902. Note the sledge flags.
(AUTHOR'S COLLECTION)

coming to Discovery on 3 February 1903. Wilson's
diary records their arrival at the ship:

> After marching 2 or 3 hours ...we saw the remains of
> our last year's depot, and before we reached it we had the
> greater pleasure of seeing two figures hurrying towards us
> on ski. Just six miles from the ship we met them –
> Skelton and Bernacchi, clean tidy looking people they
> were. And imagine our joy on hearing that the relief ship
> Morning had arrived a week or more before and that all

Section of the panorama drawn by Edward Wilson
of the mountains bordering the Great Ice Barrier entitled
'New Land. Southern sledge journey 28 Dec.1902',
from *Album of Panoramas and Sketches*.
(AUTHOR'S COLLECTION)

> our mails and parcels were waiting for us in our cabins.
> All the news was good about everything, except that there
> were still eight miles of ice floe to go out before we should
> be free to leave our winter quarters.
>
> We camped and had a good lunch and then these two
> pulled our sledges in for us. Our flags of course were
> flying and we had a very gay march in, listening to scraps
> of the world's news, and scraps of our own little world's
> news, the news of the ship...Three miles from the ship,
> we were also met by Sub Lieut Mulock, one of the
> Morning's officers, a very nice young fellow who is to
> join up with us on the Discovery. He is an RN Officer
> of the Survey Department. Next we were met by Koettlitz,
> Royds and all the rest, and a crowd of men. It was a great

Mt Christchurch

homecoming, and as we turned Cape Armitage we saw the ship decorated from top to toe with flags and all the ship's company up the rigging round the gangway ready to cheer us, which they did most lustily as we came on board...A lot of photographs were taken...and I began to realise then how filthy we were, with long sooty hair, black greasy clothes, faces and noses all peeling and sore, lips all raw, everything either sunburnt or bleached, even our sledges and the harness and our faces the colour of brown boots except where the lamp soot made them black.

Then came time for a bath, and clothes came off that had been on since November the second of the year before, and then a huge dinner. Captain Colbeck, Engineer Morrison, Lieuts Doorly and Mulock were all there and a long and tiring evening followed. But instead of drink and noise and songs and strangers, I was longing to lie down on my bunk and have a long quiet yarn with Charles Royds. I was in no hurry at all to spring at my letters, for I felt an absolute confidence that everything was well with all that I cared for most at home. ...Such was our homecoming after an absence of over thirteen weeks.

Scott described the joy of rounding the Cape, of seeing 'our beloved ship' which was still held in her icy prison, but trim and neat. She was fully prepared to face again the open seas, and her freshly painted side glistened in the sunlight.

Gerald Doorly, an officer of the relief expedition in the *Morning*, was present at the welcome-home feast and slept afterwards on board *Discovery*. He described how the southern party's hunger remained unappeased, despite the banquet. Shackleton and Wilson enjoyed the feast in their cabins. Afterwards, Scott kept

them surreptitiously supplied with more food from the pantry. Doorly relates that he had not been asleep for more than an hour when he heard Scott rousing Shackleton, whose cabin was next door: 'Shackles,' I heard him call, 'how would you fancy some sardines on toast?' This testimony is interesting, as it would tend to rule out the idea of any estrangement between Scott and Shackleton during the journey. The last entry in Scott's sledging diary, on 9 February 1903, six days after their return, recorded that all three were recovering from the strain. He ended by saying that their return was none too soon. In conclusion, he wrote:

And so our southern sledge journey came to an end on February 3 1903, when for ninety-three days we had plodded with ever-varying fortune over a vast snowfield and slept beneath the fluttering canvas of a tent. During that time, we had covered 960 statute miles, with a combination of success and failure in our objects, which I have endeavoured to set forth in these pages. If we had not achieved such great results as at one time we had hoped for, we knew at least that we had striven and endured with all our might.

This modest appraisal cloaks the achievements of Scott, Shackleton and Wilson. They had, in fact, made the first extended journey into the interior of the unknown southern continent, not merely making a bee-line towards the Pole, but altering their course so as to approach the coastline and the Western Mountains, thus enabling these to be surveyed and sketched. The recovery of geological specimens had to be left to later comers, since a great chasm blocked the way from the ice shelf to the coast. All in all, and considering the state of dietary knowledge and their lack of previous experience, it was an effort of which they could be proud.

Mounts Longstaff and Markham, named after Llewellyn Longstaff, the expedition's chief benefactor and Sir Clements Markham, its 'father and most constant friend' (Scott), from the *Album of Panoramas and sketches*.

Mt Markham

Shackleton Inlet

During the absence of the southern party, much had been going on. The most remarkable achievement was the fine pioneering sledge journey by Armitage, Skelton and party through the mountains west of the *Discovery* and on to the Antarctic ice sheet, to an altitude of nearly 9,000ft, by way of a glacier later named after the geologist, HT Ferrar. Rock specimens and photographs taken in this region gave evidence of the geology of the continent. Armitage recounted the journey in his book *Two Years in the Antarctic*, and it was summarised and praised by Scott in his narrative. Scott improved upon their route, going farther west during the next sledging season, penetrating a long way into the interior over the high plateau of ice beyond the mountain range.

Discovery had been made ready for sea, no mean task, and the boats had been recovered from their icy prisons after a great struggle. Shorter journeys to investigate Ross Island and the region adjoining winter quarters had been made in the Captain's absence by Koettlitz, Ferrar, Hodgson and Bernacchi. Royds, who was in charge of the ship, made another visit to Cape Crozier, where he was disappointed and surprised to find that the young Emperor penguins were no longer there. However, the Adélie penguins were back for the summer and were busy nesting. Royds's party gathered enough eggs for those on board *Discovery*, and brought back one very special egg, an Emperor penguin's, found by Blissett, half-buried in the snow. Royds's diary recorded these remarkable discoveries on 8 November 1902, and concluded that the young penguins had all headed for the sea. Five skuas were seen busily eating their fill among thirty dead penguins on view, and a walk along the edge of the new ice to the cliffs put some twenty Emperor penguins on the run. Bull seals were lying all along the crack against the cliffs.

A sports day had been held on 8 November 1902, in honour of King Edward VII's birthday. The programme stated that prices of admission to the floe football ground would be:

Members of the Antarctic Athletic Club, Free;
To Public. One Emperor Penguin's Egg
Children not admitted at any price

The general arrangements made by C R Ford, Hon Secretary, included: 'starts by watch and flag to be made by Lieut Armitage, with the Committee of Messrs Cross, Quartley, Whitfield and Wild on hand to assist, and cooling drinks to be supplied at the Ice-foot during the day free to members of the Antarctic Athletic Club, on presentation of their membership cards.'

The day proved a fine one. *Discovery* was dressed with flags and a great silken Union Jack was hoisted at Hut Point, the first time they had hoisted their colours in the Antarctic. The competitions comprised toboggan races, sledge-pulling, putting the weight, tug-of-war, ski-running and rifle-shooting. Skelton, Walker and Duncan came first, second and third in the exciting ski-running competition, and Duncan was awarded a delightful watercolour by Edward Wilson of the *Discovery* in winter quarters. The day concluded with a show of lantern slides by Koettlitz, Hodgson and Skelton, followed by songs by many of the others. Prizes won in the sports were distributed by 'Her Royal Highness, Princess Lobodon Carcinophagus, attended by Lord Hyperoodon Planifrons and Countess Pagodroma Nivea, prominent members of the local nobility'. A special treat afterwards at supper was sandwiches filled with mustard and cress grown by Dr Koettlitz in the wardroom skylight.

Cape Wilson

CHAPTER 6

The Relief Expedition of the Morning, 1902-03

IN LONDON the indefatigable Sir Clements Markham had set about the wearisome task of writing to the well-heeled to subscribe to the relief ship. Initially, there was little interest from benefactors or government until the King and the Prince of Wales, later King George V, expressed support, and soon £22,000 was collected, which included £5,000 each from Mr Longstaff and Mr Edgar Speyer.

It had been suggested to Sir Clements that a relief ship might be found among the Navy's obsolete gunboats, but after a report from his cousin, Admiral Markham, on the poor shape of those at the Admiralty, he resolved to buy the small wooden 31-year-old whaler *Morgen*, considered the strongest steamer in the Norwegian whaling fleet. The available Scottish whalers had been dismissed earlier as unsuitable and expensive.

With his old friend Captain Bonnevie of Lerwick, a good seaman and surveyor for Veritas, the Norwegian equivalent of Lloyd's, Markham visited Tønsberg, the whaling port on the Oslofjord, on 18 September 1901. They were accompanied by Mr

William Colbeck, RNR, chief officer of the *Montebello*, from the Wilson Line. The price of the *Morgen* was £3,880. Examination confirmed the strength and soundness of the vessel. Her engines were old fashioned but extraordinarily strong and satisfactory, likewise the boilers. A new iron boiler bed was required. A special meeting of the Council of the RGS on 2 October 1901 resolved that the Society should buy the ship, with the president as managing owner. Fearing delay, Markham accepted the price on his own responsibility and the Relief Ship Committee approved the purchase on 24 October 1901.

The *Morgen* was brought to Sheerness by a Norwegian crew, having been repainted black with her new English name, *Morning*, in white. On 4 January 1902 she was towed up-river to be refitted by Messrs Green of Blackwall, and became classed as a yacht in March 1902, through Markham's election as Honorary Member of the Royal Corinthian Yacht Club, whose Commodore presented the ship with two ensigns and five burgees. The vessel's dimensions were given as length 140ft, breadth 31ft 4in, depth 16ft 6in, and the registered tonnage was 297. The whale oil tanks were taken out and sold, and *Morning* was refitted with a large store room, a wardroom with six side cabins, a galley, a petty officers' mess with eight bunks, a sick bay and a chart room. She was given new fore- and mainmasts, bow sheathing, a spare rudder and propeller, the new boiler bed, and new shaft pumps and ballast tanks – these at Longstaff's special request and expense.

At a meeting of the Relief Ship Committee on 20 November 1901, Captain William Colbeck was proposed as commander of the relief expedition. He had been a member of the *Southern Cross* expedition, specialising in magnetism, had an Extra Master's Certifi-

Sawing the piano into pieces small enough to go below. Sketch in pen and ink from Gerald Doorly, *The Voyages of the 'Morning'*.
(AUTHOR'S COLLECTION)

ABOVE: Captain William Colbeck and officers of the *Morning*.
(AUTHOR'S COLLECTION)

LEFT: The *Discovery* ice bound in winter quarters. (frontispiece to *The South Polar Times*, Vol II 1907)
(AUTHOR'S COLLECTION)

cate and was also a sub-lieutenant in the RNR. Captain Pepper, of the Wilson Line, Hull, recommended him highly as a thorough seaman, a first-class scientific and practical navigator, a good disciplinarian and a born leader of men, imparting enthusiasm and respect. Colbeck accepted the appointment on 30 December 1901 and took charge of the ship on 10 February 1902.

The Admiralty allowed two naval officers to volunteer. These were Sub-Lieutenant G F A Mulock, RN, Fourth Officer, and Lieutenant E R G Evans, RN, later to find fame as Evans of the *Broke*. Mr R G England was Chief Officer, Dr G A Davidson the Surgeon, and Mr J D Morrison Chief Engineer. There were two midshipmen and a ship's company of twenty-nine.

The third officer, Mr Gerald Doorly, RNR, who wrote a book in 1916 about *Morning*'s Antarctic voyages, described her as 'ridiculously insignificant' after the splendid P & O liners in which he had been serving. She departed East India Docks on 9 July 1902, amid a 'bravery of bunting', ringing cheers and whistles of good luck. A last-minute item in her equipment was a piano, presented by Markham at Evans's request.

The tale of the difficulties and perse-

Morning in the ice.
(AUTHOR'S COLLECTION)

verence of the brave little *Morning* was not told in print by Captain Colbeck, but his letters remedy this to some extent. Dressed over all, *Morning* departed from Lyttelton on 6 December 1902, with bands playing amid cheering crowds and steamers firing off volleys of signal rockets. Colbeck's hopes of eating a Christmas dinner with Scott and his crew were ruled out by the contrary winds and bad weather experienced right down to the edge of the pack ice. They were very deep laden, with carcasses of mutton in the foretopmast rigging. On 13 December they lost a whaleboat, and on 22 December the first iceberg was sighted. *Morning* struck out on a new track east of all previous vessels in 178°–180°E. Colbeck was justified in this venture by being able to continue further south in open water.

He enjoyed a very special present on Christmas Day; the discovery of two unknown islands in lat. 67° 24'.50"S long. 179° 55'.50"W, one of which was later named after Captain Scott. A landing was effected with difficulty and specimens obtained of the many thousands of birds nesting on the north side, chiefly petrels. Colbeck felt his islands had nothing very special about them, but a sketch survey was made of their coasts.

From Christmas Eve, while navigating through the ice, until they reached *Discovery*, Colbeck lay down 'all standing' (ie without undressing), so as to be always on call. There was little rest for the captain.

Bad or foggy weather sometimes resulted in his being called on deck fifty times a day as the man at the helm tried to clear an iceberg or heavy piece of ice. On 28 December *Morning* hit an iceberg and lost her bobstay. However, when a boat was sent out to examine the bow plates, everything was found to be sound. A strong appearance of land was observed to the east, which was in fact King Edward VII Land, sighted by *Discovery* during her outward voyage.

On one fine day 55 miles were made through the pack to the southwest, but in thick foggy weather through close pack only 15 or 18 miles were covered, as it was necessary almost to feel the way from floe to floe and then accelerate at full speed to avoid an iceberg or escape a cul-de-sac.

Later, Colbeck grew wiser and stopped for clear weather once a fog came down. During the first week of 1903 a strong east-southeast gale and blizzard gave them many nasty knocks, but *Morning* 'took them like a brick and came up smiling'. On 8 January 1903 they landed at Cape Adare, where Borchgrevink and his *Southern Cross* party, Colbeck among them, had wintered in 1899, and picked up the record left by *Discovery*. The little *Morning* had penetrated the pack earlier than any of her predecessors, and beat *Discovery* by more than 42 hours. Proceeding south, they found no records of the main party, but left their own on Possession and Franklin islands.

On 18 January 1903 Colbeck and a small party

'Hut Point, McMurdo Sound, April 7, '11', by Edward Wilson. This watercolour was painted during Captain Scott's Last Expedition in *Terra Nova*, 1910-13, during which Wilson died. (SCOTT POLAR RESEARCH INSTITUTE)

landed on Cape Crozier, where Dr Davidson spotted the post erected by Scott's people. Colbeck wrote to his fiancée, Edith, of his relief on learning that *Discovery* was wintering in 'McMurdo Bay' in 77° 50'S. Heavy ice and contrary current caused *Morning* to make only slow progress towards Hut Point. They found open water off Cape Bird in the early evening of 23 January, and were able to proceed until the masts of *Discovery* were sighted just before midnight, at which time in these latitudes it is still daylight. They fired off rockets and dressed ship, and everyone on board was at the highest pitch of excitement. However, *Morning* was stopped in her tracks by a field of fast ice extending unbroken over ten solid miles to *Discovery*. Even so, a figure on Hut Point was seen waving arms in windmill fashion before bolting back to the ship to spread the news.

Colbeck learned later that Armitage, in command during Scott's absence in the south, had resolved not to lose his night's sleep and breakfast, though he was prepared to be called if *Morning* came alongside. Bernacchi wanted to start off straight away over the ice for his letters, and several of them were much annoyed by Armitage's indifference. However, a jolly evening, with singing after dinner, took place the following day aboard *Morning*, finishing about midight

with everyone finding a soft plank to sleep on. On the following morning, 26 January, Skelton, Bernacchi and Hodgson left with a sledge laden with letters and parcels, meat and vegetables. Colbeck tried in vain to persuade Armitage to start cutting and blasting the ice to complement *Morning's* efforts, but Armitage was confident the ice would go out, and he was acting commander of the expedition until Scott's return. Scott, Wilson and Shackleton arrived back on board *Discovery* on 3 February, just as Colbeck was preparing a scheme to release her from the ice, but everyone was too excited to do anything but talk about the farthest-south journey of the three men, and Scott was busy with his letters. After joining in the celebrations, Colbeck returned to his ship. A week later, on 10 February, Colbeck trudged back over to *Discovery*, getting caught in a gale en route. After a discussion with Scott, it was decided to transfer stores from the relief ship as quickly as possible, to enable *Morning* to depart at the end of the month. Then, if the ice broke up, *Discovery* could follow, and if not they would be prepared for another season. From 12 to

23 February the stores were sledged over the ice from *Morning* to *Discovery*. Then *Morning* went alongside a glacier snout and discharged 20 tons of coal for *Discovery* to pick up on her release from the ice. *Morning* also watered ship from the glacier.

Ten officers and twenty-two men from *Discovery* walked over to *Morning* to see her off. A dinner party on the eve of departure was held in the small wardroom, seventeen sitting down at table. The next day, 2 March, Colbeck noted that everyone's spirits were very low. At 1.30pm the sledges were loaded for the return journey to the still-imprisoned *Discovery*, and at 2pm the last of the party went over the bows, having said their adieus. *Morning* weighed anchor and backed astern, and, as she turned round, cheer after cheer broke out from both ships.

Morning departed carrying a number of men discharged by Captain Scott. The most senior of these was Shackleton, replaced by Sub-Lieutenant Mulock, RN, who was to do some good work as surveyor and map-maker to the expedition. Shackleton had been a zealous, talented, cheerful and lively officer, and his departure, much against his will, was greatly regretted by his comrades. Scott reported:

> This gentleman has performed his work in a highly satisfactory manner but unfortunately his constitution has proved unequal to the rigours of a polar climate. It is with great reluctance that I order his return and trust that it will be evident that I do so solely on account of his health and that his future prospects may not suffer.

It has been claimed that Scott used *Morning*'s departure to send home the men of the merchant service so as to make *Discovery* virtually a naval vessel. Three naval men were discharged, Macfarlane for

Captain Colbeck reading the record deposited at Cape Crozier, Ross Island by a party from *Discovery*. Lieutenant G F A Mulock, RN is on the right.
(From Gerald Doorly, *The Voyages of the 'Morning'*.)
(AUTHOR'S COLLECTION)

reasons of health, and Scott recommended his return to HM service 'under ordinary conditions'. Even though they had worked reasonably well and had earned their bonuses, Scott felt unable to recommend merchant seamen Duncan and Walker, describing them as 'of no exceptional use and a source of disturbance on the mess deck'. Young Clarence Hare, the domestic, who had worked well and had so miraculously survived a period of lengthy exposure early in the expedition, was allowed to return home to New Zealand at his own request. Herbert, Buckridge and the troublesome and unpopular cook, Brett, were not recommended for a bonus.

Scott wrote to Admiral Markham, explaining that he had found it a mistake to mix the merchant and naval services. Although both excellent in their different ways, they had never pulled together and he was sending most of the merchantmen back in addition to one or two naval men. He had given them all a chance of going. The men remaining he felt to be the best.

Scott's published diary must have caused some pain to the eight volunteers who left, when he declared the list to be precisely those he would have wished to go. Also hurtful was their omission from the list of expedition members, only Shackleton being included.

Captain Colbeck felt keenly the poignancy of *Morning*'s departure. When he wrote a few days later of the forlorn and wretched little group left behind to face another Antarctic winter, recalling them standing on the ice five miles away from their ship, and his last view of them, dragging two heavily laden sledges, he was concerned that all of the men had suffered scurvy, some worse than others. Scott had wisely, he thought, said very little about the disease in his reports. *Morning* had spared all the fruits and vegetables possible, a risky gesture, since they were left with only six months' tinned provisions and would themselves at one point be in danger of having to winter in the pack off Beaufort Island.

Scott had given the commander of the relief expedition all his official reports, unsealed so that Colbeck could read them on the way north. Colbeck wrote to

LEFT: Shackleton aboard the *Morning* on arrival in Lyttelton, New Zealand, March 1903, having been invalided home. Taken from Gerald Doorly. *The Voyages of the 'Morning'.* (AUTHOR'S COLLECTION)

BELOW: Departure of the *Morning*, 2 March 1903, from the *South Polar Times* (AUTHOR'S COLLECTION)

his fiancée that they had done *very, very well indeed* and accomplished far more than was ever expected of them. Of Colbeck's own work, Scott had written to Markham praising his outstanding efforts to further the interests of all and in hastening the despatch of stores.

Morning found some difficulty in navigating through young ice, which was rafting halfway up her side. Fortunately, a following gale from the southwest encouraged them to set all sail and start the engines full speed ahead, and after a few minutes of very anxious watching they began to forge ahead. The masts, which had been bending like wil-

lows before the gale, straightened their backs and the ship gathered way and went through acre after acre of stubborn sea ice. They were in the pack until 4 March and at last, on feeling the ship rise and fall to a good easterly swell, it seemed that the worst was over. The days shortened rapidly as they worked carefully further north, keeping a sharp look-out for icebergs, the last of which was sighted north of 63°S. They reached Lyttelton on 25 March 1903, bearing the startling news of *Discovery*'s detention in the ice, and an account of the expedition's achievements.

SCOTT'S WESTERN JOURNEY, 1903

B Y 13 March 1903 Scott had given up hope of the ice going out, and the expedition began to settle down for another winter in the south. Having resolved to stick to a diet of fresh meat, a good food supply was built up which Scott calculated would last for 275 days for the 37 on board:

116 seals to last for about 230 days
551 skua gulls for about 25 days
20 sheep for about 20 days.

THE SECOND WINTER IN ANTARCTICA, 1903

Orders were given next day for the ship to be prepared for the winter. All their care and trouble in getting ready for the sea voyage had been wasted. The boilers had to be run down again, the engines pulled to pieces, ropes unrove and coiled away and the winter awning, already in a very dilapidated state, prepared. The boats in the way of the awning were placed on the shore this time, rather than on the sea ice. Hodgson carried on collecting specimens in his fish traps under the ice and Barne his soundings and temperature observations. Hockey was played with gusto until darkness fell at the beginning of the winter nights. Bernacchi succeeded Shackleton as editor of the *South Polar Times*, for which Wilson continued his illustrations.

Scott found Sub-Lieutenant Mulock a great acquisition, possessing extraordinary natural abilities for the work. Trained as a surveyor, he was given a special table in the captain's day cabin during the winter. He first collected and reworked all the observations, and later constructed temporary charts, enabling Scott to see more clearly where efforts should be directed during the coming sledging season.

Discovery in winter quarters, 1903, depicted here by Edward Wilson disappearing in a blizzard of drifting snow.
(SCOTT POLAR RESEARCH INSTITUTE)

An album of Mulock's charts was published by the RGS after the expedition's return, with an accompanying pamphlet, also by Mulock. Of great interest was his conclusion that *Discovery* had proved that the 'Parry Mountains', sighted by Sir James Clark Ross on 28 January 1841, did not exist. Mulock believed these to have been the summits of Minna Bluff, White Island and Black Island, which *Discovery* also sighted, on 23 January 1902, to the south over the Barrier surface, when they were just to the east of Ross Island. Mulock's new Chart of the Barrier, taking in the whole length from Cape Crozier to new found King Edward VII Land, showed that the ice front had receded some 15 to 20 miles south since Ross's voyage of sixty years earlier. Wilson concluded that they seemed at last to have probed the mystery of the Great Barrier to some purpose, and that the next summer's sledging should help to unravel the question further.

Wilson provided a detailed account of the routine of their second Antarctic winter in *Discovery*. His work was indoors, drawing, reading or writing, with an hour or more in the fresh air, morning or afternoon. By the end of June he had completed the last of a number of long sheets of the southern sledge journey, later reproduced in the expedition results. Meanwhile, Scott's thoughts were on the next season's sledging, and by early July the various journeys were more or less decided. Wilson's summary of the plans, dated 1 July 1903, stated that all sledging, other than his own journey to Cape Crozier, would be over by 15 December, after which every man and officer would be put on to the ice saws, working in sets night and day. Various short journeys would be made, chiefly depot parties, in October and November, and two main parties in November and December. Barne was to take Mulock and seven men to the southwest and explore the straits they had seen the year before. The captain with Skelton, Ferrar and seven men would go west, through the mountains to the inland ice. Royds was to join Wilson on one of three trips to Cape Crozier, but from summer to mid-December, would carry out ship's work and meteorology. Koettlitz would be making a couple of short trips.

Armitage stayed in charge of the ship and the sawing camp, a sore disappointment to him, for he had set his heart on sledging over the Barrier to the south. Wilson felt that Scott had quite rightly refused Armitage's request to try to get farther south than the previous year, without dogs.

Their 'second long polar night' which had passed quietly and pleasantly ended on 21 August 1903, when the sun's rim could just be seen above the northern horizon. 'I climbed Arrival Heights and got a view of the golden half-disc,' wrote Scott. He was much cheered by the sight of the sun's

'Camping Time' from a pen and ink sketch by Edward Wilson reproduced in Albert Armitage, *Two Years in the Antarctic.*
(AUTHOR'S COLLECTION)

rays, gilding their surrounding hills. Preparations for the coming sledging season entailed repairing almost all of their gear. On one day, Wilson wrote, the wardroom became a mountain of finnesko and sennegraes, for selection of the soft Lapp footwear for sledging. Two days later he inspected the provisions for his Cape Crozier journey and reported that the food for each journey was prepared, weighed out and packed in linen bags and labelled. For a journey of three weeks a weekly bag was prepared, containing smaller bags of pemmican, oatmeal, peameal, cocoa, chocolate, red ration, sugar, milk, tinned milk frozen and cut up into small cubes, pepper, salt, onion powder and a tin of tea.

SLEDGING JOURNEYS, 1903

Two main supported parties were planned towards the west and southwest. The captain's western party aimed to study the geology of what was later called the Ferrar Glacier and to explore the inland ice sheet that Armitage had attained the previous year. The second supported party, led by Barne and Mulock, was to examine one of the extraordinary straits, some 20 to 30 miles distant, which had seemed, to the previous year's southern party, to run through the mountain ranges without rising in level. A third unsupported party led by Royds and Bernacchi was to sledge across the ice shelf in a southeasterly direction to see whether the Barrier surface continued on a level to the eastward. Some visits were to be made to the Emperor penguin rookery, to observe the habits of these extraordinary creatures from the beginning of their breeding season.

The day before the start of the new sledging season with the departure of Wilson and Royds to Cape Crozier on 7 September 1903, *Discovery* was filled with laughter and excitement, with men flying to and fro, packing sledges, weighing loads and making detailed inspections. There had been no sign of scurvy in the ship during the winter, and Scott likened the scene to boys escaping from school.

Scott's own depot-laying party left on 9 September for the lower reaches of the New Harbour, later Ferrar, Glacier. From there they found a route on the glacier's northern and smoother side, where there is less melting in summer, and which seemed likely to cut down the time to reach Cathedral Rocks, the site of their depot, from three weeks (over the hills) to a few days. Each night temperatures dropped to the minus fifties Fahrenheit, and the party marched home across the 50 miles of frozen sea to their snug ship in record time. Barne's depot-laying party to White Island met even severer temperatures, well below minus 67.7°F, at which the thermometer broke. Joyce's frost-bitten foot was saved by the officers taking it in turns to nurse it in their breasts, much to the hilarity of all.

Wilson's visit to the Emperor penguin rookery at Cape Crozier was his first. The party had set out as soon as the sun had returned, to try to observe the penguins incubating their eggs. Crampons allowed them to reach the fast bay ice, streaked and splashed with droppings from the breeding birds. A large group of them had been frightened away by the fall of a portion of the Barrier, and the party picked up sixteen deserted eggs, half of them unbroken. The main colony of about a thousand birds was standing under the ice cliff nearby. Wilson was surprised to find parents already nursing chicks, apparently as old as those brought home five weeks later the year before. He concluded that the eggs must have been laid and the chicks hatched in the depths of an Antarctic winter, in temperatures as low as the minus sixties Fahrenheit. The extraordinary life cycle of the Emperor penguin was not confirmed until Wilson, Cherry-Garrard and Bowers made their famous winter journey to the rookery during Scott's *Terra Nova* expedition of 1910-13.

The party had a tricky climb back to camp, unable to see the icy ridges they were crossing, other than what was just underfoot. Royds led with the ice axe, carrying nothing. Wilson carried a satchel containing the eight unbroken eggs, each as big as a swan's, and in his shirt he had about fifteen frozen Emperor chicks. Cross followed with a net bag of cracked eggs

CHRISTMAS MORNING NEAR THE SOUTH POLE.

["The good ship *Discovery* has been icebound near the South Pole so long that the natives are already learning to imitate the sailors in their sports and games."]

Christmas morning near the South Pole, from *Punch* 23 December 1903.
(AUTHOR'S COLLECTION).

and chicks, and a ski pole. This strange little procession of three reached camp safely, to be joined later by Whitfield, Williamson and Blissett, who had been to the deserted Adélie penguin rookery to look for specimens of dead chicks. The whole party started for home the next day with their valuable cargo. With temperatures in the minus sixties at night, camping became immensely uncomfortable, but the men's jokes and humbug made light of all the difficulties. Their clothes, wet all night and frozen all day, became so board-like that buttons were impossible to do up or undo. Their wet and frozen Burberry suits of overalls, worn from head to heel, crackled with every movement like suits of armour, and to hear their neighbour speak they had to stand rigidly still. After three painful nights in the tents they returned to the ship, with flags flying. Both Wilson and Royds greatly relished the roaring fire in the wardroom and a full feed of hot buttered toast and tea.

Wilson spent some time on his return painting and cataloguing his specimens, blowing the eggs and feeding the surviving chick, which was wayward, obstinate and vicious, losing his temper and grizzling in the most human fashion. He had Wilson out of bed twice every night, demanding chewed seal meat, and insisted on feeds every four hours during the day. The chick enjoyed looking at the candle, and struggled and chirruped in his box if put to bed early. His portly body was covered with the softest silky grey down, and his head was like black and white velvet in beautiful contrast.

In October 1903, the anniversary of Skelton's visit, Wilson made a second journey to Cape Crozier and found the chicks bigger but still in down. He took with him a record of proceedings to fix to the post at

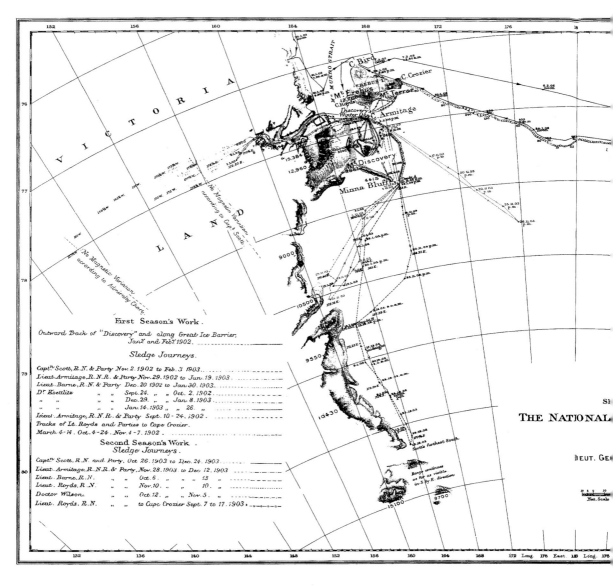

the Adélie penguin rookery, where the birds were just beginning to return after the winter to nest, but a week later not one egg had been laid. All around the disappointed egg-seekers, the Adélies waggled their flippers and stood bolt upright with their heads in the air, chortling to themselves. The birds knew they had sold the intruders a pup, and that after their departure the ground would be, literally, covered in eggs.

Scott's western journey, the great bonus to the expedition in its unexpected second year in the Antarctic, was the most significant one made in the

southern spring of 1903. He had been somewhat diffident about the achievements of the southern journey during the previous sledging season, but was to confess to some pride over the obstacles overcome, in the severest climate, on the western journey.

Armitage and his party had earlier sledged a short distance west over the inland ice sheet of Victoria Land. They had seemed to be on a lofty plateau, and their geological samples revealed the likelihood of there being sedimentary deposits. It took later expeditions, in which Discovery played her part, to

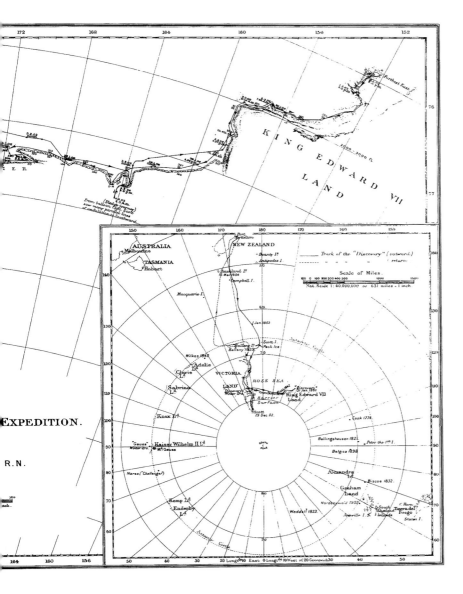

Map showing the work of the National Antarctic Expedition, 1902-04. From a drawing by Lieutenant George F A Mulock, RN in the *Geographical Journal*, 1904.

show that Antarctica is indeed a great continent, not a number of smaller land masses, overlain by ice which covers all but one per cent of the underlying rock to a depth of 8,000ft. In the absence of the eminent Professor J W Gregory, who had resigned as chief of the scientific staff, it fell to the young Cambridge graduate, Hartley Ferrar, to examine the 600 square miles of new territory in the region of the valley glacier that now bears his name.

A party of twelve left *Discovery* on 12 October 1903. First came Scott's carefully selected advance party, consisting of Scott, Skelton, Feather, Evans, Lashly and Handsley, then Ferrar's party of three and, third, the supporting party of three led by Dailey, the carpenter. The original plan for all twelve to ascend the inland ice sheet via the Ferrar Glacier had to be abandoned when it was discovered, on 18 October, at a height of 6,000ft near the Solitary Rocks, that only one of the four sledges was sound. The runners of the others, made of German silver, were split to ribbons and the wood underneath was deeply scored.

Scott found this mountainous region intriguing

and of great beauty. Camped one night on the south side of the valley, with the high sunlit pinnacles 3,000 or 4,000ft above their heads, (so aptly named the Cathedral Rocks by Armitage) and the reddish brown hills rising abruptly on the other side, Scott found it hard to imagine he was in a polar region.

Their camp on the evening of 16 October was in the medial moraine, a long line of scattered boulders, varied in shape and colour, which wound in graceful curves over the blue surface of the glacier towards the distant, pearl-grey, ice-covered sea. Looking upwards, toward the west, the formidable highway of boulders had in its centre an immense cascade of gleaming white waves, which they would need to circumvent the next day. Scott described the upper valley as their most beautiful view, with dark cliffs formed in a broad V framing the cascading glacier. Above it the distant solitary peak of Knob Head Mountain

rose beneath a patch of crimson sky.

By the following evening they were encamped in a great ice basin, looking down on the gorge by which they had entered. They could see the white slopes of Mount Lister and an ice-free summit 11,000ft above them. A feast of autumn tints from brown, red grey and yellow of the bare hillsides surrounded their camp. The horizontal layers of the hills proved of great interest to the geologist.

It was from the camp at the Solitary Rocks that the party was forced to return to the ship. The sound sledge was left with spare food and the party almost flew back to the ship, covering 87 miles in three days, another record march. From various broken sledges at winter quarters the carpenter was able to produce two sound ones, an eleven-footer for the plateau party and a seven-footer for Ferrar's geological party. On 26 October a reduced party of nine started westwards once more.

They were back at their depot above the Vale of Winds on 1 November 1903. The lid of the instrument box left there had blown open in a

gale; Skelton's goggles had disappeared and Scott found to his horror that his *Hints to Travellers* was gone. This was a serious matter, since he was depending on the data in that RGS publication to work out his sights and fix the party's position with accuracy on the polar plateau, when beyond the mountains. Determined not to return to the ship a second time, Scott consulted his companions, who agreed to risk pushing on without knowing precisely where they were or how to get back.

Using crampons made by Skelton, and benefiting from the skill of Lashly and Skelton in repairing the sledge runners, the party passed gradually from the hard, abrasive ice to snow and then, against a bitter headwind and driving snow on 2 and 3 November 1903, on to ice again in the upper reaches of the glacier. By the evening of 3 November they had reached 7,000ft where, in Scott's words, 'the masses of dark, bare rock were becoming detached and isolated, whilst the widening snowfields were creeping upward with ever-increasing

threat to engulf all between their wide mantle'. Despite being laid up in their tents at 'Desolation Camp' for a week of continual blizzards between 4 and 11 November, the party reached 8,900ft above sea level on 13 November, reaching the head of the glacier with nearly five weeks' provisions in hand. To the southeast, Mount Lister and the higher peaks of the Royal Society Range enabled Scott on a clear day to fix their latitude by bearings and to note features that would act as signposts on their return to the glacier. Scott also improvised a method of determining the daily change in the sun's declination to allow him to find the party's latitude with reasonable accuracy when out of sight of land. Ferrar, Kennar and Weller, the geological party, had separated from the plateau party on 11 November 1903, leaving Scott, Skelton, Feather, Evans, Lashly and Handsley to push on westward, facing a bitter wind at high altitude, across what Scott called the vast and lifeless plateau.

On 22 November he reluctantly resolved to divide the party, sending back Skelton with Handsley and Feather, who was later to have the mountain at the head of

Christmas camp among the ice-borne boulders, 1902, during Armitage's western journey, from Scott's *The Voyage of the 'Discovery'*.
(AUTHOR'S COLLECTION)

the glacier named after him. Through sheer incapacity they were unable to pull as hard as Evans, Lashly and Scott himself. These three were able to press on at a faster pace still farther to the west. The temperature fell each night to the -40°F, while during the day it hardly rose above -25°F, with a constant wind which cracked and cut their faces and hands. Taking observations with a theodolite was a punishing task, and even jokes in the tent were discouraged, since laughing had become very painful. The plateau rose and fell, its surface varying from smooth on the summits and eastern faces to heavy, sharp *sastrugi* (snow waves) in the hollows and on western faces. The sledge capsized often, causing a small loss of precious cooking oil each time.

Although Scott considered these three weeks of sledge-pulling the toughest physical exercise of his life, he looked back on the period with great satisfaction. His two chosen companions, Evans and Lashly, had immense strength. Evans had been a gym instructor in the navy and was an easy winner in any test of physical strength. He was chosen again by Scott to travel over this same inland ice sheet south to the Pole some ten years later, during the *Terra Nova* expedition of 1910-13, and was to die during the tragic return. Lashly, who also sailed again with Scott, was of average height only but weighed 13st 8lb and had the largest chest measurement in the ship.

Commenting on Scott's remark that sailors were best able to cope with the troubles and tricks of sledging life, Commander Ellis, the editor of Lashly's diaries, compares Scott's experience with that of Nansen in 1895 in the north. Nansen, a scientist, found his sailor companion, Johansen, unable to give him any sort of intellectual companionship, and Ellis reckoned that Scott would not have chosen Lashly and Evans only for their practical value. In his accounts of their journey Scott always uses *we*, never *I*. They even shared a three-man sleeping bag, and a very real bond of affection and loyalty existed between them.

On 30 November they thankfully finished the westward march in long. 146° 33'E. Travelling up the last slope, Scott hoped against hope to find a different view, but all they saw was a further expanse

of their desolate and terrible plateau, where they reached the end of their tether. But, inside the tent, his companions were cheerful and busy, with jokes and singing. They wondered at supper whether future explorers would travel further over this inhospitable country. Far beyond the reach of human help, the little party in their threadbare tent had the great ice sheet to themselves. They were not to know that men would one day explore Antarctica from the air, and that even under-ice topography would be ascertained by instruments carried in aircraft high above the land surface. The next parties to 'leg it' over 'South Victoria Land' were making for the South Magnetic Pole: David, Mawson and Mackay, during Shackleton's *Nimrod* expedition of 1907-09 and Bage, Webb and Hurley during Mawson's Australasian Antarctic Expedition of 1911-14. To Scott, the month spent on this vast plain remained a continuous strain on mind and body, lightened only by the unfailing courage and cheerfulness of his companions. They began the 300-mile journey back to *Discovery* on 1 December 1903.

The biting wind was at their backs while marching, but still plagued them at camp sites. An overcast sky caused them to lie up for a time on 2 December because they could not see the surface in the dark. Further delay caused Scott to fear they would soon be forced to make long marches on short rations. Mercifully, his companions proved invincible, always finding something to jest about. In the evenings they had long arguments about naval matters, and generally agreed they could rule the service far better than any Board of Admiralty. Scott also learned a great deal about life on the lower deck.

A gritty, sand-like snow surface and southerly wind cut the pace to one mile an hour on 9 December. Scott's anxiety grew as they approached the plateau edge. On the afternoon of 10 December Evans sighted land, which was cheering. However, navigating by 'rule of thumb', there was no certainty that they would hit their own glacier first when so many others flowed down through the mountains from the plateau. Overcast weather hid the tops of the mountains that should have been their landmarks. Ten hours' daily pulling on a heavy surface reduced them to

Emperor penguins at Cape Crozier, Ross Island,
painted by Edward Wilson.
(SCOTT POLAR RESEARCH INSTITUTE)

ghosts of their former selves, yet they remained fit, despite acute hunger pains and numerous frostbites, particularly to Evans's nose. Pushing steadily eastward on 13 December, they began to descend.

Next day they rocketed down an ice fall on what all three agreed was the most adventurous day of their lives. In the morning the clouds still covered the mountain tops, so they continued their eastward march, soon coming across a rough area which they were unable to circumvent. Preferring the dangers of pressing on in whirling snow to trying to sit out the blizzard, they threaded their way round hummocks and across crevasses on to a smoother, steeper surface for which they donned crampons. Scott guided the sledge in front, with the two men holding it back in the rear. Suddenly Lashly slipped, and in an instant he was sliding downward on his back. Evans, too, was thrown off his feet. The two men and the sledge hurtled past Scott, who braced himself to stop them, but with the first jerk he too was whipped

off his legs, and all three lay sprawling on their backs flying downward at ever-increasing velocity. Soon all three had ceased to slide smoothly and were bounding over a rougher incline, sometimes leaving it for several yards at a time, coming down with tremendous force on a gradual slope of rough, hard, wind-swept snow. Its irregularities brought them to rest in moments, and they staggered to their feet dazed, bruised and shaken but all sound in limb. They had descended some 300ft of the highest of the 'ice cascades' of the glacier they had been seeking. At this lower level many familiar features were in view, including the plume of smoke from Mount Erebus. After nearly a month without seeing any landmarks, Scott's rule of thumb navigation had none the less proved astonishingly accurate.

They packed their scattered belongings and scanty food and marched farther down the glacier, descending the second ice fall without mishap. Five miles from the depot, Lashly saw the captain and Evans disappear down a crevasse. He managed to secure the damaged sledge, supported by two skis, and hold on to it above the crevasse where Scott and Evans were dangling below. Scott was in the better position to move first, and groped about on every side with his cramponed feet, but found only the same slippery smooth wall. Eventually, by swinging from side to side, he located a projection and by raising himself he was able to gain a foothold on it and transfer some of his weight. He found himself standing on a thin shaft of ice which was wedged between the walls of the chasm, and he proceeded to get Evans's feet firmly guided on to the same bridge. All this took some time, and only then did Scott see the outline of the frail support of the broken sledge, some 12ft above their heads. While Lashly held on grimly to the sledge with one hand, his other was busily employed withdrawing their ski. There remained no other course for Scott and Evans but to climb out by their own unaided efforts, and without delay. The chill of the crevasse was already attacking them, and their faces and fingers were close to freezing. Scott went first. He had not swarmed a rope for some time, and reaching the top in thick clothing and heavy crampons and with frostbitten fingers seemed unlikely, but swinging his mittens over his shoulder, he swung off their bridge and climbed and climbed. With two of them on top and one below, Scott was able to unhitch his own harness and lower it once more for Evans, who was guided and hauled to the surface.

They wasted no time in the chill discussing their escape, but trudged on, pulling the broken sledge, keeping a sharp lookout for crevasses and harnessed so that only one of them could disappear at a time. Early in the evening they reached the depot, where there was enough food to carry them on to the main depot some miles down the glacier. There they found not only food, but sunshine, calm, rest and peace. The steam from their cooking rose straight upward in the still, warm air. Evans's astonishment at their escape grew deeper, marvelling at the one solitary snow bridge which had saved them. Scott had to agree with him that it had indeed been a close call.

The little party was further cheered during the descent of the glacier by finding notes at various pre-arranged points containing good news of Skelton's and Ferrar's parties. Before making for the ship, Scott, Lashly and Evans spent a long day on 17 December 1903 exploring the north arm of the Ferrar Glacier, later to be known as the Taylor Glacier after the geologist of the *Terra Nova* expedition. They made the remarkable discovery that the glacier, instead of discharging its icebergs into the sea, was withering away, ending tamely in a strange, steep snow-free valley where there were frozen lakes and long muddy moraines. As they lunched on a sandy spot next to a stream, Scott found it incredible that they were less than a hundred miles from that terrible plateau.

Then they climbed to a wild and beautiful vantage point of some 700ft, but steep winding gorges obscured their view of the sea. By the time they returned to camp and supper they had spent 14 hours walking and climbing over very rough country. Scott reflected on their discovery. The wonderful valley revealed all the indications of colossal ice action and considerable water action, yet none of these agents

Castle Rock near the *Discovery*'s winter quarters. Watercolour by Edward Wilson.
(SCOTT POLAR RESEARCH INSTITUTE)

was still at work. There were no living things, not even a moss or lichen; even the great glacier that once pushed through this valley of the dead had withered.

The valley is one of three forming the McMurdo oasis, the most extensive area of ice-free land in Antarctica. Named the Taylor Dry Valley after geologist Griffith Taylor, it is still studied by modern geologists, naturalists and limnologists.

On the homeward journey the travellers were dismayed to find the ice in McMurdo Sound as fast as ever. Late on Christmas Eve they saw the masts of *Discovery* and were welcomed by Koettlitz, Ford, Handsley and Quartley, the only four on board. They spent a snug and secure Christmas Day enjoying the delights of a civilised existence after so long without them. Scott later worked out his observations quietly at his desk and was relieved to find that his watch was accurate, for their longitudes on the plateau depended on its accuracy. He had calculated that, during the western journey, he, Evans and Lashly had averaged 15.4 miles a day over 81 days' absence, during which time they had sledged 1,098 miles and climbed heights totalling 19,800ft, a very fine achievement perhaps rivalled only by Shackleton's southern journey 1907-09.

During their absence a number of other journeys had been accomplished. Skelton and Ferrar had returned before them from the west, where Skelton had used the half-plate camera to good effect. Ferrar's observations showed that the Royal Society Range had a simple geological structure, the rocks comprising mainly thick horizontal layers of sandstone, with basalt and granite also present. Ferrar named this formation Beacon Sandstone. He was delighted to find some seams of coal running through the sandstone from which he collected specimens. Fossils of the fern *Glossopteris* and a gymnospermous wood indicated that in earlier geological times the climate of Antarctica must have been warm with abundant trees and plants.

Owing to southerly gales, Barne and Mulock had been able only to reach the entrance – Barne Inlet – of what was later called the Byrd Glacier. Here they found progress so impeded by crevasses and ice ridges that they were compelled to return without

exploring the glacier itself. Mulock was tireless in surveying this area of Victoria Land. With his theodolite he was able to ascertain the positions and heights of some 200 peaks. They also accidentally discovered that Depot A on the ice of the Great Barrier – the Ross Ice Shelf – off Minna Bluff, had moved over 600 yards in just over a year. The vast pressure ridges against the slopes of Mount Terror and elsewhere, earlier in the expedition, had shown that the Barrier was not only afloat, but moving. Barne and Mulock returned to the ship after 68 days out.

Royds, Bernacchi and party were 31 days out, sledging to the southeast and accomplishing a fine journey over what Scott called 'the unutterably wearisome plain' of the Great Barrier. Bernacchi wrote a lighthearted account of both the journey and the nightmare of the 'hygienic daily ceremony' performed in biting winds and drifting snow.

Bernacchi and his party achieved their main objective in discovering that the Barrier continued level to the southeast. Bernacchi's observations with a Barrow dip circle in perfect conditions, free of magnetic interference, were an important contribution to understanding the region's magnetic conditions. Armitage, Wilson and Heald examined and surveyed the Koettlitz Glacier during this second sledging season. Wilson made a third visit to the Emperor penguin rookery at Cape Crozier, where he solved the mystery of how the chicks had vanished the previous year while still in down and unable to swim. Batches of chicks and old birds sail out to sea on the ice floes released each spring. Wilson, Hodgson and Croucher later investigated the strand crack between land ice and floating ice on the south side of Ross Island.

The journeys accomplished during this second fortuitous summer in the Antarctic added greatly to the knowledge of the continent. In his review of the 1903 sledging work, Scott concluded that no polar ship had ever wintered in a more interesting spot than *Discovery*. After their first season there remained still many important gaps in their knowledge. Fortune had given them another chance, and by the end of their second sledging season they considered that the main part of their work was done.

CHAPTER 8

THE SECOND RELIEF EXPEDITION
AND RELEASE OF DISCOVERY, 1903-04

AFTER RECUPERATING AND FEASTING for a few days on board the snow-bound *Discovery*, a dyspeptic Scott with Lashly and Evans, both visibly gaining weight on Ford's savoury dishes, went north over the sea ice to the sawing camp. This had been set up by Armitage on Scott's order, to saw through the fast ice of the strait between *Discovery* and the open sea. Scott found the thirty men there in good condition and high spirits. They looked like tramps in tattered clothing, with faces burnt by the sun and enormous appetites. Penguins, seal meat and other supplies were brought from the ship by the dog team, and the main party slept in turns in a large tent near the Dellbridge Islands. Scott was pleased to be with his men again, and declared New Year's Day 1904 a holiday. As he lay in bed that night he listened to the chorus of noises from the hundreds of Weddell seals on the ice, like an orchestra tuning its many instruments. Above was the harsh, angry cawing of the skua gulls quarrelling over food and the distant squawk of penguins. From the main tent came the snores of the men and the occasional yapping of the dogs in their dreams.

A visit to the edge of the sea ice next day confirmed the depressing news that twenty miles of ice lay between *Discovery* and open water. Astonished at the small amount of progress made in ten days, Scott ordered the sawing to stop. Ice saws had been used during the British naval expeditions to the Arctic in the nineteenth century, and this occasion must have been one of the last on which such a cumbersome, back-breaking apparatus was employed. Aware that the expedition might have to remain in the Antarctic for a third year, Scott ordered four men to lay in a stock of penguins for the winter to vary the usual diet of seal meat. He and Wilson made their way up to the north, Scott to watch for the break-up of the ice and Wilson to

study the wildlife. This was to be a journey with no hard sledging, and they pitched their tent on the sand alongside a penguin rookery at Cape Royds.

They later walked to the north side of the cape, where a lazy sea was lapping the sandy beach. After a wash in a small stream and a supper of penguins' liver and seal kidneys eaten from the frying pan, they concluded that life in the Antarctic Regions could be very pleasant. If only *Discovery* could be lifted up and deposited twenty miles north they would feel themselves to be in Antarctic clover. This idyll was soon to be disturbed. Scott and Wilson were writing in their tent when they saw *Morning* barely three miles from them, followed to their amazement by a second relief ship, the *Terra Nova*, a Scottish steam whaler.

The *Morning*, under Captain Colbeck, and the *Terra Nova*, skippered by Captain Henry MacKay, an experienced master with the Dundee whaling fleet, arrived on 5 January 1904. As Wilson and Scott approached the ships, everyone was below. The watchman failed to see them until they were quite close, and then each ship thought they were stragglers from the other. Eventually four Scots whaling men, who spoke such 'perfect Dundee' that Scott and Wilson found them hard to understand, realised they were strangers. They learned that the Government had stepped in with the *Terra Nova*. After shaking hands all round, the commander of the National Antarctic Expedition and its second surgeon, sun scorched, unwashed, unshaven and in rags, boarded *Morning* and were made very welcome.

ARRIVAL OF THE RELIEF SHIPS
They learned both through Captain Colbeck and the orders and letters he carried that the two societies in London had been unable to raise the funds them-

ABOVE: Captain Harry MacKay and the crew of the *Terra Nova* during the voyage to relieve the *Discovery*, 1903-04.
(DUNDEE ART GALLERIES AND MUSEUMS)

LEFT: The relief ship *Terra Nova* in the pack ice.
(SCOTT POLAR RESEARCH INSTITUTE)

selves for a second relief voyage, and had been obliged to appeal to the Government. An Admiralty Committee had been formed which despatched *Morning* and the more powerful *Terra Nova* to relieve Scott, whose orders left no doubt that, due to the expense, he must abandon *Discovery* rather than spend another year in the Antarctic. This harsh mandate left Scott sadly unwilling to abandon his ship. The ties that bound the expedition members to *Discovery* were far beyond the ordinary and involved a depth of sentiment and gratitude to her for providing so comfortable a home in all the rigours of the southern region.

The *Terra Nova* had been quickly and well equipped for the voyage to the Antarctic. Because of the need for haste she was towed at speed through the Suez Canal by a relay of cruisers, and by the end of November 1903 she lay off Hobart, Tasmania, to be joined by *Morning*, which had wintered in Lyttelton. The two ships departed from Sandy Bay on 6 December 1903 on a wearying voyage to the south. Colbeck had given MacKay written instructions amended from those he had received from the Admiralty, and changed their track farther east. He also acted independently with stores, coal and gun cotton, informing the Admiralty afterwards of what he had done.

The relief ships had met their first iceberg on 23 December and entered the pack early on 26 December in lat. 62° 35' S long. 179°W. MacKay and some of his officers came on board *Morning* for Christmas dinner. Earlier, on Christmas Day, Davidson, *Morning's* doctor, who was making a representative collection of birds from the voyage, added to these a number from an iceberg nearby. Many toasts were drunk in the evening to those at home, and the party continued until about 3am. MacKay had told the second mate to keep a good lookout in his absence, and that he would be back before dark. Colbeck noted that it would not be dark until 22 February!

Captain Colbeck attributed the ships' good run through the pack to his decision to follow the easterly course, and to his experience during the previous voyage. They reached the open water of the Ross Sea in lat. 70° 22'S, resulting in a happy New Year's Day 1904 after less than four-and-a-half-days' actual steaming, and a week earlier than any previous expedition. They passed a hundred miles east of Cape Adare, giving the land a wide berth until Franklin Island, where a party landed to search for a record from *Discovery*. None was found. On 4 January they left the island and steered for McMurdo Sound, through open water as far as Beaufort Island, where they worked through loose pack for 18 hours. They then proceeded

Captain Colbeck, at left, and Captain Scott aboard the *Morning*. January 1904. Scott is wearing finnesko (reindeer skin) footwear; from Doorly's *Voyages of the 'Morning'*.
(AUTHOR'S COLLECTION)

'Dog post ready to start'. The team carried mail across the miles of sea ice between *Discovery* and the relief ships, from Scott's *The Voyage of the 'Discovery'*.
(AUTHOR'S COLLECTION)

at full speed through open water to the edge of the fast ice, which they sighted at 12.40pm on 5 January, three weeks earlier than the previous voyage.

From the ice edge in McMurdo Sound, despite sudden gales and looming icebergs, sledge parties transported mails, meat and vegetables across to *Discovery* from the relief ships. Killer whales were a menace, and badly frightened one of the men on his way to *Discovery* by swimming underneath the ice on which he was walking and cracking it.

On 13 January 1904 Captain Scott wrote to Captain Colbeck, telling him that the sawing work of *Discovery* was a waste of time and that, if the ship were to be abandoned, there was much equipment that needed to be transferred. He planned to begin the transfer as soon as possible, and to use the main camp on the sea ice as the entrepot for the sledging parties. The various articles would be sent in order: scientific collections and notebooks, instruments, scientific library and books of value and, finally, private effects. Royds and two men would be sent to try to clear the ice with explosives. There were still nearly twenty miles of ice between *Discovery* and the open sea.

Blasting (at which Captain MacKay was particularly skilled) began at the ice edge on 15 January, with the ice going out or not, almost of its own accord. As Scott became increasingly pessimistic about freeing *Discovery*, the scientific records and collections were sledged over a poor ice surface to *Morning* and *Terra Nova*. On 11 February Colbeck received a copy of Scott's arrangements for abandoning *Discovery*, although by then the ice was going out consistently. Colbeck expressed his optimism about her chances when Scott went to see him. There were still two-and-a-half miles of solid ice between the two ships, and three weeks before their orders obliged them to leave her. It was simply a question whether the ice would break up faster than the season would close in. The ice was 8ft thick, no easy task to bore. On 13 February 1904 the two relief ships were still almost two miles from *Discovery* but the next day, amazingly, saw the excitement of her release.

THE RELEASE OF DISCOVERY

Aboard *Morning*, Captain Colbeck described 14 February as the *day of days*, with a strong east-northeast wind and light northwest swell, the best of all conditions for their work. About 600 yards of ice was dislodged before noon, and the two captains of the relief ships had the pleasure of seeing it drift northwards, leaving a clear ice face for the swell to act on. In the afternoon the ice broke away as quickly as they could fire the charges, and by 4.30 they had crossed the 8ft bridge of ice and were working on ice 3 to 4ft thick. It seemed they might reach *Discovery* before midnight. Slowly and steadily, inch by inch, the two vessels

Vince's Cross.
Watercolour by
Edward Wilson.
(SCOTT POLAR RESEARCH
INSTITUTE)

worked towards her, then a fanatical yell burst forth and cheer after cheer went up on all sides. The Union flag was unfurled at Hut Point. Scott came on board as soon as *Morning* came alongside, and was so excited he could scarcely speak. It meant all the difference between complete and comparative success to him, and there was not a happier man living than Scott that night.

In *Discovery* the excitement had begun while dinner was being eaten, earlier that same day, with a shout down the hatchway to the captain of 'The ships are coming, sir!'. There was no more dinner. In one minute all were racing for Hut Point, where a glorious sight of ice rapidly breaking up right across the strait met their view. For long intervals the small community in their tattered garments remained almost spellbound, then a burst of frenzied cheering broke out. By 11 o'clock all the thick ice had vanished and a few minutes later *Terra Nova* forged ahead, crashing into the open, to be followed almost immediately by her stout little companion. Soon both ships were firmly anchored to the last wedge in *Discovery*'s bay of imprisonment.

The ice that encased her was finally cracked by

Ice-saw at work, depicted in a pen and ink sketch by Edward Wilson, reproduced in Albert Armitage, *Two Years in the Antarctic.* (AUTHOR'S COLLECTION)

explosive charges two days later. The last one shook the ship from stem to stern. The cracks widened, and there was a gurgle of water and a creaking aft. *Discovery*'s stern rose with a jump as the keel was freed from the ice that had held it down. Then, as the great mass of ice on their port hand glided slowly out to sea, the ship swung gently round, riding peacefully to her anchors with blue water lapping against her sides.

Scott concluded his account of these memorable days: 'Thus it was that after she had afforded us shelter and comfort for two full years, and after we had borne a heavy anxiety on her behalf, our good ship was spared to take us homeward. On February 16, 1904, *Discovery* came to her own again – the right to ride the high seas.'

That evening the ship's company landed at Hut Point and assembled round the cross erected earlier to the memory of their shipmate, George Vince. Captain Scott read the prayers, while all stood bareheaded. He thought the cross should endure for centuries in a climate where nothing decays. He was not to know that nine years later another cross to his own and his companions' memories would stand nearby, in full view of *Discovery*'s winter quarters.

Terra Nova and *Morning* reach the *Discovery* in winter quarters, 14 February 1904, after six weeks of blasting and charging the sea ice. (ROYAL GEOGRAPHICAL SOCIETY)

HOMEWARD BOUND, 1904

THE ANTARCTIC did not part lightly with *Discovery*. Steam was raised on the 17 February, just in time to prevent her striking the icefoot broadside on, after dragging her anchor. In attempting to round Hut Point in a gale at 11am the same morning, the ship crashed head-foremost on to a shoal and stopped dead with her masts quivering. Scott described the hours that followed as truly the most dreadful he had ever spent. Each moment the ship came down with a sickening thud which shook her from stem to stern. It seemed she could not long survive such awful blows. An attempt to force her over ended in failure, and the engines were pronounced useless as their inlets were choked. By 3pm Scott decided nothing more could be done until the gale abated. Their situation was horrifying.

During an almost silent evening meal, with the ship aground below the summit of Hut Point with its cross erected to Vince, the officer of the watch burst in and reported her working astern. The current had turned and was running strongly in the opposite direction. The inlets were freed, the engines began to revolve and *Discovery* slipped free. The solid structure sustained very little damage, but, as Scott remarked, their little bay had tendered a treacherous farewell.

Discovery coaled 50 tons from *Terra Nova*. Colbeck unselfishly spared 25 tons from *Morning*, an action much appreciated by Scott. It meant that, before making for New Zealand, *Discovery* could

try to venture to the west of Cape North and the Balleny Islands, in the event sailing over land mistakenly charted in 1840 by the U.S. Exploring Expedition. The three ships had a rendezvous at the Aucklands, a group of uninhabited islands south of New Zealand. *Discovery* arrived first, on 15 March 1904, with only 10 tons of coal remaining. She was followed some days later by *Terra Nova*, from which more coal was obtained, and twenty-four hours later *Morning* joined them. Here the ships' companies were able to enjoy the beauty of green earth after the desolation of the Antarctic. Off Cape Adare *Discovery* had been obliged to ship her spare rudder. On departing from McMurdo Sound all hands, officers and men, had to labour extremely hard to get the ship coaled, watered and into sea trim. At one point the pumps failed. Scott was able ruefully to contrast his own ship's continual rolling with the steady *Terra Nova*. Wilson reported that a roll of 48° to starboard caused wonderful upsets and lapfulls at the dinner table.

The three ships proceeded in company from the Auckland Islands to Lyttelton, New Zealand, where they received a tremendous welcome on Good Friday, 1 April 1904. *Discovery* completed her circumnavigation by sailing east from New Zealand through the Straits of Magellan, largely in the latitude of the fifties south, finishing her magnetic survey in the Falkland Islands and searching for the non-existent 'Dogherty Islands' en route. The

Sunset with two ships under sail. Woodcut from *The South Polar Times*.

first high-latitude soundings were taken in the South Pacific Ocean, showing an average depth of over 2,000 fathoms.

Edward Wilson's diary entry for 26 July 1904 in the South Atlantic, some days out of Port Stanley, pays a fine tribute to *Discovery* as she battled with seas of 40 and 50ft in hurricane force squalls, when the roar of the storm in the rigging drowned every scrap of thunder. Man makes nothing more wonderful, he declared, than a sailing ship tried to her utmost.

HOMECOMING AND EXPEDITION RESULTS

Discovery made slow progress to the north, this being especially felt in the tropics with a decomposing sea elephant carried on the skid beams. A more pleasant feature of the return voyage was a visit to the Prince of Monaco's yacht, *Princesse Alice*, in the Azores. *Discovery* arrived at Spithead on 10 September to a hearty welcome from Sir Clements Markham, Sir Allen Young and cheers from all the men-of-war. Markham sailed round in *Discovery* to the

Silhouettes of expedition members from *The South Polar Times*.

Thames, where she berthed in the East India Dock on 15 September. Shackleton was there, and dined with Scott and Markham after everyone had gone off with friends. The indomitable *Morning* eventually arrived in Plymouth towards the end of the month, her engine and boilers in a wretched state.

The members of the National Antarctic Expedition were reunited on 7 November 1904, when a nervous Captain Scott gave a memorable lecture at the Royal Albert Hall to a full house. Medals were awarded to Scott, and a silver loving cup, in the form of a globe showing the tracks of the *Morning*, was presented to Captain Colbeck. Sir Clements Markham received a silver sledge from the officers and men, a gift he valued immensely. It is depicted beside him in the portrait that hangs in the RGS.

HOME

Discovery had completed a rewarding first voyage, and the expedition she carried made a splendid contribution to Antarctic geography and science. The interior of the unknown southern continent had been explored for the first time. Scott's narrative of *The Voyage of the the 'Discovery'*, published in 1905, was a notable addition to polar literature, as were the two delightful volumes of the *The South Polar Times*, reproduced in facsimile in 1907.

Bernacchi later summarised the achievements of the National Antarctic Expedition in a fair evaluation:

The expedition had returned after more than three years' absence with the richest results, geographical and 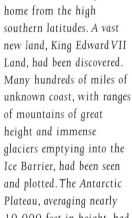 *scientific, ever brought home from the high southern latitudes. A vast new land, King Edward VII Land, had been discovered. Many hundreds of miles of unknown coast, with ranges of mountains of great height and immense glaciers emptying into the Ice Barrier, had been seen and plotted. The Antarctic Plateau, averaging nearly 10,000 feet in height, had been found and partly traversed where, subsequently, the South Pole itself was found to be situated, proving that the Antarctic Continent was almost all under ice without any vegetation or animal life of any kind. Never had a polar expedition come home with so great a harvest of original research work...*

The specialists of Discovery were lone-handed and encountered many difficulties. Hodgson must be regarded as a pioneer of Antarctic marine biology...Ferrar is the pioneer of Antarctic geology. The extensive physical work, part of an international programme, for which I was responsible, was one of the principal objects of the expedition. It was completed. In due time the scientific work was reduced, discussed and published in many large volumes by the Royal Society.

Sir John Murray paid the expedition a fine tribute on its return, particularly welcoming the evidence it furnished for the existence of the Antarctic continent. His appreciation of the excellent work accomplished and the great contribution to human knowledge was an especially welcome endorsement after his disagreement with Sir Clements Markham early in its history.

It was not long before Shackleton and Scott himself were to return to the Ross Sea area of the Antarctic, in what is called 'the heroic age of Antarctic exploration'.

The *Discovery* seen with parhelia under sail in the pack, by Edward Wilson. Frontispiece to Scott's *The Voyage of the 'Discovery'* (AUTHOR'S COLLECTION)

Southern Cross hut, Cape Adare. February 25, 1904. Led by C E Borchgrevink, the *Southern Cross* expedition of 1898-1900 made the first intentional wintering on the Antarctic continent. The hut still stands. Watercolour by E A Wilson.
(SCOTT POLAR RESEACH INSTITUTE)

CHAPTER 10

PURCHASE BY THE HUDSON'S BAY COMPANY

To the north of the mainland of North America is an archipelago of Arctic Islands extending to within 200 miles of the Pole. Discovery of a sea route or Northwest Passage from Atlantic to Pacific, through the maze of often ice-bound waterways surrounding the Arctic islands, was the objective of a number of British naval expeditions in the first half of the nineteenth century. This aim was eventually achieved only with tragic loss of men and ships. Today these channels are being considered again as shipping routes for companies interested in the exploitation of the natural gas, oil and mineral reserves of the far north. The improved design of icebreakers and ice-strengthened ships, more-detailed charts and greater knowledge of ice and its distribution plus improved aids to navigation have enabled modern vessels to operate in certain of these ice-infested and hazardous waters for longer seasons and in higher latitudes than ever before.

Many great merchant expeditions set out in the last four centuries from the shores of these Islands and materially altered the lands to which they sailed. Of these, none was more prominent than the HBC. Its resounding title, The Adventurers of England Trading into Hudson Bay, aptly conveys the spirit which has imbued it from its Royal origins in the 17th century to the present day. Its interests have swelled from the early trading posts, where furs were the principal article of trade, to the vast commercial undertakings of the 20th century, when the company is active in so many spheres of exploration and development in every province of Canada.

SIR WINSTON CHURCHILL

THE HUDSON'S BAY COMPANY

For two-and-a-half centuries the icy waters of one passage north of 60° were navigated yearly by wooden sailing ships, beginning with *Nonsuch* in 1668 and ending with *Discovery*. This was the Hudson Strait, which leads into the great basin of Hudson Bay, both first entered and explored in 1610-11 by Henry Hudson in an earlier *Discovery*. The successful voyage of *Nonsuch* opened up a sea route for fur trading with the North American Indians. This led to the incorporation in 1670 of the Hudson's Bay Company (HBC) by royal charter, granted by King Charles II, under the governorship of Prince Rupert. This gave the company 'sole Trade and Commerce' as 'true and absolute Lordes and Proprietors' of this vast territory, to be known as Rupert's Land. The adventurers were effectively given the modern provinces of Ontario and Quebec north of the Laurentian watershed and west of the Labrador boundary, Manitoba, most of Saskatchewan, the southern half of Alberta, much of the Northwest Territories and part of Nunavut, an area of 1,486,000 square miles comprising 38.7 per cent of modern Canada.

The fur trade proved profitable in the early years of the company, and three wooden forts were built on James Bay, the southern arm of Hudson Bay. These were Fort Charles, later called Fort Rupert River and Rupert's House, Moose and Albany, all established before 1685. Wars in Europe against the French had their repercussions in the Bay, where there was at least one naval engagement. By the late eighteenth century many lengthy inland journeys had been made by Kelsey, Stewart, Henday and Hearne with the aim of stimulating peaceful trade with the Indians. British rivalry with the French continued until the conquest of French Canada in 1759, that *annus mirabilis* or year of victories. Ten years later the North West Company, based in Montreal, began to emerge as a competitor, and by 1776 it had become a power in the land. The rivalry was based on the competition of two routes, Hudson Bay versus the St Lawrence River, for the trade of the fur regions to the north. Each side established posts in the interior and endeavoured to wrest trade from the other. After years of violence, bloodshed and lawsuits the two companies eventually began to unite in 1821, under the name of the senior enterprise.

A great period followed in the history of the enlarged and reorganised HBC. In 1821 parliament confirmed the charter that extended the territory to the rest of the northwest, north to the Arctic Ocean and west to the Pacific, on condition that the company assumed responsibility for law and order and acknowledged its duties towards the Indians. For half a century of almost unbroken peace the company had control of trade over a vast area, from the boundary of Labrador to the Pacific, and from the lower reaches of the Mackenzie River to the American passes over the Rockies, while from time to time wars resulting almost in extermination broke out south of the border.

The officers or chief traders, often known as wintering partners, were given a share of the profits of the fur trade. For 40 years after the merger this fur empire was dominated by Sir George Simpson, known formally as the Governor-in-Chief from 1839. Nicknamed the 'little Emperor', this tough Scot travelled the length and breadth of Rupert's Land and the northwest. The officers of the company were men of integrity with a tremendous sense of duty towards the Indians and towards others in the company's employ. Many of their names are well known in the history of Arctic exploration, and include at least one writer of adventures stories, namely R M Ballantyne.

The flag and Coat of Arms of the Hudson's Bay Company.
(AUTHOR'S COLLECTION)

By the mid-nineteenth century the need for change became apparent as immigrants from Britain and Europe sought to settle in the west. With the Deed of Surrender of 1869 the General Court of the company gave back to Queen Victoria the lands given to their forebears by Charles II. The company left a record of achievement that facilitated the task of the new Government.

The transformation from monopoly to open competition in the new Dominion of Canada, a land of pioneering settlements and migrating peoples established in 1867, was successfully made by the old company. The fur trade continued, but assumed a lesser importance as a chain of large retail stores was set up in the cities to meet the needs of the settlers and to diversify the company's interests. These changes were of little advantage to the native peoples, and with the opening of the north to free traders, trappers and adventurers the Indians became demoralised because game herds and some fur bearers were destroyed. The hitherto orderly existence they had enjoyed when the HBC held a monopoly was replaced by uncertainty and breakdown.

The years that *Discovery* was in the company's service in the north, 1905-11 and 1918, were among the last before the railways, motor transport, aeroplanes and radio shortened both time and distance there. For a century the lifestyle of the post managers at many of the northern trading posts had scarcely changed. Summer transport and communication were by York boat and birch-bark canoe; in winter by the carriole and dog sled. In the proper season the annual visit of the ship from England was awaited eagerly by the posts on the shores of Hudson Bay. From 1905 to 1911 that ship was *Discovery*. She has the distinction of being one of the last of a line of wooden sailing ships which, for well over two centuries, made the stormy transatlantic voyage from London, through the ice-infested and uncharted waters of the Hudson Strait and Bay, to the company posts at the mouths of the Churchill, Hayes, Albany, Moose and Rupert Rivers in the southern portion of the Bay.

Discovery in HBC Ownership

The Honourable Company became the owner of *Discovery* in January 1905. Hopes that she would continue as an exploring ship after the return of the National Antarctic Expedition in 1904, or even as a government vessel pursuing fishery investigations in the North Sea, were dashed when it was announced in the Press that the Joint Committee of the Expedition had been forced to sell a vessel which had cost £50,000 to the HBC for £10,000, despite Captain Scott's claim that she was a better ship than when she was launched. The *Morning Post* newspaper reported that it was to be hoped that her special scientific equipment would not be removed, and that future subsidiary scientific work in the Arctic regions

might present itself.

Late in 1904 the company was seeking a replacement for the *Stork*, which had been forced to winter off Charlton Island, James Bay, from October 1904 to August 1905, arriving in London on 4 October 1905 and thus missing a year's shipment or 'outfit'. Messrs Williams and Sage, Engineering and Nautical Experts of Bishopsgate, in the City of London recommended *Discovery* as a steamer which might be adapted for service by the HBC, and they were authorised to take formal possession of her on 17 January 1905.

She was placed in a graving dock the following week, so that she could be examined, repaired, refitted and adapted swiftly and more cheaply than if she were afloat at a distance. The lifting propeller was considered unnecessary, and was replaced by a new tail shaft. *Discovery's* windlass, winding engine, galley stove, skylight, ladders, gun metal and brass were sold for scrap or re-use. By mid-April 1905 the vessel was ready to be undocked and placed in the com-

pany's berth in the West India Docks, London. Only the painting, graining, cleaning and varnishing, reeving the rigging and bending the sails had still to be done. Messrs Williams and Sage calculated that 180 tons of special double screened Welsh steam coals would be sufficient to make the journey down the Thames and across the Atlantic under sail, through the Hudson Strait to Charlton Island and back.

Discovery had effectively been converted from a scientific and exploring ship to a cargo vessel for the HBC. There seems to have been no attempt to retain her scientific gear. The magnetic and dredging laboratories at the sides of the vessel had been extended to accommodate the officers below the bridge. The wardroom and other accommodation between decks had been removed to provide space for the holds. The crew had quarters in the forecastle, and there was one small passenger cabin with four berths. A steam windlass had been erected on the forecastle head, the cross timbers and bulkheads being cleared out for cargo.

The ship was to continue in HBC ownership for the next 18 years. The years 1905 to 1911 were spent on the yearly run from London across the Atlantic to Hudson Strait in northern Canada, then westwards through the ice-infested strait into Hudson Bay and south to James Bay to unload at Charlton Island. Here the 'returns', mainly furs, were shipped and a few passengers taken on board for the homeward voyage. These voyages have been called dull and routine, but the navigation of Davis Strait, Hudson Strait and Hudson Bay was neither. The strength of *Discovery*'s bow and the power of her engine were much needed during this passage. Most of *Discovery*'s log books kept during these voyages have survived in the company archives, now in Winnipeg, after their transfer from London in recent times.

1905 HBC Voyage

No log for the 1905 voyage has yet been found, and details are scarce. The command of *Discovery* was given

Native birchbark canoes, some as long as 45ft and paddled by *voyageurs*, were used by the Hudson's Bay Company to carry furs downstream and supplies back up. This evocative painting, by Frances Ann Hopkins, dates from the mid-nineteenth century. (GLENBOW MUSEUM, CALGARY)

ABOVE: Captain J G Ford, Master of the *Discovery*, during her voyages to Hudson Bay, 1906-11. (AUTHOR'S COLLECTION)

RIGHT: The *Discovery* in 1911, when owned by the Hudson's Bay Company, painted by Thomas G Purvis. (COURTESY THE HUDSON'S BAY COMPANY, WINNIPEG)

to Captain Alexander Gray, then aged 65, master of the *Pelican*, with A Cleveland Smith as mate. It was agreed that Captain Ford, beset in the ice in *Stork*, should relieve Captain Gr ay of the command of *Discovery* the following year. In this first year of HBC ownership *Discovery* left West India Dock on 15 June 1905 and called at Aberdeen from 21 to 22 June, where the carpenter and two Able Seamen deserted and for whom replacements were signed on.

She anchored at Charlton Island on 27 August and began her return trip on 8 September, passing the Lizard in Cornwall on 1 November and berthing in West India Dock two days later.

Captain Gray was an experienced sailor in polar seas Sadly, one of the substitute Able Seamen, A Curley, lost his hold on the yard and drowned on a dark night with a tremendous sea running. This tragedy cast a gloom over the ship, which also suffered bad weather for days after.

1906 HBC VOYAGE

Captain John Graham Ford took command of *Discovery* in 1906 and remained her master until 1911. He had previously commanded the barque *Lady Head* before being beset in *Stork*. The *Discovery* cast off from the West India Dock at 5.30am on 14 June 1906, and

at noon she anchored at the Powder Ground, off Gravesend. After being inspected by the Government Inspector, the Powder Barge came alongside and 85 barrels and kegs and two cases of gunpowder were taken on board. The anchor was weighed and the ship proceeded at full speed. Sea watches were kept and regulation lights strictly attended to. Peterhead, the port in the northeast of Scotland, was reached on 18 June and some chickens were taken on board as stores.

The log records 118 nautical miles on 20 June, 119 on the 21st and 123 on the 23rd. The engines were then stopped, the intention being to make the passage of the North Atlantic under sail alone. *Discovery* was by then due west of Shetland and to the south of Iceland. The winds and weather were variable, and the daily distance travelled varied accordingly. Gales in early July produced a heavy cross sea, causing the ship to labour and strain heavily, sometimes shipping a quantity of water. The clip hooks of the main fore topgallant sail sheet carried away at 7.45pm on 8 July, causing the sail to split. The following day the gale continued strong, with hard squalls and heavy rain. Seas were shipped fore and aft, washing away the starboard light screen. The position on 9 July was given as well to the south of Greenland. Foggy weather was recorded on 10 July, followed by clearer weather but with decks continually awash. On 13 July a hard gale in gusts and squalls caused the clew iron of the foresail to carry away.

Steam was ordered in *Discovery* on 16 July, and all sail was furled when southeast of Cape Farewell (Kap Farvel), the southern tip of Greenland. All fore-and-aft sails were set for some hours during the evening of 17 July. Several pieces of ice were seen next day, the temperature of the air being 39°F and of the water 43°F. Next day the pack ice was skirted in foggy weather and, later, all square sail was set, with engines slow. Oil bags were hung over each bow to prevent the sea breaking on board in a strong gale on 19 July. The main topgallant and foresail were handed (furled) during the day. The gale moderated on 20 July, but the ship continued to take heavy seas on board. The upper fore- and main topsails and jib were set.

The south cape of Greenland was rounded and a passage made to the north and west under sail or steam, as the ship crossed the 700-mile-wide Davis Strait. Resolution Island was sighted on 26 July at the entrance to the Hudson Strait, which is some 400 miles long and 100 miles wide. The ship was able to work slowly to the west through heavy pack ice. On 29 July she was beset and no open water could be seen from the crow's nest. Later, the ice opened out and the freshwater tanks were filled from the pools on the floe, the ship being moored to the ice.

By 31 July *Discovery* was roughly halfway through the Strait. Cape Pembroke, Coats Island, was sighted on the afternoon of 3 August as the ship proceeded south through the shallow waters of the Bay, steaming through scattered pack ice. During the afternoon of 7 August the ship was stopped several times and sound-

ings of 10 fathoms, 12 fathoms and 100 fathoms were made. A few hours later, soundings of 17, 20 and 23 fathoms were made, and by 5.30pm on 8 August Lisbon Rock was abeam, five miles distant. At 9.25pm the ship dropped anchor off Charlton Island, her destination at the southern end of James Bay.

Next morning at 6am the anchor was weighed and *Discovery* proceeded at half speed towards the bar, a seaman at the lead sounding in. She anchored near the bar buoy in 10 fathoms at 8.45am to await the tide. The crew worked at rigging cargo gear and making ready for moving alongside the wharf. At about 11am the manager of the HBC post of Moose Factory, Mr McKenzie, arrived. He left at noon with a Mrs Cockram and her child, who had been passengers from London, and the Second Engineer, Joseph Love, who was to join the *Inenew*, a small vessel used to transport goods in James Bay. Amid rain, lightning and thunder *Discovery* anchored abreast the wharf at Charlton Island in 40 fathoms to wait for the tide. The night watch was set. The following morning, 11 August, the anchor was hove up and she steamed closer in, anchoring in 60 fathoms.

All hands worked at mooring ship, which was hove alongside the wharf and moored ahead and astern by noon. The main hatches were taken off and the bulk of the cargo broken. The crew were at work in rainy, unsettled weather, washing the decks, clean-

Charlton Island 1905, with the *Stork* offshore. (COURTESY HUDSON'S BAY COMPANY, WINNIPEG)

ing the ship and pumping her out. Her draught on arrival was found to be 17ft 2in fore and 16ft aft. Just over 104 tons of coal or patent fuel had been used for the 58-day outward passage, leaving 76 tons in the bunkers. No work was done the next day, Sunday, which instead was spent ashore exploring the low sandy wooded island.

CHARLTON ISLAND AND ITS HISTORY

A modern visitor to Charlton Island, the late Dr W A Kenyon of the Royal Ontario Museum, Toronto, Canada, has described this uninhabited island with great charm. He tells us that it is some 18 miles long, dotted with small shallow lakes, much of it open parkland and meadows, sprinkled with occasional evergreen and spruce around most of the ponds and along many of its streams. Two short ridges rise to about 100ft, but otherwise the island is a low, undulating, sandy plain. Extensive reefs and shoals extend from its shores. Blueberries and strawberries are scattered about in profusion, and the geese and ducks which nest all over the island are quiet and unobtrusive. Beaver are plentiful on the ponds and streams, and the tracks of foxes and lynx frequently appear. To Kenyon there seemed to be a contradiction between the silence and solitude on one hand and the richness and vitality of living things on the other.

A compelling, fiercer impression of northern Canada is given by P G Downes, who describes the lashing, screaming wind and sudden vengeful bursts of cold rain which mock the consuming restlessness affecting all dwellers in the north. The weather is never constant for a day and the animals, birds and fish are never still, always moving, migrating, wandering. The lakes are retreating and the rivers devour their banks. Man too, he wrote must catch this strange beat of everlasting flux and change, or he will perish.

It was at Charlton Island that Captain Thomas James of Bristol, after whom James Bay is named, wintered in 1631-32, during his 'strange and dangerous voyage' in the *Henrietta Maria*, searching for a northwest passage into the South Sea. The island was

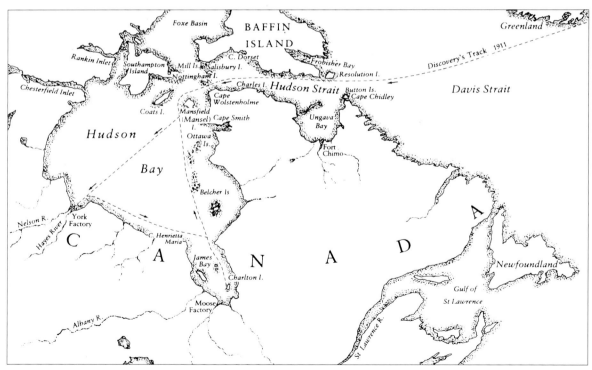

Map showing the *Discovery's* voyages to Hudson Bay and James Bay, 1905-11 and 1918-19, with the track of the 1911 voyage to York Factory and Charlton Island approximately plotted.

visited in 1672 by the men who established the fur trading post of Rupert House, near the mouth of the Rupert River, and in 1679 warehouses were built on Charlton Island to store furs in the spring and, in turn, to receive cargo from London. After two centuries of changing fortunes, Charlton Island again became the HBC's depot in James Bay and continued to be used until the railway from the south reached Moosonee in 1932. The warehouse was built at what is now known as House Point, opposite Danby Island.

Moose Factory, at the southern end of James Bay, had been the earlier port of entry for the London ships. A large establishment was maintained in the nineteenth century at Moose, to unload and distribute cargo, but the difficulties of local navigation and the complicated transport system there persuaded the Company in 1900 to adopt Charlton Island again as a port of arrival and departure.

Discovery was to carry a much larger cargo, estimated at 850 to 900 tons, than had previously been sent to Charlton in one vessel. With a draught of 16 to 17ft she would draw more water than the *Lady Head* (15ft 6in), which had occasionally touched bottom when at the wharf at low tide. It was thought that *Discovery*'s bilges might be damaged if this ever happened to her. There was no permanent jetty at Charlton Island: the structure had to be wholly removed each winter because of the ice. Spars and planks were therefore sent out in the ship with which to build an additional length of jetty, so allowing the vessel to moor in at least 20ft of water. The officer in charge of the James Bay District was in fact able to extend the wharf before *Discovery*'s arrival. He reported on 10 September 1905 that she was unloaded in five-and-a-half days, then reloaded and ballasted in two-and-a-half days, eight days in all.

From 13 to 17 August the crew discharged cargo and tarred down the rigging and backstays. The company's small steam vessel *Inenew* was loaded during the week. On the afternoon of the 17th the crew began shifting patent fuel from the fore lower hold into the bunkers aft, and also put five tons of coal from the shore into the bunkers. Twenty-six casks of oil were taken on board that day. The crew worked from 6am to 6pm in temperatures of 80°F. It had been 58°F three days earlier. On the Saturday, besides moving the patent fuel, they cleared the 'tween decks rigging gear for taking in ballast and loaded logs on board for shifting boards, and took a further five tons of coal from the shore, all by 9am.

The ship's moorings were then slacked up and she was hove off from the wharf. Seventy-two tons of ballast were then taken on board because the return cargo, largely of furs, was light. This was often sand, which could be sold in London. Some of the crew were sent away to get fresh water on the Monday and Tuesday, and the ballast was topped up to 160 tons. All the cargo was taken in and stowed on the Tuesday, 21 August. It comprised 102 bales, 69 cases, 26 casks of oil, 45 bags of feathers, 30 packs, 2 kegs, 2 casks and 16 private packages. Four tons of patent fuel were shifted out of the after trunking into the bunkers. The vessel was shifted on Wednesday and anchored again away from the wharf.

The following morning the HBC barque *Stork*, commanded by Captain N E Freakley, was in sight off the bar, having departed from the Thames in June. Meanwhile, *Discovery*'s crew were bending sail, trimming ballast and making ready for sea. The main hatch was battened down, the anchor was weighed and she proceeded at half speed down river to the bar, where she anchored in 8 fathoms of water close to the *Stork*. The boat was lowered to take the pilot on board the *Stork*, it being afterwards placed in chocks on the main hatch of *Discovery*.

On Friday 24 August 1906, after new wire wheel ropes had been rove to replace the old ones partly stranded, the anchor was weighed and the ship steamed at full speed to the west-southwest. At noon, in sight of Lisbon Rock, all square sail was set, with a moderate breeze and clear weather. *Discovery* arrived off London's South West India Dock on 5 October 1906, awaiting tide. At 1.30am she entered the dock and was hauled into the basin. The vessel was moored and the crew discharged at 2.30am, her draught being 12ft 8in forward and 15ft 6in aft. G F Lovegrove, Chief Officer and keeper of the log, made his last entry: 'This ends this log'.

VOYAGES
1907-11

LOVEGROVE TOOK UP his pen again the following year, on 20 June 1907. The crew were mustered as the ship steamed down river out of the West India Dock, when it was found that one man had failed to join. Before leaving the Thames 68 kegs and 4 boxes of gunpowder were loaded, and at Peterhead on 24 June 5 cases of cargo from London, stores, chicken, beef and mutton were taken on board. The course followed was again north of the British Isles, giving the southern tip of Greenland a wide berth as before. The crew went about their tasks as always. On 18 July they were occupied making a canvas screen for the engine-room and canvas cask covers for the stores, while the carpenters decked over the 'boats skidds' on the starboard side.

After crossing the Davis Strait, between Greenland and northern Canada, Cape Resolution was sighted on 24 July and *Discovery* entered the eastern entrance to Hudson Strait, meeting pack ice the next day. The crow's nest of a polar ship in those days was a barrel, situated high above the decks on the fore- or mainmast, entered from a trap door below, from which the ship could be navigated through ice. A modern ship has a more sophisticated version of the old barrel, the masthead conning position, sometimes called the 'spotting top'. A speedy passage brought Cape Wolstenholme, at the western end of the Hudson Strait, in sight on 31 July, and on 9 August *Discovery* was hove alongside the jetty at Charlton Island and moored ahead and astern with offshore and onshore moorings.

The crew were at work at 6am the next day, rigging cargo gear, hauling the ship's boat up on shore and discharging and landing cargo. Two hands were filling up fresh water from the shore, while one hand helped the carpenter in caulking, paying and painting the new half-round abreast the engine-room. After Sunday off, Monday was spent tarring the rigging, filling up with fresh water and landing cargo. Discharging and landing cargo continued for twelve hours every day until 6pm for a week. The carpenter fitted shelves in the steward's store room and repaired the jolly boat. The powder magazine was taken down in the 'tween decks.

The *Inenew* arrived and went out to tow the *Stork* to anchor close to the company post. By 8am on 16 August all cargo was out of *Discovery*'s main hold. The gear was then shifted and at noon coaling the bunkers began. Coaling continued for three days, to a total quantity of 80 tons; 54 tons of ballast were loaded and 54 tons of patent fuel.

York Factory, Hudson's Bay Company post, 1910. For many decades the company's principal depot, it was abandoned in 1957, but the main building became an historic site in 1968. (COURTESY HUDSON'S BAY COMPANY, WINNIPEG)

During 20 August the crew continued to take in and trim the sand ballast. The SS *Inenew* came alongside at 10am and discharged twelve barrels of oil, skins, and 48 bales, as well as seven tons of ballast by 11.30am. After this the homeward cargo was taken aboard, consisting of 74 bales, 29 cases of fur, 7 cases of missionary goods and a keg. The carpenter repaired the 'tween deck fore and aft of the main hatch and later the bridge deck, while the crew trimmed the ballast and took on a further 200 gallons of fresh water.

On 22 August *Discovery* was unmoored and her anchor hove. The *Stork* was then taken in tow and dropped down the tide to an anchorage close to the wharf. New main-topgallant clew lines, 26 fathoms each of 2in manilla, and new jib halyards, 38 fathoms of 2in manilla, were rove, while the fore-topgallant clew lines were turned. More water was obtained on Saturday 24 August 1907, the crew being sent away in the large boat with a tank and pumping gear. The Woodall family of four arrived as passengers in the SS *Inenew* and their luggage and nine cases of fur and five bales were unloaded. By 5pm the main hatches were put on and battened down and the ship was ready for sea.

A third Sunday was passed at Charlton Island, as usual without work being done on the Sabbath. In a moderate gale the next day the crew washed the decks and cleared up the after store rooms and forepeak. A new weather cloth was made for the bridge. The anchor was weighed at 5am on 27 August, and the homeward voyage began. Cape Wolstenholme was rounded on 2 September. Three days later icebergs surrounded the ship in the Hudson Strait. The lifeboats and gear were overhauled and cleaned by the crew as *Discovery*, rolling and lurching heavily at times, proceeded towards London. During the passage the crew painted the bridge, cleaned the ship, scraped the pins and rail, put anchors over the bows and scraped, oiled and painted the masts. *Discovery* berthed in London's South West India Dock on 27 September, after a homeward voyage of 32 days.

1908 HBC Voyage

The mate wrote the first entry in the log for the next voyage in *Discovery*, still commanded by Captain Ford, on 13 June 1908. The ship was ready to depart from the West India Dock, her draught of water being 16ft 4in forward and 18ft 6in aft. The customary call was made to take on gunpowder downriver. The vessel anchored in Peterhead Bay and took on stores on 17 June, then proceeded north and west on her usual course south of Cape Farewell towards the Davis Strait and Hudson Strait. The pumps were 'strictly attended to' each day, an entry not previously made in the

logs. This was obviously necessary as the decks flooded fore and aft in the high cross-seas, heavy rain and hard squalls.

On 12 July, when nearing the Hudson Strait, *Discovery* entered open pack, the engines turning at 'slow ahead'. Several icebergs were in sight, and solid pack stretched across the entrance to the strait as the ship approached 'Cape Resolution' and 'Hatton's Head'. This year proved to be particularly bad for ice, and the passage through the Hudson Strait took 28 days, from 13 July to 10 August. Because of the ice, *Stork* was detained and lost that season. Log entries for those days record fog, ice 'closed in all round', mooring the ship to a large floe with two anchors, hard gales with rain, and no open water visible among the heavy pack ice. On 10 August at Cape Wolstenholme the entry proclaims: '10pm. Open water, clear of the pack'.

Passing between Digges Island and Nottingham Island next day, through ridges of scattered ice, they were clear of the pack at noon and able to advance 123 nautical miles in the next 24 hours into Hudson Bay. The usual cautious approach was made to Charlton Island, where a fortnight was spent unloading cargo, including a boiler which had to be slung over the side into a specially prepared boat, coaling the bunkers and obtaining fresh water and ballast. One hundred bags of flour were put aboard the schooner *Pride*. The SS *Inenew* came alongside as usual, being loaded from the shore across *Discovery*'s deck, leaving afterwards for Rupert's House. The homeward cargo consisted of 21 casks of oil, 90 bales, 26 cases, 25 bags of feathers, 25 packs, 2 kegs, 2 boxes and 3 bundles. This year's passengers were Mr and Mrs Donald Gillies and their three children. The ship began her homeward passage on 3 September. Oil bags were again used during gales to prevent the sea breaking on board. She proceeded up the English Channel in early October and berthed in the South West India Dock on 7 October.

No log survives for 1909. However, we know that Captain Ford was still her master. *Discovery* left the West India Dock on 19 June and arrived at Charlton Island on 12 August. She departed from the island on 25 August, berthing on 2 October at the West India Dock.

1910 HBC VOYAGE

Captain Ford again commanded *Discovery* in 1910, with G F Lovegrove as Chief Officer and keeper of the log. The ship unmoored from the South West India Dock on 21 June 1910, all crew being on board. She again took on gunpowder before proceeding to Peterhead, where she anchored from 25 to 27 June. The customary gales were endured during the outward passage. A sudden shift of wind on 5 July in lat. 58° 45'N, long. 25° 15'W increased to a violent gale and brought all hands on deck to reduce sail by lowering topsails and foresail. The upper fore topsail and inner jib were split, and deck cargo was washed adrift. Resolution Island and 'Hatton's Head' were sighted on 21 July, when the crow's nest was sent aloft, ice anchors brought on deck and a ladder rigged to the foretop to reach the crow's nest. The ship was able to work with much less difficulty than two years previously through the ice of the Hudson Strait, and she moored at Charlton Island on 4 August.

Discovery spent some three weeks at Charlton, not departing until 28 August. Another boiler was lifted out of the hold soon after arrival, and the crew discharged cargo on to trolleys on the jetty. The usual repairs to rigging were made, water was taken on board, the forepeak was pumped out and the carpenter payed the seams of the bridge deck to prevent leaking. The crew coaled the cross-bunker from the lower main hold, 28 tons, on 12 August, and the limber boards were taken up and examined and the gear shifted for taking on ballast.

The carpenter also worked on the schooner *Pride* on 15 August, cutting away her main deck to make room for taking the boiler, which was lowered into the hold. A cargo of 18 casks of oil and 71 packages and bales was taken on board *Discovery* from *Inenew*. Eight tons of coal were put on board from the shore, as well as the funnel smoke box and boiler gear.

Unloading and loading were complicated this season. *Discovery* had cargo for the HBC post of York Factory, all of which had to be first landed on shore so that the boiler could be removed and then re-stowed on board afterwards. Four canoes had also been landed for the same reason, and were re-stowed and stored on the skids the same day, 23 August. A total of 236 cases, bales and packs were taken on board from the shore for London, as well as 73 from *Inenew*, plus 18 barrels of oil.

The *Mooswa*, a small steam vessel of 80 tons, had to be taken in tow by *Discovery* to York Factory. On 24 August she was hauled alongside, her deck gear unrigged and stowed away. Twenty tons of coal were put into her hold and bunkers, plus a spare propeller, boiler tubes and ten gallons of oil. Her hatches were battened down and her boat taken aboard *Discovery*. The following day she was made secure and all made ready for sea. *Inenew* arrived from Rupert's House to deliver a further 14 packs of fur. Further preparations for sea were made on 26 and 27 August.

Anchor was weighed at 5.50am on the 28th, then *Discovery* steamed full speed ahead out of the sound. The pilot was discharged at 7am and the *Mooswa* passed astern with the towlines secured.

On 30 August the ship was under sail some miles off Cape Henrietta Maria when the steel towline of the *Mooswa* parted. Two towlines were secured again, but parted almost immediately. The deteriorating weather prevented another attempt, and the *Mooswa* drifted away. At daylight next day she was nowhere to be seen. The lead was cast while the wind increased to a hard gale with a confused heavy sea that filled *Discovery's* deck. The spanker split up the leech and across the cloths. In the afternoon the squalls rose to hurricane force, with the ship labouring and straining heavily.

The *Mooswa* was not in sight at dawn the next morning, 1 September, by which time the wind had moderated to a fresh breeze. Steam was ordered at 5.30am, and an hour later the ship steered to the east-northeast in search of the missing vessel in a strong breeze and ugly sea. At 9.30am *Discovery* came up to the *Mooswa*, dodging close to her until the sea moderated. The log records that at 1pm all hands were on deck and the port lifeboat out. Volunteers were invited, but only three men offered, so the master ordered the boat to be swung in and landed on skids until the sea subsided. At 4pm the master offered a gratuity of £1 per man if they succeeded in getting the *Mooswa* to York, and at 4.30pm the port

lifeboat was swung out and manned by a crew in charge of the mate, and the perilous retrieval was performed without accident.

The next three days were trouble free, apart from occasional dense fog, during which the lead was cast. Land was made out in mid-morning of 6 September, and after a cautious approach, still casting the lead, *Discovery* was anchored in 7 fathoms at 5.30pm in a choppy sea and northeast swell. It was found impossible to keep the *Mooswa* clear of the ship, so the anchor was hove up and the ship steamed round to make a lee side. Three men then got on the *Mooswa* and the towlines were cleared. She was anchored with a 3.5in wire hawser astern of *Discovery*, for fear she would be smashed alongside. Lovegrove wrote in the log that by 8pm they had managed to steam clear and had anchored in 7 fathoms, with all hands on deck. Three rockets were fired from the roadstead to signal the vessel's arrival to the York Factory Post, some 20 miles away. For the watching traders at the fort, the sight of the rockets meant that, at last, the long-sought annual ship from England had arrived with supplies and letters from the outside world.

Discovery's crew cleared the canoes and the jolly boat from the main hatch and rigged cargo gear for both sides of the ship. One cargo boat from York Factory came alongside and was loaded and away by 10am. The second was half-loaded when it had to leave the ship's side, and by midday the three remaining coast boats had to seek shelter, as the wind had increased to a gale. At 5pm the *Mooswa* was found to be dragging her anchor. She drove past *Discovery* and brought up suddenly 200yd astern of her. Much of the next day was spent manoeuvring the tow vessels so that they did not smash against each other.

By 12 September wind and sea had moderated sufficiently for the *Mooswa* to be towed further inshore towards the York Factory beacon, with a seaman at the lead, sounding. Four boats from Fort York were loaded next day. The *Mooswa* was hove alongside *Discovery* and 12 tons of coal were taken out of her into the ship's bunkers. The *Mooswa* also took aboard 450 bags of flour and five cases.

At 8pm on 20 September two rockets were sent

up to signal the Post for boats, and the lights of the *Mooswa* were seen in the distance. She arrived alongside *Discovery* at 4am, and three hours later steamed away for the post with 348 packages of general cargo on board. By 11am three boats had also come alongside and been loaded, thus emptying *Discovery* of her York Factory cargo. A Mr Moir, passenger for London, joined the ship with his luggage. The following day all hands were working on deck taking the Charlton cargo out of the lower hold and re-stowing it in the 'tween decks. The crew painted the combings of the main hatch and the 'tween deck hatch, stowing away hauling lines, warps and fenders. The main hatch was battened down and the jolly boat put in the chocks on the hatch and secured. The ship was made generally ready for sea at 6pm. Snow was falling as the night watch was set.

Discovery was kept waiting by the late arrival of the Second Engineer and two hands from York Factory. They arrived at last by boat at 6.30am on Saturday 24 September, and an hour later the ship steamed full ahead out of the bay, homeward bound towards London. No doubt the three of them would have told their shipmates about their visit to the post in the wilderness, which had once been the heart of the HBC's inland trade. The large mess room in the officers' quarters, whose walls were adorned with oil paintings of Lord Nelson and Trafalgar and the dusky Cree squaws, gaudy in their tartan dresses and embroidered moccasins, waiting upon the officers, would certainly have made a lasting impression upon young Morgan, the Second Engineer.

Sir John Franklin, who died in 1847 off King William Island during the British naval expedition searching for the northwest passage, was landed at York Factory in 1819 and described the Post in detail. It stood on the west bank of the Hayes River, about five miles from its mouth, on a flat, marshy peninsula that was covered with trees, except in the vicinity of the post, where all wood had been expended as fuel. The principal buildings of York Factory were placed in a square, and were two storeys high with flat roofs covered with lead. The officers lived in one portion of the square, and in the other parts merchandise was stored. The servants' houses were ranged around the outside of the square, and the whole was surrounded by a stockade 20ft high. The bank of the river was about 20ft high, but frequently flooded with spring water. A platform was laid from the house to the pier on the bank, to transport stores and furs.

The logistics of HBC and York Factory involved getting the furs from the vast Mackenzie District of northern Canada on board sea-going vessels at York Factory, and the trade goods back. It was impossible to make a return run within the ice-free months. In

York boats, so called because their most usual destination was York Factory, were based on the old Orkney pattern, and were introduced after the 1740s. Bigger than the native birchbark canoes, they could carry considerably larger cargoes of furs and supplies. From Isaac Cowie *The Company of Adventurers* (AUTHOR'S COLLECTION)

the mid-nineteenth century the solution was to collect the furs from everywhere west of Lake Superior in Norway House, from where they were taken down in a large brigade of York boats in August, in time to catch the ship at York Factory. The new shipment of trade goods was picked up and carried to Norway House, to be stored and sorted over the winter. This transport system, with York Factory as its focal point, was in part superseded by the St Paul-Red River route in the 1860s, and by 1870 the importance of York Factory had greatly waned. It was abandoned in 1957, but acquired by the Federal Government some ten years later as an historic building.

Discovery's passage to London from York Road, Nelson Bay, is recorded in the log with familiar entries regarding the gales, the oil bags, and the ship straining heavily and flooding her deck. On this return voyage there was trouble with the steering gear. Despite fall tackles having been put on the tiller to check the heavy strain on the wheel the day before, on 13 October, in a hard gale, the big cogwheel of the steering purchase on the bridge broke in two with the heavy jerking strain of the rudder. The rudder was secured by tackles, and steering tackles were got on the wires, enabling the ship to be steered until the engineers could repair the broken parts the following evening. Discovery was moored to the quay and the crew discharged at the West India Dock by 3.30pm on 5 November 1910. Pasted at the end of this log book is a sworn Protest by John Graham Ford, master of Discovery, for all 'losses, costs and damages' caused by the cables having parted at York Roads, when Mooswa was in tow, dated and signed at Dunfermline in the County of Fife on 27 January 1911.

1911 HBC VOYAGE

The voyage of Discovery from London to the Bay in 1911 may have been Captain Ford's last command, as he was then 62 years old. G F Lovegrove, Chief Officer from 1905 to 1910, was replaced by G R Redfearn, who, as mate, kept the log. This voyage differed from others in that the ship called first at York Factory, from 1 to 5 August, and then at Charlton Island from 14 August to 12 September. The SS Beothic,

of about 3,000 tons displacement, was chartered this season by the HBC to deliver supplies to York Factory and to Charlton, presumably from Montreal, where she was in port from 4 to 19 July.

Despite a seamen's strike, Discovery departed the West India Dock on 17 June 1911, making her usual calls at the Powder Ground off Gravesend and at Peterhead. A first-hand account of this voyage was written by Captain A R Williamson, DSC, who sailed before the mast as an able seaman. Each seaman bought a straw-filled mattress and pillow, a 'donkey's breakfast', at the ships' chandlery's outside the dock gates, and these were delivered on board by the chandler's boy, pushing a handcart. After the port and starboard watches had been picked from the crew by the two mates, these mattresses, plus blankets, were spread by each man in his chosen bunk and a regular ship routine of watch and watch, four hours on deck and four below, was established.

After all sails had been set on 2 July, the engine was stopped, the boiler fires drawn and Discovery proceeded under sail alone, being then some 500 miles east of Cape Farewell, with the Denmark Strait between Greenland and Iceland open to the north. The usual 'fair winds and foul, moderate seas and rough' were encountered, and the seamen went about their duties happy and contented, remembering the four-and-a-half gold sovereigns piling up month by month while the voyage lasted. Captain Williamson described Captain Ford as the happiest man on board. He had been in command of the company's ships for more than 20 years, and was experienced in all the hazards and difficulties encountered during a Hudson Bay voyage. This was his sixth voyage in Discovery, and he was wise to the barque's peculiarities. He was a sailor of the old school, and while at the wheel it was a pleasure to see him study the set of the sails at every turn and hear him chanting his orders in an old fashioned manner: 'Well the main yard! Be-lay there; Oh, Be-e-lay!'

By 19 July Discovery was some 140 miles from Resolution Island at the eastern entrance to Hudson Strait, during a day of fog patches, rain showers and moderate winds. On the previous day the cables had been shackled to the bower anchors, ready for instant use. Able Seaman Williamson was sent up aloft at midnight with three other members of the starboard watch to furl the fore and main topgallant sails. A shout from the Captain: 'Hang on, aloft, Hang on!', gave them a timely warning of a large ice floe right athwart the bows, into which the ship crashed, lifting the bows and whipping the foremast under impact.

Captain Williamson explains how the secret of the entrance into Hudson Strait is to keep to the north, where a branch of the Labrador current turns west. *Discovery*'s auxiliary engines and Captain Ford's skill in ice navigation enabled her to follow leads among the ice floes and bergs to within ten miles of the southern point of Resolution Island. Here the westward-flowing current carried the barque, together with polar pack ice and bergs from the north, in the right direction. Once past Resolution Island they worked their way towards the centre of the Strait, where thinner one-season ice allowed easier going. When the ice was too heavily packed the barque was manoeuvred alongside the adjacent floe to await a lead opening up, rope ladders were put over the side and the crew descended on to the ice with long iron rods with chiselled-off ends. Holes were dug in the ice opposite the bow and stern, into which ice anchors were inserted, thus securely mooring the vessel until they were able to proceed. On these occasions the opportunity was taken to water ship from the pools of fresh water in hollows on the floes. Williamson's account also noted the wildlife of the region: seals, a lone walrus and half-a-dozen magnificent polar bears, their peace disturbed by the bumping and crashing of *Discovery*'s stem thrusting aside the loose pieces of ice in the leads.

More difficult ice conditions were met south of Big Island, where the Strait narrows to 60 miles and the Labrador current peters out. Far heavier ice was then traversed, where the hardened ice of several seasons is carried into Hudson Strait towards Charles Island. By 29 July they were passing Cape Wolstenholme at the western end of the Strait, and the next day, with open water ahead, the officer of the watch was able to descend from the foretop to his usual position on the bridge. Passing between Coats Island

and Mansel Island, the barque proceeded southwest towards York Factory, off which she anchored on 4 August 1911.

A launch came to take Captain Ford ashore, and the crew, apart from the nightwatchman, enjoyed a good night's rest after seven weeks of watch-and-watch. *Mooswa* brought lighters alongside, and a clerk from the Post to receive the 45 tons of cargo. After a spell ashore Captain Ford was in good form, with his barque once more under sail, chanting his orders cheerfully to the crew. *Discovery* anchored off Charlton Island at 8pm on Sunday 13 August, at the end of her outward voyage.

Captain Williamson described the last Sunday evening on Charlton Island, Sunday 10 September 1911. He and his watchmate, Clifford, had paddled over to Danby Island in a borrowed canoe. They strolled back through the woods, enjoying the wild strawberries growing there in profusion, on a beautiful, peaceful and calm evening. Midway across the strait they stopped paddling and sat quietly, breathing in the pure, unpolluted air and admiring a scene they would never forget. The light was fading fast, and ahead of them the black hull of their ship was becoming indistinguishable from the dark woods behind. A flickering light appeared ahead which quickly became a blaze, and they joined their shipmates and the stevedores, who had lit a campfire and were spending a farewell evening yarning and singing.

The following day the barque was made ready for sea, and a small black bear arrived by boat in a rough cage and was embarked as passenger and placed in the large hen coop, apparently not unduly perturbed. *Discovery* sailed for home on 13 September, berthing at the West India Dock on 29 October. The bear, full of life and in good shape after his rough passage, was taken to the London Zoo. The crew received their sovereigns the following Tuesday, watched by Captain Ford, now in a smart city suit. Captain Williamson recorded his own and his shipmates' great respect for this 'Master of the Sea', 'a prime and wise seaman, experienced in commanding and handling a ship in all the hazards and dangers of navigation in northern latitudes'.

CHAPTER

12

TO NEW YORK AND
ARCHANGEL, 1915

I N 1912 *Discovery* and *Pelican* were replaced as supply ships by a steamer newly constructed for Arctic navigation, in which the HBC had a majority interest. This was the legendary *Nascopie*, 2,600 tons, which was to make 36 voyages through the Hudson Strait before sinking off Baffin Island during her last one in 1947. In October 1913 the company agreed to sell *Discovery* for £9,500 to an Antarctic expedition that never sailed. Its leader was J Foster Stackhouse, a Fellow of both the Royal Geographical Society and the Royal Scottish Geographical Societies, who paid £1,000 deposit on the purchase. By 1915 the enterprise had assumed the title of the 'British Antarctic and Oceanographical Expedition', with offices in London and the support of Sir Clements Markham. The aim was to survey as much as possible of the Antarctic coastline, 'to determine what lands are insular and what lands are continental'. Winter quarters were to be established firstly in Graham Land and afterwards in King Edward VII Land. Stackhouse was unable to raise enough money to pay the other instalments on the ship. He died in

1915 aboard the torpedoed *Lusitania*, apparently returning from a fund-raising visit to North America. The £1,000 deposit was kept by the HBC, which maintained that the expenses entailed in retaining the steamer at the expedition's disposal in the South West India Dock amounted to more than that sum.

THE FIRST WORLD WAR, 1914-1918

Discovery was to play a small part in the great conflict that brought to an end on 4 August 1914 the *Pax Britannica* that had existed since the defeat of Napoleon a century before. She was one of a merchant fleet of some 300, purchased and financed by the HBC, acting as agents for the French Government. Managed by the specially formed Bay Steamship Company, these vessels were to transport munitions, food, raw materials and manufactured goods for the army and, later, for civilian needs. The agreement came about as an initiative of a young brandy merchant, Monsieur Jean Monnet, who had traded for several years with the HBC. Years later he wrote in his published memoirs: 'We needed furs, the trappers liked cognac'.

In August 1914, at the very beginning of the First World War, Monnet suggested to the London directors that they should become the purchasing agents for the French Government, and also proposed to the French Premier that France and Great Britain should co-operate over supplies and shipping during the war. His scheme was endorsed by both nations, and the experience gained by Monnet during these negotiations led to his being the architect of the European Common Market, now the European Union, after the Second World War.

Thus it was that the HBC came to play a crucial and hazardous role in Allied shipping and supplies during the four years of the First World War. The com-

SS *Nascopie* loading munitions of war at Brest for Archangel, from Sir Wm Schooling. *The Governor and Company of Adventurers*
(AUTHOR'S COLLECTION)

pany signed some 6,600 separate contracts with various agencies of the French Government, in addition to many with the Romanian, Russian and Belgian governments. It employed 145 agents in various countries throughout the world, and a merchant fleet of several hundred ships was organised. Some of these were purchased, while others were chartered or managed for the various governments. More than 13,000,000 tons of goods were transported, as well as a substantial number of soldiers, refugees and escaped prisoners of war. During this time the HBC lost 110 vessels, primarily to enemy submarine action.

The Governor of the HBC, Robert (later Lord) Kindersley, called in Charles Vincent Sale to run this far-flung network. Born in 1868 into the big business world of the family shipping concern, Sale & Co, Sale had a distinguished career and was decorated with orders by Japan, Belgium, France and Denmark. He was an impressive and able man, and to some extent a visionary. His eagerness to introduce modern trading methods to the company's ventures did not endear him to the long-serving wintering partners or fur traders; however, historians and scientists have reason to be grateful to him for centralising the HBC's archives in London.

Discovery became part of this great enterprise in 1915, the year described by Winston Churchill as 'disastrous to the cause of the Allies and to the whole world'. The lost opportunity in Churchill's opinion was not to have used Britain's supremacy at sea to relieve the isolation of Russia by forcing the Belts into the Baltic, or Dardanelles into the Black Sea. This was the background to *Discovery*'s voyages to north Russia later in 1915, and to the Russian Black Sea ports in 1919-20.

TRANSATLANTIC VOYAGE TO NEW YORK, 1915

Having spent four years in her lying-up berth in the West India Dock, the barque needed refitting. She was assisted into dry dock in the spring and re-rigged in the London docks for £55 11s 0d, an inconsiderable sum. The boats were repaired and equipped to Board of Trade regulations, and medical items were provided. Fresh, dried, pickled and preserved provisions and three dozen live chickens were taken on board.

In its letter of 17 April the company trusted that *Discovery* had been satisfactorily fitted out and told her master, Captain Williams, to look to Mr N Bacon, the Fur Trade Commissioner, on arrival in New York. It wished him a speedy voyage and safe return. *Discovery* sailed in ballast. She was forced to put back into Falmouth on 25 April 1915 because of a bad leak in the rudder truck, and then suffered a rough transatlantic passage, with twenty-seven days of strong headwinds. With only eight tons of coal left in her bunkers she had to put into Halifax before arriving at New York on 9 June 1915. Writing from the Empire Building, Broadway, on 15 June, the company agent reported to London that almost all of the foremast rigging would have to be renewed, while work on the lower rigging was already in hand. The decks were in a very bad shape and would have to be recaulked in a number of places before cargo could be properly carried. The engine-room also required some repairs. The agent considered that many of her fittings had been removed to SS *Pelican*, and that she had been sent from London with undue haste. Despite several enquiries, he had been unable to sell *Discovery*, and asked for the lowest figure the Board was prepared to accept. He hoped to despatch her on 16 June with a full cargo of 415 tons of caustic soda, 360,000 empty bags and 22,000 yards of corduroy.

On 21 June 1915 *Discovery* sailed from New York for La Pallice, the outer port of La Rochelle. Captain Williams wrote from La Pallice, confirming his arrival there in a letter received in London on 20 July. The first few days of the passage had been fine, but after five days at sea the ship had sprung a bad leak. Provision stores were destroyed, rooms and cabins were flooded for four days, and 35 tons of coal were lost off the deck in a heavy gale. He reported that the ship was still leaking badly and that he had to keep the pumps going every watch, fearing damage to the lower part of the cargo. He considered it a mistake that she 'had not had a caulking iron put into her, inside and out, when in dry dock in London'. The fore topsail yard was gone altogether, and the yard was now strung with chains.

The cathedral and quay at Archangel, c1895. The cathedral was later blown up by the Bolsheviks.
(AUTHOR'S COLLECTION)

Having discharged her cargo, *Discovery* sailed from La Pallice for Falmouth, where she arrived on 30 July and awaited orders. There Captain Williams resigned and was succeeded for the passage to Swansea by the Chief Officer, G F Bush. Captain Williams's report, dated 17 August 1915, records that neither the decks nor the outside of the ship had been touched in London before her departure for New York. Certain parts were suffering dry rot, and he considered the ship had been damaged under the stern. The crew had refused to continue before they put into Falmouth on the outward voyage, and the repairs were not satisfactorily carried out there due to pressure from London. She sailed with a plank still out of position, and on arrival was too low in the water for anyone to get near it. During the return voyage another leak developed, in the centre of the provision store. There were insufficient tools on board for the engineers to carry out the work, and neither evaporator nor condenser, so that salt water was used in the boilers, which had to be scaled out in New York.

On 4 February 1915, when *Discovery* was still in dock, the German Admiralty declared the waters surrounding Great Britain and Ireland, including the whole of the English Channel, a war zone, and stated that from 18 February 'every enemy merchant vessel found within this war zone' would be destroyed, 'without it always being possible to avoid danger to the crews and passengers'. The German submarine attacks did not begin to bite hard until 1917, and on her first wartime voyage *Discovery* seems to have been in far greater danger of foundering from tempests of the deep than from enemy action. Attention must have been given to improve her state of repair in Swansea during August 1915, from where she departed for Manchester under Captain William James Bartley, arriving on 7 September. Bartley was to be her master during her next two voyages, the first to Archangel and the second to the Atlantic ports of France.

Voyage to Archangel, 1915

The Russian Empire was part of the old order destroyed by the First World War. The Imperial Russia of Tsar Nicholas II was almost sealed off from the rest of the world, not by an Iron Curtain, but by the accident of geography. Peter the Great's famous 'window to the west' in the Baltic was closed by German naval supremacy, and the south Russian ports on the Black Sea by the entry of Turkey into the war on the German side.

Before the First World War, Russia had paid for her imports of farm machinery and manufactured goods by the export of wheat, eggs, other foodstuffs and raw materials. But when the Bosphorus became blocked by Turkey, and the Baltic by Germany, neither exports nor imports could move. The only remaining large port was Vladivostok, on the Pacific Ocean, linked with St Petersberg over vast distances by the Trans-

Siberian railway. This left Archangel on the White Sea as the main port of entry for vital munitions and equipment for the Russian army and the export terminal for food and other products, including the wood alcohol used in the manufacture of explosives.

Archangel was frozen in the winter months and had extremely limited facilities for handling goods. The quays were too small, with insufficient warehousing, and the railway station was on the wrong side of the river Dvina. Only a single line of narrow gauge, without adequate rolling stock, ran south from Archangel to Vologda, where goods had to be rehandled.

The main prewar trade of the other White Sea ports had been the export of timber, floated down-river to the sea. None of them was linked by rail, so they were unable to relieve congestion at Archangel until the Murman railway was built. Nevertheless, some efforts were made, and reindeer carried light ammunition across snow-bound country during the winter.

Unfortunately, there was not one first-class icebreaker stationed in the White Sea. Russia had the world's most powerful icebreaker, *Yermak*, 10,000 hp, but she was imprisoned in the Baltic. The Russian authorities therefore negotiated the purchase of a number of Canadian icebreakers, including the fine-lined *Earl Grey*, which was renamed *Canada* on her arrival in Archangel in October 1914. Orders were also placed for new icebreakers from British yards, then pre-eminent in shipbuilding and repair.

Ice was not the only enemy to be faced by merchant ships. The Germans recognised the importance of the White Sea route to the Russian war effort, and in early June 1915 despatched the auxiliary cruiser *Meteor*, escorted by a submarine, to lay 285 mines. In the next three months ten vessels, British, Russian and neutral, were damaged or lost to mines. A minesweeping expedition of six trawlers and two supply ships sent from Lowestoft by the Admiralty destroyed 150 mines. Minesweeping stopped in November 1915, at

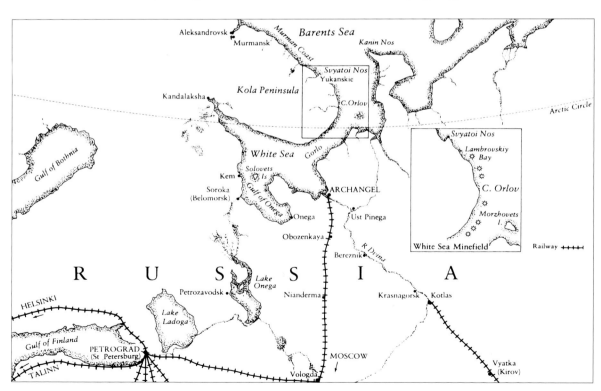

Map of North Russia, illustrating the *Discovery's* voyage through the White Sea to Archangel in 1915.
(VERA BRICE).

the onset of a particularly severe winter.

The Royal Navy's White Sea or Arctic Squadron operated in these waters, its Commodore being senior naval officer in Archangel. A second senior officer was stationed at Murmansk, in command of the old battleship *Albemarle* and of the cruisers and smaller vessels within his jurisdiction. He also dealt daily with Russian officials in the vicinity. Stationed at the mouth of the channel leading to the White Sea, a third senior officer commanded in 1916 HMS *Intrepid*, her sister ship HMS *Iphigenia*, four armed boarding steamers, two yachts, sixteen trawlers, plus colliers and smaller vessels. It was the duty of the Arctic Squadron, and particularly of the British minesweeping

At the market Archangel. c1915.
(IMPERIAL WAR MUSEUM).

trawlers, to keep a safe channel swept for shipping sailing inward and outward. Hundreds of ships passed through each season, laden with coal, guns, and munitions, many with single cargoes valued at more than two million pounds. It was only the old *Intrepid* and the other units of the British Arctic Squadron which made this traffic possible, by keeping open the mouth of Archangel, through which the Russian bear was fed.

Further south, the Tenth Cruiser Squadron Northern Patrol was engaged in the blockade of Germany. Its ships operated on the high seas in all weathers, despite the presence of submarines, in an area of 22,000 square miles that formed a rough triangle between Iceland, Norway and Scotland. By the end of 1915 over 3,000 vessels had been intercepted, of which more than 700 were sent to British ports because they carried contraband or suspicious cargoes. In charge of the Tenth Cruiser Squadron was Rear Admiral Dudley de Chair, whose flagship was *Alsatian*. Her record of being at sea for 262 days of the year 1915, steaming 71,500 miles and using

over 40,000 tons of coal, was typical of the work of each ship of the squadron.

These were the seas through which *Discovery*'s voyage to north Russia would take her in the autumn of 1915. Under Captain Bartley she departed from Manchester on 8 September, calling at Nantes and Bordeaux before visiting Brest. Here, from 1915 to 1917, goods from French factories and American ports were piled up for shipment to Russia. *Discovery*'s freight account shows that she carried a cargo of munitions from Brest to Archangel, arriving on 22 October 1915. Her exact route is uncertain, as the log for this voyage is missing, but she must have sailed north from Brest and rounded the North Cape of Norway, probably at some distance from the coast, where it was thought there was less danger from submarines. She would then have been escorted by minesweepers from Yukanskiy with other cargo ships to the Gulf of Archangel and the mouth of the Dvina River, some 30 miles downstream from Archangel, where the HBC had a representative, Mr C Fuog. He had travelled to north Russia with the French Vice-Consul to implement the agreement with the French Government to transport wheat from Archangel to the French ports. The HBC was to supply the steamers, but the responsibility for finding the cargo and labour was that of the French. Fuog was there to 'smooth the way'. German mines and poorly charted waters made it impossible to keep to schedule. Apart from winter ice, there was a shortage of labour and the port lacked adequate facilities. For four years, until the British Government ordered the removal of all British subjects, virtually all munitions from France for Russia and Romania were transported to Archangel under the company's flag. On the return voyages more than 350,000 tons of wheat, carried by rail and river from Siberia, together with timber, ore, flax, hemp, beetroot seeds and other cargo, were taken to French ports.

Steamer No 141 – *Discovery* – discharged her 500 tons of cargo at the Russian government berth of Bakaritsya. During the outward voyage bad weather had caused the ship to labour and strain heavily. The decks were rotten in parts and had leaked a lot, making a great deal of water in the bottom. Thirty-five tons of coal had been lost in a storm at sea and, afraid that some of the cargo might have been damaged, Bartley extended a legal protest against the weather encountered on the passage. The ship's company was paid a war bonus for this voyage, a monthly extra £5 for the Captain, £3 for the Engineer and mate, and £1 for the firemen and sailors. There was much to do in port: manoeuvring the vessel for discharge and loading, taking on coal for the return voyage, dealing with various officials and getting *Discovery* swung in the ice to ascertain the deviation of her compass. Visits ashore were possible too, to Archangel, a city of gleaming domes, wide streets and wooden houses, each with a geranium, fuchsia or oleander at its window. Apart from handling the timber, the women seemed to do all the work, even the boating. They washed their linen in the river and were accustomed to living a hard life in an inhospitable climate.

Discovery loaded 557 barrels of wood alcohol, of which 364 were iron drums and 193 wooden barrels. The loading and stowage proved difficult because only one hatch was big enough to take in cargo, and the drums had to be rolled the length of the ship. She was fortunate to depart for Le Havre before the freezing of the Dvina and the White Sea.

Bartley discharged his cargo of wood alcohol in northern France, thus contributing to the Allied war effort. He was instructed to take the East Coast route home and to call at Dundee for orders. From there he wrote to London on 19 November, before leaving for Le Havre, to report that the top tier of barrels had come adrift when the between-deck stanchions gave way in a heavy northerly gale, and that he was having them re-stowed. He suggested that the addition of 'bilge pieces' to the hull would stop the vessel labouring so much, and that with a four-bladed propeller she would do an ordinary tramp speed. The construction of a fore hatchway for delivering and taking in cargo would save much in labour, he added.

Discovery was lucky both to escape being frozen in at Archangel and to miss a violent storm with dense snow squalls and a tremendous sea in the North Atlantic on Christmas Eve 1915, when the old Scottish whaler *Active* and the brave little *Morning* were both lost. The story of PQ17 and other convoys to Russia during the Second World War is deservedly well known. Perhaps this account of *Discovery*'s voyage to north Russia in 1915 will draw attention to their predecessors in the First World War.

The icebreaker *Canada* formerly *Earl Grey*, at Archangel, North Russia, February 1919.
She was bought from Canada and arrived in Archangel, October 1914.
(IMPERIAL WAR MUSEUM)

13

THE SEARCH FOR SHACKLETON, 1916

A S RECOUNTED EARLIER, Lieutenant Ernest Shackleton, RNR, had been a member of the National Antarctic Expedition of 1901-04, but was invalided home in the *Morning* at the end of the first year, to his own intense disappointment and to the regret of his friends. Having drunk these bitter dregs, his roving and adventurous spirit would not let him rest until he had returned to the Antarctic, this time as leader of the *Nimrod* expedition of 1907-09. He sledged with three companions to within 97 miles of the South Pole, ascending the great Beardmore Glac-

ier, named after his patron, and discovering some 500 miles of new mountain ranges bordering the Ross Ice Shelf. The following years saw the attainment of the South Pole by the Norwegian explorer Roald Amundsen, and the deaths of Captain Scott and the British Pole party during the *Terra Nova* expedition of 1910-13.

Shackleton next set himself the heroic task of crossing the Antarctic continent from the Weddell Sea to the Ross Sea, as leader of the Imperial Trans-Antarctic Expedition, which was financed very largely by the great Dundee jute manufacturer Sir James

Seeing off *Discovery* at Devonport, August 1916. The boy is Peter Scott, son of Captain Scott, with his mother behind him. Emily Shackleton is leaning on the capstan while Rear Admiral Sir Lewis Beaumont is on the left.
(TOPHAM PICTURE LIBRARY)

Caird. Its Weddell Sea party in *Endurance* sailed from London on 1 August 1914, only three days before the outbreak of war. Shackleton offered to place the ship, crew and stores at the nation's disposal, but received a telegram from the First Lord of the Admiralty, Winston Churchill, which read 'Proceed'. After consulting King George V and his benefactors, Shackleton resolved to carry on.

THE DEMISE OF THE ENDURANCE

Endurance sailed south and became beset in the ice at the head of the Weddell Sea. The dog teams trained for the crossing of Antarctica never ventured on to the continent. They remained with the ship, which drifted north until she was crushed and sank on 21 November 1915, some 200 miles east of the Antarctic Peninsula, south of the Antarctic Circle in the northwest

MAIN PICTURE: *Endurance* heeling over in the ice of the Weddel Sea, Antarctica, during Shackleton's Imperial Trans-Antarctic Expedition, 1914-17. Photograph by Frank Hurley.
(SCOTT POLAR RESEARCH INSTITUTE)

INSET: Shackleton's men marooned on Elephant Island after the sinking of the *Endurance*. Photograph by Frank Hurley.
(SCOTT POLAR RESEARCH INSTITUTE)

Ross Sea party, had been landed from *Aurora*. Their duty was to lay depots to the southward that could be picked up by the crossing party on the second half of their traverse, from the South Pole towards Mount Erebus and McMurdo Sound.

Shackleton's men from *Endurance* continued to live in squalor under two of the upturned boats on a grey beach above high water, below the cliffs of Elephant Island, surviving on a diet largely consisting of penguins, other birds, seals and shellfish. News of their plight reached the world from the Falkland Islands. Transported by the small whaler *Southern Sky*, Shackleton had gone ashore at Port Stanley from South Georgia, which he reached at the end of his epic voyage from Elephant Island, in the third of *Endurance's* boats, the *James Caird*. His telegrams reached England late on 31 May 1916, claiming public attention before news began to arrive of the Battle of Jutland. Elephant Island is well north of the Antarctic Circle and does not suffer winter darkness, but it can become ice-bound. Shackleton was anxious to rescue his men before they had to endure much more of the winter. His first attempt, in the *Southern Sky*, was unsuccessful because of the sea ice.

Despite the exigencies of war, a Shackleton Relief Advisory Committee had been set up by the Admiralty in London *before* any news came from Shackleton. Its chairman was Admiral Sir Lewis Beaumont, and among a strong committee were two with recent polar experience, Dr W S Bruce and Sir Douglas

quadrant of the Weddell Sea. The party camped on the floes, which continued to drift northwards. When at last they reached the open sea, three ship's boats were launched and, after great deprivations suffered by their crews, beached safely on desolate Elephant Island, to the north of the Antarctic Peninsula. Meanwhile, on the opposite side of the continent, the other half of the Imperial Trans-Antarctic Expedition, known as the

Mawson. The Government approved the Relief Committee's report of 16 May 1916. This recommended the despatch of *Discovery* to examine the shores of the Weddell Sea, having been equipped with dogs, tents, and sledges and provisioned for two years.

The work of the Committee stopped briefly after Shackleton's arrival in the Falkland Islands, since it was thought a rescue vessel would be found there. However, it appeared that no ship suitable for use in the ice was available in South America or at the Cape, so Shackleton urged the despatch of a relief expedition from England. The HBC offered to lend *Discovery* free of charge, and the committee agreed to equip her for six months to send her south under the command of an experienced Ice Master. On arrival, they recommended, the relief ship 'should be placed at the disposal and under the orders of Sir Ernest Shackleton'. *Discovery* was manned and equipped at Devonport with great dispatch. She was ready to sail by 5 August, but lost a further five days because of 'war delays' to the collier that was to tow her south.

The man chosen to command her was Captain James Fairweather, aged 63, who had been master of the whaler *Aurora* in the northern whale fishery throughout the 1880s. Fairweather was granted a temporary commission as Lieutenant Commander, RNR. He was described as a man of genial personality, with a great fund of Scottish humour. Photographs taken on departure show him holding a black cat. His sailing orders, dated 2 August 1916, stated that when *Discovery* was 'in all respects ready for sea' he should leave Devonport, in tow of the collier *Polesley*, for the Falkland Islands. If Shackleton was at Port Stanley, the

Elephant Island rescue was to be thought out with him, in accordance with the letter to be given to the explorer. Shackleton was to be taken on board, and his wishes were to be carried out 'as far as possible'.

Directions were also given for the treatment of those rescued, and for the marking of graves. No bodies were to be embarked. On their return to Port Stanley, the rescued men should be landed and transferred to the charge of Shackleton. However, a passage home in *Discovery* might be offered to those willing to accept the accommodation and certified fit to undergo the long voyage. If Sir Ernest was not at Port Stanley, or was unable to accompany him, Captain Fairweather was to proceed with the rescue to the best of his ability.

The letter and enclosed copy of Captain Fairweather's orders addressed to Shackleton repeated these instructions. In contrast to the Advisory Committee's recommendation, it stated that command of the ship, any action taken and responsibility for all on board must belong in Fairweather's hands.

Portrait of Captain James Fairweather who took command of *Discovery* during the Shackleton Relief Voyage, 1916.
(TOPHAM PICTURE LIBRARY)

THE VOYAGE SOUTH

Discovery began her voyage in the early evening of 10 August 1916. A hawser from SS *Polesley*, the collier ordered to tow her to the Falklands, was shackled on in Plymouth Sound. An armed trawler escorted her on each bow for the first 100 miles towards the Cape Verde Islands. A motor launch was carried on deck, and barrels of salt pork were stowed in the forepeak. The potatoes quickly began to go bad at the start of the voyage. More than 200 miles were covered in each 24 hours, much farther than *Discovery*'s unaided power would have allowed. The log does not record any difficulties with the tow, despite a great deal of rough weather, but in the tropics on 1 September the upper main topmast staysail was carried away and, two days later, the ship was 'diving and jumping heavily'.

After 20 days' passage from the Cape Verde Islands the two vessels arrived at Montevideo on 11 September. Here the hawser was slipped from *Discovery*'s chain-bridle and she proceeded with *Polesley* to the anchorage. The crew were employed scrubbing down *Discovery*'s side where grass had grown, and removing barnacles under the stern.

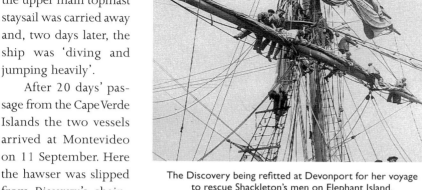

The *Discovery* being refitted at Devonport for her voyage to rescue Shackleton's men on Elephant Island.
(AUTHORS COLLECTION)

Shackleton, meanwhile, had been far from idle, organising further rescue attempts in various South American craft. The last of these, in the *Yelcho*, a small Chilean naval vessel, was successful. On 30 August 1916, with their bay free of ice, the Elephant Island party, ably led during their months there by Frank Wild, embarked by boat from the beach in less than an hour, for fear the ice should return. Shackleton's delight at finding them all alive was equalled by theirs at seeing him. *Yelcho* returned in triumph to Punta Arenas, with Shackleton immensely pleased that he had managed to organise the rescue trip without the Admiralty. Inevitably, he would have resented their Lordships' stipulation that Fairweather, and not he, should command *Discovery* after her arrival in Port Stanley. It is stated in the Advisory Committee's Final Report that the Admiralty only heard of his success through the newspapers.

At Montevideo the purpose of *Discovery*'s voyage was negated, since the marooned men had been rescued. The surgeon, Dr G M Martin, wanted to get home, and was paid off and discharged. While orders were awaited, fresh-water tanks were refitted and some painting done. The crew were allowed liberty ashore one day, with a steam-launch to take them there and back. *Discovery* was next piloted to Buenos

Aires to take on a cargo of grain. Bad weather plagued them *en route*, and on arrival they had to be towed into harbour on 21 September.

The next day, Flynn, the Second Cook, was arrested on Fairweather's orders and taken to gaol, no reason being given. A hundred tons of coal were landed. The sails were loosened, dried and furled, and a squad of caulkers worked on the vessel's seams. The holds were cleaned for cargo, as were the decks. On 28 September, after a squad of carpenters had made ready the hold, the wheat was loaded in bags. On 30 September *Discovery* departed Buenos Aires under her own steam, homeward bound. The deck log records that engines were stopped on 11 October, 'to see how the ship would act under canvas'. However, the trial proved a failure even with the helm hard over, so full speed had to be rung.

On 16 October *Discovery* berthed at Pernambuco, where water and coal were taken on and the cargo was shifted. Bad weather still harassed the vessel in the lower latitudes, and she berthed on 31 October in a gale at St Vincent, Cape Verde Islands. On 3 November Captain Fairweather, in the words of the log, called the crew together and explained to them that he had been invalided home and that the chief officer, J Cumming, would now become Master. He was replaced as mate by H Moar. Perhaps Captain Fairweather, an elderly man, was exhausted by the responsibilities and disappointment of the voyage.

Discovery departed St Vincent on 8 November, all fore- and aft sails being set. More gales were encountered on passage and the decks, engine-room and officers' cabins were all flooded as *Discovery* rolled, shipping heavy seas. On 28 November the Eddystone Light was abeam and the vessel anchored later in Plymouth Sound, entering the basin next day.

14

LAST WARTIME VOYAGES

THE ADMIRALTY HANDED *Discovery* back to the HBC, then operating the Bay Steamship Company, at Devonport on 18 December 1916. Her new master was Captain L Hiles. After coaling and signing-on crew she crossed the English Channel to Lorient on the south coast of Brittany, where she joined an extensive coasting service for transporting grain and other supplies from incoming ocean steamers to the smaller ports of France. A system of convoys was in operation to combat the menace of German submarines. Most of *Discovery*'s logs have survived from these war years, and the following narrative is largely based upon these.

FRENCH ATLANTIC PORTS,
DECEMBER 1916 TO JULY 1917

In Lorient *Discovery* discharged the 5,943 bags of South American wheat taken on in Buenos Aires and departed towards Bordeaux on 12 January 1917. At Pauillac, a small port on the south bank of the Gironde to seaward of Bordeaux, she loaded 350 tons of wheat, which were discharged at Bayonne from 23 to 26 January. There was an embargo in force at Bayonne, as there had been at Pauillac, and the ship was not allowed to proceed until 28 January, with a pilot on board. At Rochefort she moored alongside the French ship *Laennec* on 31 January 1917 and took on 350 tons of wheat, which she discharged at Bayonne. Here she loaded a cargo of zinc plates, presumably for batteries, and departed for Nantes, escorted by a French gunboat. On 12 February, 'following Admiralty instructions' and under convoy escort, she proceeded to Saint Nazaire and then up river to Nantes, where the zinc plates were unloaded and 300 tons of sugar and 30 tons of bunker coal were taken on. On 19 February dense

fog stopped all navigation in the River Loire, and a day later there was further delay owing to a large quantity of drift ice in the river. The following day she proceeded downstream and towards Brest, where she discharged 3,700 bags of sugar and coaled again from 24 to 28 February. On 13 March *Discovery* took aboard 853 bags of wheat and received orders from the French Admiralty to sail early the following morning.

Under convoy from Brest she proceeded to Lorient, where she discharged from 18 to 22 March. From there she continued in snow squalls towards Nantes, calling in to discharge and load at Saint Nazaire and Rochefort. On 30 April she reached Bordeaux, where Captain F Gray became her master. Sugar was her main cargo for the next few weeks as she steamed her way between the French Atlantic ports. While proceeding towards Bordeaux under convoy a shock was felt in the after part of the ship, which appeared to have struck some sunken wreckage. Water began rising in the engine-room bilges, and pumps were used to keep it under control. On 21 June 1917 *Discovery* steamed into Brest harbour and was shifted with three tugs, first to the military dock and then to the dry dock. Once she was pumped dry, workmen began the repair work. Mr Nicholls, the owner's superintendent, visited the ship and found several treenails loose and the vessel's bottom leaking badly. Repairs and the caulking of her bottom took several days, but she eventually left the dry dock for Commerce Dock, assisted by tugs. Much of *Discovery*'s log of this time records anchoring in bays or harbours, awaiting instructions to join a convoy. Even so, a steady progress of discharging cargo and reloading was achieved. She berthed in Barry Dock, South Wales, in late July 1917.

BARRY TO MADEIRA AND BORDEAUX, AUGUST – NOVEMBER 1917

Captain Gray continued as master of *Discovery*, with G Pearce as mate, during this voyage to Madeira. A larger quantity of coal than usual, 144 tons, was taken on for bunkering, plus a cargo of coal of 569 tons. The embargo in force at Barry was lifted on 31 August, when the vessel proceeded down the Bristol Channel under Admiralty instructions. At Milford Haven she awaited permission to leave for several days, proceeding as instructed on 6 September, and arrived in Funchal on 15 September. Coal was discharged over three days, and the hold washed out. A general cargo, which included heavy guns, was loaded before departing for Bordeaux. Fresh gales and heavy seas caused her to strain severely during the return voyage, and she put into Bilbao for bunkers in early October, finally arriving at Bordeaux on 16 October. She discharged between 18 and 22 October, when it was found that several casks were broken in the Number 1 hold. She loaded again at Pauillac and proceeded in heavy seas and gales towards Barry, sheltering in Mousehole Bay before discharging, first at Barry and then at Cardiff, where a new mate, A J Bills, took over and concluded the log on 15 November.

FRENCH ATLANTIC PORTS, NOVEMBER 1917 – APRIL 1918

Discovery departed Cardiff on 19 November 1917 and returned there on February 1918, having called at Saint-Nazaire, Nantes and Bayonne, her master again being Captain Gray. The next and last of these French coastal voyages began at Cardiff on 23 February 1918 and terminated there on 25 April 1918. While *Discovery* lay at anchor in Brest Bay, a destroyer patrolling the harbour damaged her port bow. The log also recounts that on 12 March, when the pilot came on board alongside the wharf at Bayonne to shift her to the discharging berth, the crew could not turn out to move her because they were all drunk. Gray had to engage five men from a Spanish vessel to move the ship on the next tide, as five of *Discovery*'s had gone ashore without leave. One of the seamen,

Map showing convoy routes in the Bay of Biscay, 1917-18.

D. Adamtzevitch, was imprisoned in the town gaol for three days after being questioned about his behaviour, and responding by using abusive language and throwing buckets about. He was eventually paid off in Bayonne in mid-April.

LAST VOYAGE TO HUDSON BAY, 1918-19

Discovery's voyage of 1918 to Hudson Bay was her last to the north and her last wartime voyage. Her master was Captain G H Mead of Cardiff, who was making his first voyage as master to the Bay. She sailed under the flag of Sale and Company, which firm provided a gun and two gunners for the Atlantic crossing. She left Cardiff on 6 June 1918, provisioned for 12 months and carrying 304 tons of coal for her bunkers and some 400 tons as cargo, and arrived safely in Montreal on 30 June after what Mead called 'a very good passage out, being twenty-two days from Pilot to Pilot'. A bonus of an extra month's wages was to be paid to all who completed the Bay voyage satisfactorily.

Discovery departed Montreal for Charlton Island on 13 July 1918, with a cargo of Welsh coal plus Canadian goods comprising flour, pork, fats and eighteen canoes, totalling some 700 tons. She was equipped with a motor boat. News of the war was scanty in the north, and came mostly as rumour. The original purpose of *Discovery's* voyage was to land cargo at Charlton Island only and to return in ballast, but it was later decided that she should bring the Charlton 'returns' as far as St John's, Newfoundland. Special stowage and dunnage (packing and wedges) were necessary to protect her cargo from leaks. Mead received his instructions from the Fur Trade Commissioner of the HBC in Montreal, Mr N H Bacon, urging him to take all precautions in navigating the ship by making proper use of the lead, so as to avoid untoward misfortune. *Discovery* vessel had a long and difficult passage of the Hudson Strait, probably because of Mead's lack of experience. He failed to enter the Strait close to Resolution Island, to take advantage of the current flowing west along the north shore, and his diary records that his ship was set in towards Cape Chidley. This area is dan-

gerous for shipping, owing to the convergence of the southbound Labrador current with the current flowing east along the south shore of the Hudson Strait, both carrying masses of ice. Fast in the ice and right under the cliff, she was only half a ship's length from destruction. If the cliffs had not been steep-to and the ship had taken the ground, she would have been lost. Fortunately, the ice eased up before she was again beset.

The chief officer's log records ice-inflicted damage to rudder and steering gear on 28 July. Two weeks later, after a period of fog and heavy snow falls, another awkward situation was encountered at the western end of the strait, to the north of Salisbury Island, when she should have been south of it. The vessel was trapped by heavy ice from Foxe Basin flowing to the east towards Charles Island. The ice loosened and *Discovery* was eventually worked into Hudson Bay. James Bay was found clear of ice, and she anchored at last at Charlton Island on 10 September. Captain Mead sent aloft a topgallant mast and yard at Charlton Island. The mast was cut there, but he had to buy the yard from the HBC post because he could not find a sufficiently large tree from which to make it.

Discovery departed Charlton Island on 24 September, reaching St John's, Newfoundland, on 13 October. Mead reported to the HBC that the ice damage was not great, and suggested that the vessel should remain in eastern Canada for the seal fishery in the spring and for voyages to Hudson Bay. The worldwide Spanish influenza epidemic attacked a number of the crew in both St John's and Halifax, Nova Scotia, including the engineer, who proved difficult to replace. Meanwhile, the war had ended with the signing of the Armistice on 11 November 1918. *Discovery* sailed at last for England from Halifax on Christmas Eve, bound for Liverpool. She carried a cargo of some 2,000 cases of canned goods, 113 cases of bronze powder, 1,035 kegs of nails and a sample case of fish. The pumps had to be kept going continually throughout the voyage to keep the leaks under control, and Mead was forced to put into Queenstown (now Dun Loaghaire), Ireland, for bunkers and to get the ship on an even keel again. This long-drawn-out final voyage terminated in Liverpool on 16 January 1919. Mead sent an abstract of his diary to the RGS, summarising the voyage and observing that *Discovery* was still afloat and earning her keep.

COASTING THE FRENCH ATLANTIC PORTS AND THE LOW COUNTRIES, 1919

The voyage to Hudson Bay was followed by two coasting voyages to France and the Low Countries during the first half of 1919. There was a shortage of shipping immediately after the war, and *Discovery* continued to act as a small cargo vessel, presumably very largely under steam.

The first of these voyages, again under Captain G H Mead, started in Liverpool and terminated in Kingston-upon-Hull. Her ports of call were Antwerp, London, Antwerp and King's Lynn. She left Liverpool on 20 February, sighting a floating

Discovery beset in Hudson Strait.
(COURTESY HUDSON'S BAY COMPANY, WINNIPEG)

mine in the North Sea en route for Antwerp, where her cargo was discharged at the Old Dock. She proceeded by way of Orfordness, south of Aldeburgh, on both the outward and return passages. Next, she steamed up the London River to Blackwall, where she began loading barrels of petroleum from lighters and bunkering, the cargo amounting to some 2,059 casks in the hold and 1,341 cases of fish on deck. The oil was safely discharged at the Continental Petroleum Company's wharf, Antwerp, as was the fish, on 16 and 17 March.

Discovery then crossed the North Sea again, taking on a pilot off Orfordness as usual and another at King's Lynn for Hull on 21 March. Strong gales and heavy snow squalls prolonged the voyage.

During her second coasting voyage of 1919 the vessel's master was Captain D D Richards. This began

and ended at Hull, with two calls at Bordeaux, three at Rotterdam, one at Dunkerque and two at Le Havre. During one of the passages to Rotterdam a strong wind and rough head sea caused *Discovery* to 'plunge'. She put into Dartmouth, perhaps for shelter and certainly to coal, and proceeded to Rotterdam, where a tug helped her to dock on 26 April.

From Rotterdam, assisted by a tug, she proceeded towards the Hook of Holland in the early morning of 30 April but was unable to stem the tide and had to turn back. She crossed the North Sea to Orfordness the next day and anchored in the Downs off Deal early on 3 May in dense fog, entering the dock at Dunkerque later that day to wait for orders and to bunker. From Dunkerque she was sent to Le Havre to load cases of bacon. Some of this was discharged in Rotterdam on 2, 3 and 4 June.

On the afternoon of 4 June the vessel proceeded towards the dry dock, assisted by pilot and tugs. Once she was in dry dock, workmen started repairs to the deck and engine-room. The crew took the anchor cable out of the locker, pumped water out of the forepeak, cleaned out the chain locker and the cable chain and whitewashed the holds. Caulking the ship's bottom, overhauling the cable chain, putting in deck planks and replacing the ceiling in the hold were among the repairs completed by tradesmen. On 14 June the cable chains were taken on board, the chief officer being on duty for nine hours and the carpenter for eight while this was done. The crew were next employed painting the funnel, whitewashing the 'tween decks and cleaning out the holds. *Discovery* was ready for sea on 18 June, when she departed from Rotterdam for Hull, where the voyage officially terminated on 7 July 1919.

SOUTH RUSSIAN VENTURE, 1919-20

IN THE SUMMER OF 1919 two elderly square-rigged vessels might have been observed slowly sailing and steaming from Yorkshire through the Mediterranean, Bosphorus and Black Sea towards a Russia torn apart by civil war and bloodshed following the Revolution of 1917. One of these vessels was of course *Discovery*, while the other was the former naval gunboat and anti-slaver *Pelican*, both chartered from the HBC by the Merchant Trading Company of London.

In the years before the First World War the wheat exports of Imperial Russia were harvested in vast quantities, and there existed what was known as 'coal out and grain home' trade from the British Isles. Because most steamers were coal burners, a network of coaling stations throughout the world enabled ships to replenish their bunkers. One of the most important of these was Port Said, at the entrance to the Suez Canal, and between early summer and late autumn, after discharging her coal cargo at Port Said, a steamer would proceed via the Dardanelles to Con-

stantinople (now Istanbul), cleaning her holds *en route*. Orders would await her at Constantinople, stating to which south Russian port she was consigned. The Russian grain was eventually distributed throughout northern Europe from Antwerp, Rotterdam or Hamburg. Before the war, Russia had provided Great Britain with huge quantities of raw materials and food, including one eighth of British grain imports. This lucrative trade came to an abrupt end with the First World War and the alliance of Turkey with Germany.

It was the collapse of Russia, and not anti-Bolshevism, that in the first instance brought about armed Allied intervention to the north, east and south of the small new Soviet state. What began as an effort to reconstruct the Eastern Front against the Germans became thoroughly bound up with the White Russian cause. Added to this was fear of the spread of Bolshevism at a time when Germany, in defeat, also seemed to be turning Bolshevik. The struggle in south Russia forms the background to the Black Sea trad-

General view of Novorossiysk on the Black Sea, from an undated old Russian postcard.
(COURTESY JOHN MASSEY STEWART)

ing voyages of Discovery and Pelican in the autumn of 1919. Although it cannot be said that they took part in any major events, the fact that they were present is noteworthy. For it was during those two years of civil war in 1919 and 1920 that the destiny of Russia was settled, in what was truly the aftermath of the First World War.

The Allies had divided south Russia into sectors of interest, and both the British and French navies were active in the Black Sea. A small Volunteer Army gradually and painfully came into being in south Russia, harassed not only by the Red Army but also by insurgent peasants led by local brigands comprising the 'Green Army'. Reports sent back to the Admiralty in London concerning the situation in south Russia emphasised the importance of trade, especially in the wake of advancing White armies. Most of the original peacetime businessmen had left, but a Minister of Shipping and Trade had been appointed. Even so, the discharge of imports and distribution of cargo would remain difficult until reliable agents and land communications were re-established. The people of Russia were said to have no money and nothing with which to trade. To establish links with this part of the world would require merchants to combine business with charity.

These observations released in the City of London led to a proposal by a Lieutenant Gurland to the Merchant Trading Company for 'an expedition to the Black Sea for an exchange of goods' in June 1919. The HBC agreed to charter Discovery and Pelican and to take a 20 per cent stake in the venture. These two old-fashioned auxiliary barques thus became two of the eleven merchant ships in Novorossiysk in late September 1919. Fortunately, the logs of both survive in the HBC archives.

The master of Discovery was George Wetherill. The two vessels did not sail in company, but met in the south Russian port of Novorossiysk, on the northeast coast of the Black Sea. They followed a roughly similar course outward and homeward, departing from Hull in July 1919, both having first loaded coal and general cargo. On 28 July Pelican fired at and sank a

floating mine off the Aegean island of Lemnos. They must have been among the first British merchant ships to pass through the Dardanelles and Bosphorus since the 1914-18 war. The two vessels anchored off Constantinople in early and late August respectively.

Pelican took on water and embarked passengers at Batoum (now Batumi), on the east coast of the Black Sea, important as the terminal of the oil pipeline from Baku. She berthed on 30 August at Novorossiysk, a pleasant port by all accounts, at the foot of wooded hills. The year before it had witnessed the dramatic scuttling by the Bolsheviks of the battleship Svobodnaya Rossiya and eleven destroyers. Discovery joined the Pelican from Constantinople on 1 September, and the two remained in the vicinity from late August to November 1919, the critical three months that saw the advance of the White Army, under General Denikin, to within 250 miles of Moscow. By the end of the year the Red Army had counterattacked and defeated Denikin's armies in a ghostly and ever-fluctuating civil war.

One of the last signs of the sway of the old regime can be seen on the pages of the official log of Discovery: the Imperial two-headed eagle stamped by the port authorities of Novorossiysk.

On 4 September 1919 stevedores began discharging cargo from Pelican into Discovery. A superintendent and six labourers had already shifted cargo from Discovery's 'tween decks to her lower hold the previous day, while the crew was employed painting the lifeboats and the donkey winch. Working cargo during the period the two vessels were at the quay seems to have been intermittent, probably due to general disruption and shortage of labour. Reports about the town at this time describe the place as wallowing in mud, vastly overcrowded with troops and with its streets 'full of penniless refugees and indescribable beggars'.

The crew was employed at various jobs, including setting up Discovery's topmast rigging and painting the ship outside. Pelican departed for Constantinople on 27 September, after discharging 100 tons of boots, clothing, drugs and woollen garments. On 4 October Discovery left after discharging a similar amount of boots, clothing and linen goods. The official log records that 1,688 roubles and 81 kopeks were paid in quarantine and customs dues on 21 September, which authorised *Discovery* to depart for Rostov with a foreign cargo of 23 pieces, duty paid.

The commercial and industrial centre of Rostov-on-Don had grown up in the nineteenth century at the mouth of the Don, one of the great rivers of Russia, which flows through the Russian steppe, the

The *Pelican* off York Factory
(AUTHOR'S COLLECTION)

country of the Don Cossacks. Cossacks had originally settled in the wilder southern and eastern areas of the Russian Empire, but they became the instrument of the Tsarist state, each horseman having to leave home and serve 20 years with the colours in return for a plot of land. The changes brought about by the trade in coal and iron resulted in the rise of Rostov. The world demand for grain in the later nineteenth century encouraged the Cossacks to turn 90 per cent of their pasture into arable land. In addition to grain, the production of grapes and tobacco also increased significantly, causing the price of land to rise, and this led to discontent among the Don Cosssacks. The First World War of 1914-17 and the civil war devastated

their communities and countryside.

Discovery's log records that she proceeded with a pilot towards Taganrog roads after receiving *pratique*, (permission to continue), presumably from the British warship stationed in the narrow Strait of Kerch, the gateway to the Sea of Azov. She met strong headwinds and sea the next day, 6 October, the vessel pitching heavily and shipping much water as she progressed past navigation lights and markers. On the following day she came to anchor at Taganrog roads in 17ft of water. Only shallow-draft vessels were able to reach Rostov; those with a deeper draft anchored some 40 miles away, awaiting the transfer of their cargo to lighters. On 9 October at 6.30am the steam lighter *Nichole*, No 973, came alongside and her labourers went aboard, discharging all cargo by 4.30pm. In happier days, before the cataclysm, *Discovery* would have loaded a consignment of grain from lighters sent out from Taganrog, but now she had to wait five days for orders. The crew was employed shifting coal from the lower hold to the bunkers. On 15 October at 5.30am she hove up anchor and proceeded towards Novorossiysk in dense fog, with a pilot in charge and her whistle blowing. She came to anchor in Kerch Strait, no doubt to drop the pilot on 16 October, before continuing to her destination against a strong breeze and head sea. The following day the pilot came aboard and she proceeded to the quay berth, where *Pelican* joined her five days later.

A shortage of wagons, heavy rain and strong northeasterly or southeasterly gales interrupted the work of the stevedores. Fenders had to be continually renewed as the two ships chafed against the wharf and one another. Extra springs were put out fore and aft, and *Pelican's* log records 'a considerable amount of minor damage'.

After nearly three weeks awaiting orders, *Discovery* proceeded on 8 November with the pilot and moored at the loading berth alongside the Cement Wharf. Between 15 and 21 November stevedores and labourers loaded a full cargo of cement in 3,936 barrels. Despite bumping and rolling, 25 tons of coal were bunkered from *Discovery* to *Pelican*. Delays to

Map showing Russia during the Civil War, 1919, to illustrate the *Discovery*'s Black Sea voyage.(South Russian venture), 1919-20. From a map in W.S.Churchill, *The Aftermath*.

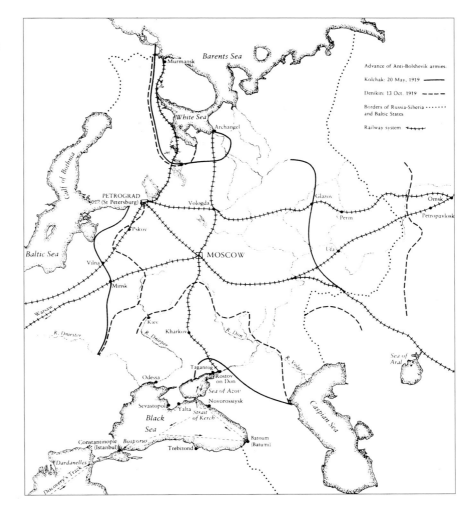

the discharging and departures of the steamers were described as 'ruinous' by the merchant companies, and conditions in the port as 'perfect chaos'. The situation in Novorossiyski continued to worsen. Thousands of men, women and children, including whole train loads, died from typhus or exposure. From the bay, British and French warships shelled the approach roads to the city to slow down the advancing Red cavalry. The evacuation to the Allied ships was limited mainly to White troops and their families, while the waterfront, the foreshore and the streets were thronged with people, camels, horses, perambulators, wagons and handcarts as the 'wreckage of a whole nation' was swept towards the only remaining seaport in the area.

Discovery departed for Constantinople with her cargo of cement in mid-Novemeber 1919, having paid the requisite dues and taxes. She arrived at the Piraeus on 1 December, where the cement was eventually unloaded in late December and early January. The crew were fumigated on arrival, while the vessel was in quarantine. On Christmas Day, Able Seaman Cloudsdale was taken prisoner aboard a Greek warship after a drunken fight with another seaman. After the cement had been discharged, on 6 January 1920, the fumigating boat came alongside and pumped liquid sulphur down the holds.

At Constantinople, between 26 January and 8 February, *Discovery* loaded a general cargo for London. This comprised nearly 2,000 bags of nuts, more than 1,000 bags of linseed, 15 cases of gum, 213 bales of rugs, 62 casks of copper, 52 cases of caviar, 43 barrels of mohair, 8 bales of carpets and over 800 cases of other cargo. Snowstorms and rough weather delayed departure for three days. The pilot came aboard on 11 February and *Discovery* proceeded towards London, having anchored in the Bosphorus the same day for clearance by the Examination Officer. She coaled in Malta on 18 February, received *pratique* and bunkered at Gibraltar on 27 and 28 February, and with fresh water on board progressed towards the Channel, rolling and pitching heavily in the March gales. Off Dungeness she stopped to receive the London pilot on board. At Gravesend on 11 March, where *pratique* was received, the sea pilot was discharged and the river pilot took charge of the run up the Thames to the East India Dock. The crew signed off that day. The cargo was discharged between 12 and 16 March, when it was found that the contents of nearly a whole barrel and two cases of caviar had been stolen.

There were no more south Russian ventures, owing to the conditions of the time. Doubtless the cargoes carried by *Discovery* and *Pelican* were valued by the individuals who were able to buy or purloin them, but they and other trade goods made no difference to the course of the Civil War in what Winston Churchill called 'the wreckage of the Empire of the Czars'.

W R Colbeck, the son of Captain Colbeck of the *Morning*, later to serve in *Discovery* during her BANZARE voyages of 1929-31, was in one of the earliest merchant vessels to reach south Russia under the trade agreement signed by the two nations when trade between Great Britain and the new Soviet state started in the early 1920s. He was in Novorossiysk during April and May 1922, and found the port derelict and the people starving. A crowd of forty or fifty would fight over galley swill brought down to the quay by the ship's cook. The rate of exchange was 13 million roubles to the pound, with postage stamps overprinted to serve as money. While he was there, another British ship came in with a cargo of grain. The grain was put into sacks which men carried on their backs across the quay to a line of railway wagons. One of the carriers stumbled and dropped his bag, which burst open, causing the large crowd of starving spectators to rush in and fill their hats with grain. The guards yelled and shouted, then opened fire. The bodies of a young girl and two men were thrown on to a handcart and taken away. On another afternoon the dockers were found to be searching the bilges for the remains of a previous cargo of copra, which was found to be edible. Work was not resumed until every scrap had been removed.

Laid up in London, 1920-23

A press report headed 'The *Discovery* in the Thames', announced her return from south Russia in mid-June 1920. Apparently a coal charter had failed, and the decline in the shipping boom caused the Bay Steamship Company to consider whether she should be laid up. The 'little *Discovery*' had been lying at a buoy off Deptford for some weeks, waiting for a charterer.

A formal proposal to lay her up at a buoy berth in the South West India Dock was made to the managing director, CV Sale, on 23 June. The costs of this, some £800, would include annual dock dues and a salary of £260 per annum to a watchman, an elderly master, living on board, and the expenses of shifting to the berth, pumping out the water, additional dismantling, emptying and drying boilers, and greasing the engines. All moveable gear was to be stored on shore and all navigating gear, apart from the lamps, was to be handed over to Messrs Kelvin, White and Hutton. Ropes should be unrove and all brasswork covered with white lead. A complete inventory would have to be taken of all gear landed or left on board. All hands would be paid off.

This is indeed what happened to SS *Discovery*, a vessel of peculiar design and limited cargo space and speed, unable to compete in the 1920s with modern merchant ships. However, she did not remain entirely deserted. Early in 1922, through the kindness of the HBC, the barque became the temporary headquarters of the 16th Stepney Sea Scout troop. Perhaps this precedent influenced the decision to hand her over to the Boy Scouts Association once her seagoing had come to an end, some ten years later.

CHAPTER 16

THE PLIGHT OF THE
GREAT WHALES

THE FRIENDS OF THE EARTH, Greenpeace, the World Wide Fund for Nature (formerly the World Wildlife Fund) and other conservation societies have been very effective in publicising the plight of many of the great whales, whose numbers have been reduced through overfishing, to a very low level. The practical beginnings of the conservation movement arose before the First World War, when a British government committee on whaling and the protection of whales was established in London to collect information and a biologist was despatched to study whaling operations in South Georgia during the 1913-14 season.

Whales had been hunted for some 300 years in the northern hemisphere, from small boats operating from sailing vessels, and later steamships, until the early twentieth century. Only the slow Right whale and the Sperm whale could be caught using the prevailing methods, as neither sank on being killed by the harpoons and lances thrown from the small boats. It was not until 1864, when the Norwegian Svend Foyn invented an explosive harpoon that could be fired from the bows of a ship, that the faster, larger Rorquals and Humpbacks could be attacked. They were inflated on capture so that they did not sink, having died a terrible death on the immensely strong lines linking the harpoon and the whale catcher.

Many accounts of whaling voyages were written in the nineteenth century, the most authoritative of which was William Scoresby's *Arctic Regions*, published in 1820. Because of his studies and observations of the sea, Scoresby is acknowledged as a pioneer in the science of oceanography. The small

Badge of the *Discovery* (Oceanographic) Expedition, 1925-27.

steam vessel that would be specially built to complement the work of *Discovery* and later research ships was named after him.

When it became clear that the northern waters were almost depleted of whales, attention turned to the south, where fast whale catchers with explosive harpoons caught vast numbers of Humpback and the larger Fin and Blue whales. The Compañia Argentina de Pesca, formed by Norwegian and Argentine interests in 1904 to operate in the Antarctic, was soon followed by other companies, also operating in the Dependencies of the Falkland Islands, between the meridians of 20°W and 80°W. The Norwegians recognised British sovereignty and paid for licences to set up shore whaling stations on the islands of South Georgia and the South Shetlands. These and later taxes on whale oil processed allowed the Falkland Islands government to build up a substantial research and development fund. The prosperity of the industry can be seen from the statement of receipts from the Dependencies, which in 1917 amounted to £15,366. This money paid for the purchase of *Discovery* in 1923 and her refit as an oceanographic research vessel.

The archives of the British Museum (Natural History), now the Natural History Museum preserve a brief but significant correspondence of 1910 between Norwegian chemical engineer J A Mörch and Dr (later Sir) Sidney Harmer, then Keeper of Zoology, in which Morch suggests that records should be collected from the whaling grounds under British jurisdiction. He felt that a journal kept by each licensed whaling steamer, recording details of each whale killed, the presence of plankton plus meteorological observations, including water temperatures, in certain locations, would greatly enhance scientific knowledge. The data could then be presented on large-scale maps to some 'British scientific institution', to provide a 'graphic view' of the situation each year. Mörch went on to point out that the catch from a single 'floating factory' at Deception Island was worth £50,000, while the cost of a licence was only £200. He suggested that a proportion of each licence fee should be put aside for scientific research, and that licences should be limited to avoid depletion of whales in any one locality.

Harmer was encouraging in his replies, and recommended that as much as possible should be done on the lines suggested by Mörch to prevent the extermination of the whales. One immediate result was the first of a series of Whale Reports submitted to his Trustees in November 1910, based on information from the whaling stations sent via the Colonial Office to the British Museum. Another practical step taken was the despatch of an Irish zoologist, Major G E H Barrett-Hamilton, to South Georgia in October 1913 to investigate the whaling and sealing there, and also to report on the fauna of the island.

Barrett-Hamilton had been a friend and fellow-student of Edward Wilson at Cambridge and was the author of their joint publication, with Wilson's illustrations, The History of British Mammals, which was currently being issued in parts after Wilson's death on return from the South Pole in 1912. Barrett-Hamilton began his investigations at Leith Harbour in South Georgia, measuring his first whale on 15 November 1913, and continued to work there until his sudden death on 17 January 1914.

The Interdepartmental Committee on Whaling and the Protection of Whales sat on 10 December 1913 in London. Its purpose was to consider whether whales needed protection and, if so, how this should be done. Under the chairmanship of H G Maurice it sat for five sessions until 7 May 1914. Eight witnesses gave evidence: three scientists, including Dr Harmer; the Governor of the Falkland Islands, Mr W L Allardyce, CMG, after whom the

Allardyce Mountains in South Georgia are named; two company directors involved with whaling; the managing director of a company which marketed hardened whale oil, in soap and chemical manufactures, who hinted at a future 'edible product' which we now know as margarine; and most authoratative of all, Dr Hjort, the Norwegian oceanographer and marine biologist, then Director of Fisheries in Bergen, who produced a useful summary on the Distribution of whales in the waters about the Antarctic continent. Papers left by the late Major Barrett-Hamilton were also published as appendices. A careful reading of the report and appendices reveals that scientists knew relatively little about the growth, reproduction, feeding habits and general behaviour of whales, their species identity, breeding grounds, migrations and seasonal distributions, and in particular whether the same stock might be hunted off both southern continents and near the ice. The views of the whalers were also recorded, as to overfishing, licensing, the utilisation of the whole carcass, close seasons, the prohibition of attacks on mother and calf, and the enforcement of regulations.

A significant summary by M A C Hinton of the British Museum (Natural History), written in 1915, not very long after the start of whaling in the Antarctic, concluded: 'On its present scale, and with its present wasteful and indiscriminate methods, whaling is an industry which, by destroying its own resources, must soon expire'.

The outbreak of war frustrated an Anglo-Swedish Antarctic Expedition, which was scheduled to run from 1915 to 1920 and had research on the protection of whales as one of its principal objectives. After suspension during the war, the earlier Interdepartmental Committee on Whaling was reformed and replaced by the Interdepartmental Committee on Research and Development in the Dependencies of the Falklands Islands, which had a wider brief. A postwar research expedition to the Falklands was proposed and planned. Harmer advised his Trustees to approve the expedition on 1 August 1917 and, soon after, a second advisory committee considered what could then be done to speed up action at the

Discovery under trials after her refit.
(AUTHOR'S COLLECTION)

conclusion of the war. Information was needed regarding the economic significance of the whaling industry, the provision and employment of a research vessel, and the scientific investigations most required within these regions.

Port Stanley's extensive ship repair business was in decline following the demise of the windjammer and the opening of the Panama Canal, so the search for other industries was paramount. The second interdepartmental committee appears to have begun its meetings early in 1918, and met twenty-one times before publishing its report in April 1920. Its plan of operation was to obtain memoranda from experts and then discuss these with their authors. The broader brief of the second committee is reflected in its reviews of whales and whaling from 1909, when regulations were first imposed, seals and sealing, potential fisheries, and even penguins and reindeer. The sciences of hydrography, meteorology, geology, botany and magnetism were considered in relation to the Dependencies. The phenomenal rise in the use of whale oil during the war for the production of glycerine, for explosives, was recorded. The steep decline in the catch of Humpback whales at South Georgia and the subsequent concentration of the whalers initially on Fin and then Blue whales was also noted, and statistics provided.

The Committee's interviews and investigations led to the publication in 1920 of a Parliamentary Report. Its priority was to provide a scientific basis for whale regulation; there was at that time no question of abolishing whaling because of its cruelty.

An Executive Committee of nine, chaired by E R Darnley, was appointed in 1924 by the Secretary of State for the Colonies, to carry out the report's recommendations. The committee became known as the *Discovery* Committee. The Ship's Sub-Committee proposed the employment of two vessels, both wooden three-masted topsail schooners, with steam power and wireless. One vessel should be some 700 tons net, and her consort would be just over 200 tons. The two should work in close co-operation, the larger being ice-strengthened and the other more fully protected for work in heavy ice. Besides cabin accommodation, each should have two laboratories, a chart-room, also serving as a study and scientific library, and a dark-room for photography. Motorboats with a speed of 9-12 knots should be provided for each vessel, for the marking of whales. Portable huts, double tents and sledges should be carried. Despite the recommendation of three-masted topsail schooners, *Discovery*, a barque, was purchased and converted. Her tender, the *William Scoresby*, was designed as a small fully powered steamship with a foresail, jib and spanker for use when these would help to drive or steady the vessel. She was built at a cost of £33,000 to assist in the oceanographic research, to mark whales and to make exploratory trawls off the Falkland Islands.

SALE TO THE CROWN AGENTS
AND REFIT BY VOSPER

After *Discovery*'s completion of her Black Sea voyage of 1919-20, and her subsequent removal from the East India Dock to the West India Dock, an agreement was drawn up between the HBC and the Crown Agents for the vessel to be sold for £5,000. This was subject to the inspection, in dry dock, of hull and engines by the purchasers, and the HBC was allowed first option to buy her back, to forestall any rivals in the fur trade. From London she transferred to Portsmouth, where a great deal of reconditioning was carried out by Messrs Vosper to turn her from a cargo into a research vessel.

Captain Scott's criticisms of *Discovery*'s sailing qualities were taken into careful consideration in the drawing-up of the specifications for what was, in effect, her rebuilding. Extensive alterations were made in her masting and in the general sailing plan. The foremast was placed 4ft further forward, and the mainmast 8ft. More headsail would be carried and the overall sail area was increased by over 20 per cent. It was intended that she should thus carry an easy helm and be a much improved sailer. The single topgallant was split into upper and lower topgallants for easier handling. The hull was replanked inside and out, while new decks were laid and new deckhouses fitted.

A wardroom was provided once again, with cabins for the officers and scientists. Accommodation for the rest of the crew was in the crew space on the main deck. Chemical and biological laboratories were built, and she was provided with a large trawl winch and three powered reels for use with vertical nets and water bottles. Water bottles, sounding machines, outboard platforms, and other oceanographic equipment fitted *Discovery* for her new life as a Royal Research Ship in the Southern Ocean. As she was owned by the Government of the Falkland Islands, her port of registry was changed from London to Port Stanley. The vessel was to fly the Blue Ensign emblazoned with the Arms of the Falkland Islands.

The *Hampshire Telegraph* of 8 May 1925 carried an article headed 'Ready for research work: Scott's ship as she is today'. The writer described numerous features of the reconstruction, including the replacement of the larger part of the keel with timber from Quebec oak, after five trees from north Somerset had been sawn up and found wanting. The total cost of the purchase and reconstruction of *Discovery*, excluding scientific equipment, was nearly £114,000.

On 2 July 1924 Dr Stanley Kemp had been appointed leader and Director of Research of the *Discovery* Expedition. One of his first duties was to sanction the design of *Discovery*'s badge, which combined a whale, the ship's name, the Imperial Crown and the waves of the sea. A man of great physical stature, Kemp was modest, beloved of his staff, whom he was able to inspire, and sometimes exasperate, through his own devotion to the task, in the often trying conditions on board the ever-rolling ship. He had gained experience in both Ireland and India, and occupied himself 'in planning, organising and carrying out one of the most comprehensive schemes of oceanographical research ever undertaken by any country in the world'. One reason for the *Discovery* Expedition being comparatively little known was that publicity was shunned by its leader and the Committee. Kemp was a scientist first and foremost, and he stressed that the voyage would be strictly concerned with routine traverses of the sea to provide data, the raw material of research.

Before leaving England, Kemp informed the scientific world about the forthcoming oceanographical expedition of 1925-27 in RRS *Discovery* through two articles in *Nature*, emphasising that it would pursue 'the solution of a particular economic problem...a biological one, occasioned by the rapid expansion of the southern whaling industry in recent years'.

The new master of *Discovery* was, in contrast to Kemp, a burly sea dog and romantic from the heroic age of Antarctic exploration. Commander Joseph Russell Stenhouse, DSO, DSC, OBE, Croix de Guerre, RD, RNR, came from a family of shipbuilders in Dumbarton, famous for their clipper ships. Born in 1887, he had served in the Antarctic in 1914-17 as captain of Shackleton's *Aurora*, and was well acquainted with the perils of navigation under sail in high southern latitudes. On his return from the Antarctic he had served in wartime 'Q ships', armed merchant vessels. His DSO was awarded for ramming and sinking a German submarine with the patrol boat PC61, commanded by Frank Worsley, in September 1917. He next served under Shackleton with other old polar comrades in the North Russia Expeditionary Force of 1918-19, and was in charge of organising the winter transport of troops by horse sledge between Murmansk and Archangel.

Stenhouse was appointed nautical advisor to the *Discovery* Committee in 1923. Frank Worsley called him 'one of the most efficient seamen of this century', and duty was said to be his watchword. However, the relationship between the captain of an expedition ship and the scientists he carries is not an easy one, and this was true of Kemp and Stenhouse. Stenhouse wanted to feel that he was taking part in a great venture, but Kemp, the dedicated scientist, was not prepared to give him this assurance. The team of eleven scientists comprised zoologists and hydrologists. The Admiralty lent a surveyor who sailed as second officer.

The large 4.5 metre net.
(SOUTHAMPTON OCEANOGRAPHY CENTRE.)

Naturalist A C Hardy, later Sir Alister, first heard of the *Discovery* Expedition in 1923, when he read an article by Rowland Darnley entitled 'A new Antarctic expedition'. He joined the expedition in 1924 and could recapture, decades later, the excitement the article had given him.

Before *Discovery* set sail, Hardy had been invited by Professor Johan Hjort to join him aboard *Michael Sars* on the very first whale-marking cruise. The Norwegians fired a shoulder gun, while Hardy would try out the cumbersome crossbow designed by C V Boys, which was intended to be noiseless, so that the whales were not scared by the sound of a gun. Sir Sidney Harmer, a friend of Boys and by then Director of the British Museum (Natural History), had taken a particular interest in this. Hardy recalled that at one time Harmer had a large oil-cloth model of a whale behind the Museum, and in morning coat, striped trousers and bowler hat would excitedly watch Hardy fire the first shots with this 'barbarous-looking medieval weapon'. The contraption failed to work effectively and caused some hilarity on board ship. The three weeks' cruise in the North Atlantic was meant as a preliminary to Hjort's major investigations of the stocks of northern whales. Hardy obtained valuable insight into the equipment and methods of this famous oceanographic research vessel, especially the large nets that could be closed at the end of their tow in different depths of water, *before* being brought to the surface. This ensured that the catch represented the marine life at a particular depth only. It was agreed that *Discovery*'s plankton nets would be made to the same design as Hjort's, so that results from both ends of the world could be compared. Sadly, in the end, Hjort was unable to carry out his project and the co-operation came to nothing.

No full-length account of the 1925-27 *Discovery* (Oceanographic) Expedition appeared until the publication in 1967 of Sir Alister Hardy's book, *Great Waters*. This is not only a narrative of the expedition, written from his diary and beautifully illustrated with his own watercolours and sketches, but it is also a commentary on events and scientific work in the light of subsequent voyages and research. Hardy includes a detailed description of the general arrangement and equipment of RRS *Discovery*. He guides the reader over the ship, beginning at the forecastle head, 'where there are the most glorious views of the sea imaginable; we have a feeling of soaring up over the waves like a bird, whilst behind us are the great towers of sails, filled with the breeze and brilliant in the sun, like outstretched wings'. Hardy also writes of the joy of 'seeing and *hearing* square-rig sails set' to the chorus of an old sea shanty sung by the crew, and of the massive wooden bulwarks, breast-high, with lengths of step here and there on both port and starboard, that enabled the scientists to jump up and lean over the side when, in the tropics, beautiful jellyfish went by and the ship might be slowed down to allow them to be caught in hand nets or other devices.

VOYAGE TO THE CAPE, 1925

The voyage started badly. The reconstruction of the ship in Portsmouth by Vosper took far longer than anticipated, and towards the end the job was very hurried. The original intention had been to reach the South Atlantic by the beginning of the Antarctic whaling season in November. In July 1925 *Discovery* sailed from Portsmouth for the Bay of Biscay, to try out the experimental echo-sounding gear developed by the Admiralty scientists who were on board, but she did not leave the Channel. Vosper's workmanship failed to withstand a prolonged gale and the ship put into Dartmouth, where she lay for two months while extensive repairs were made. Here the expedition scientists, under Kemp's expert guidance, worked in teak to produce racks for test tubes and bottles, and shelves for books and other loose items so that these would remain in place when the ship rolled.

On the evening of 24 September 1925 *Discovery* steamed slowly down the river Dart towards the sea and the voyage really began. She put into Falmouth to land the two Admiralty scientists, after a successful trial of their apparatus in deep water on 29 September. The fine old clipper ship *Cutty Sark*, now preserved at Greenwich, lay in port, and *Discovery* anchored nearby, departing finally for the south on 5 October. Once again Hardy's narrative brings their voyage to life, as he writes of tropical nights with a shining wake of phosphorescence near Ascension Island, the 'fishing out of treasure after treasure' from the gently swelling sea, and the mysteries of the old-

Outline plan of the upper deck and forecastle of the RRS *Discovery*. From Sir A Hardy *Great Waters*.

1 Anchor davit
2 Capstan
3 Searchlight
4 Deepwater hydrographic reel
5 Sounding platform
6 Lucas sounding machine
7 Companion ways to galley and crew's quarters
8 Wing of bridge (above deck house)
9 Chart room
10 Survey store
11 wireless cabin
12 Deck cabin
13 Upper deck laboratory
14 Companion way to ward room
15 Stairways up to bridge
16 Two shallow water hydrographic and plankton reels (with outboard platforms)
17 Wardroom skylight
18 Main winch house
19 Auxiliary winch drum
20 Accumulator springs for use with towing warps
21 Deepwater plankton winch (with outboard platform)
22 Auxiliary steering wheel
23 Officers' heads
24 Armoury and lamp store
25 Grating platform
26 Stern fair-leads for the warps from the main winch
27 Kelvin sounding machine

time sailing ships 'crossing the line' at the Equator.

Things were different in the engine-room. Young George Gourlay had been appointed junior engineer, and the rolling and pitching of the ship made him very seasick. He worried that he would become drowsy and miss attending to some part of the machinery which threatened to go wrong all at once, with the water level flying up and down in the gauge glasses on the boilers, the circulating pump slowing down and the vacuum falling back.

Gourlay found the heat of the Tropics almost unbearable. The CO_2 freezer compressor failed and all the fresh meat had to be dumped. The hotel chef engaged as caterer could not keep yeast in the hot temperature, so there was no bread. Rejecting the salt beef and pork beloved of the bosun and other old salts, he survived on sardines and ship's biscuits.

The youngest of the three cadets on board, John Bentley, aged 15, had joined the ship from the training ship HMS *Worcester*. His letters home describe his first impressions of the maze of ropes and rigging, brails, halliards, buntlines, sheets and braces, and the beauty of a tropical moonlit night, with the flying fish jumping right out of the water, some of them landing on deck. 'They are delicious fried' he wrote, a welcome addition to their restricted diet.

Another young scientific member of the expedition, E R Gunther, found the crow's nest, high up on the mainmast, a refuge from the tuneless singing or whistling of his shipmates. His daily diary provides many personal impressions of these same shipmates, and also his first impressions of the master of *Discovery*, Captain Stenhouse.

> I am a bit surprised by the culture of our Captain. True his knowledge is superficial, but he takes an interest in almost everything and uses the general library more than anybody. He is an authority on horses: today he told us a lot about harness and how it varied in different parts of the country; he knows a trifle about pictures, is always interested in old customs, Archaeology, Botany and Natural History. As in the development of any Captain he is convinced that a sailor's idea of a bird is the truth...when a man has to live with the bird for months on end, what right has an old fossil at home to call it something else?

Gunther came from a family of 'old fossils'. His grandfather, Albert Gunther, had been Keeper of Zoology at the British Museum, while his father, R T Gunther, founded the Old Ashmolean Museum of the History of Science at Oxford.

Gunther's cabin, like those of the other scientists, opened off the wardroom and allowed him to hear their conversation over dinner if he did not eat with them. His comments on the harmony and good humour that existed between the members of the expedition, and the respect they gave to one another's views, underline the smooth running of the venture.

Discovery called to bunker at Ascension Island. As the scientists went ashore in the whaler they were surprised to see how much the ship was rolling. The hydrologist, H F P Herdman, who was to return to the Antarctic time and again, found the ship a good cure for seasickness, since she rolled 'even in the calmest weather'. Writing to a friend from near the Equator, he described his daytime rig of 'boiler suit, topee and sandals', and said everyone could wear what they liked. In fact, uniform regulations for colder weather and more formal occasions, including special cap badges and buttons, had been drawn up by the Committee, modified by the Admiralty and approved by the King. Kits were issued free to officers and men, but not to cadets.

Trials of the experimental echo-sounder designed by the Admiralty scientists continued during the passage south. Echo sounders of both shallow- and deep-water patterns were fitted in *Discovery*, enabling the ocean bed to be charted not only with greater accuracy, but while the vessel was under way, which resulted in an enormous saving of time. Deep-water sounding was pioneered more extensively at this time by *Meteor* during the German Atlantic Expedition of 1925-27, with soundings made every 20 minutes. Hardy described the Admiralty instrument as complicated, though it was based on a simple principle. A hammer struck a metal drum, while a microphone placed in the bottom of the ship picked up the echo from the sea floor, timing it by electrical means. As the speed of sound in seawater is known, the depth can be measured and recorded to the nearest foot. Trials were also made of the oceanographic gear, including the very large deep-water tow-nets, 15ft in diameter.

The westerly winds were picked up at last some 800 miles from Cape Town, resulting in good progress under sail, and *Discovery* entered Table Bay on 20 December 1925, in time for Christmas and Christmas mail. The passage from England had taken nearly five weeks, and, towards the end, water had to be rationed. Because time was short, investigations off the coast of Africa were left for the homeward voyage.

TO SOUTH GEORGIA AND THE FALKLANDS, 1925-26

ALTERATIONS TO THE WINCHES were completed at the Cape, coal was taken on, and *Discovery* finally sailed for South Georgia via the lonely Atlantic Island of Tristan da Cunha on 17 January 1926. She carried 15 tons of supplies, parcels and mail, the first shipment for the 140 islanders for over two years. Tristan da Cunha was sighted early on 30 January, and the anchor was dropped off the tiny settlement of thatched stone cottages overlooked by the great volcanic peak, a spur of which was to erupt in 1961, causing the evacuation of the entire population. Two of the island's frail but seaworthy longboats, made of oiled canvas stretched on a wooden frame, approached the ship, and their crews came aboard wearing a variety of old clothes, including an engine driver's hat and island moccasins laced with knotted string. With high-pitched voices and kitbags over their shoulders, they came to beg and to barter furs, skins, moccasins and socks for any clothes, food and soap. The women ashore wore old-fashioned long skirts and blouses, with brightly coloured plaid headscarves and shawls. Dr E H Marshall, *Discovery*'s surgeon, landed with Dr Kemp and made a medical examination of the islanders. Later, everyone gathered outside the little church to hear Captain Stenhouse, in uniform, read a message from King George V and a proclamation from the British Government in answer to the islanders' petition for a regular steam mail service. He also presented a portrait of the Duke of Edinburgh from the Queen of Roumania, whose father, the Duke, had given his name to the settlement. Formalities ended with the singing of the National Anthem.

The anchor was weighed on 1 February. Much biological work had been done, including examining the fronds of giant kelp, and catching fish and other sea creatures, which were either preserved or eaten. One of the fish and two shrimps were new to science, and were pickled for posterity. Another particularly rare fish, keenly sought by the British Museum, was eaten for supper by mistake. A breath-taking collection of tree-like corals, looking like branches torn from trees laden with spring blossom of many different colours, was taken in the dredge.

The main oceanographic work of the expedition began with a series of 'standard vertical stations' on passage towards the sub-Antarctic island of South Georgia. The tools or instruments used to take the samples of minerals and plant and animal life had been devised and modified over the previous century. The Nansen-Pettersen water bottle was used for sampling water down to 100m, and the Ekman reversing bottle at greater depths. Each measured the temperature of the sea at the moment the sample was taken. Plankton samples were collected using conical nets, like giant stockings without heels ending in small 'buckets' similar to those used by the famous oceanographers Hjort and Murray in the North Atlantic. Vertical stations regularly punctuated the ship's passage. Written reports of the work stress the constant difficulty of retaining the ship in position to keep the wires carrying the nets and water bottles vertical. Immediately the ship stopped, the sounding party sent away the lead on thousands of meters of fine piano wire. The depth-sounding machine was so designed that it would automatically stop as soon as the lead struck the bottom and took the tension off the line. While the sounding was being taken, water samples were collected from shallower depths using the engine amidships, and plankton net hauls were made using the aft engine. The routine temperature readings and water sam-

Personnel of the *Discovery*, the *William Scoresby* and the Marine Biological Station at South Georgia, with Dr Stanley Kemp, scientific director and Captain J R Stenhouse, Master, *Discovery* (Oceanographic) Expedition 1925-27. Alister Hardy is on Captain Stenhouse's left.
(SOUTHAMPTON OCEANOGRAPHY CENTRE)

ples were taken at the surface and at 5, 10, 20, 30, 40, 50, 75, 100, 200, 400, 500, 1,000, 2,000 and 3,000m, or as deep as the sounding would allow. The vertical plankton net hauls were usually taken in six stages: from 50m to the surface, from 100 to 50m, from 250 to 100m, from 500 to 250m, from 750 to 500m, and from 1,000 to 750m, and sometimes even deeper.

These long sessions of 'fishing for knowledge in this deep water world we cannot see' lasted for six hours or more. Station No 10 in lat. 46° 11' 30"S, long. 22° 27' 30"W yielded the first ocean-bottom sample of Radiolarian ooze, taken at 4,402 m depth. It was different from the usual Globigerina ooze, and more characteristic of the Indian and Pacific Oceans. It had never before been recorded from the Atlantic.

These oozes on the ocean floors are made of microscopic shells rained down from the surface of the sea.

The expedition's first iceberg was sighted at dawn the following Thursday, 16 February 1926. It was a flat-topped tabular iceberg with beautiful sculptured sides, broken off from an ice-shelf on the coast of the Antarctic and typical of the Southern Ocean. The Captain steered the ship through pieces of ice, which they heard scraping musically along her bows and sides for the first time. Just as *Discovery* came directly opposite, the berg calved with a thunderous noise and a flat portion broke off to go its separate way, melting in the warmer waters to the north.

At Station No 11, a few miles past the berg, in lat. 50° 26' S long. 30° 27' W, a cold layer of water at a depth of 100 or 200m between two warmer

King Edward Cove, South Georgia. *Discovery* in foreground.
(SOUTHAMPTON OCEANOGRAPHY CENTRE).

layers showed that they were in Antarctic surface water. In summer there is a temperature minimum which marks the limit, generally 100 to 150m down, of surface warming, where there may be a movement of colder water from higher latitudes, sandwiched between the warmer upper and lower layers. The Antarctic Convergence, at about 50°S in the Atlantic Ocean and farther south in the Pacific, where the Antarctic water sinks below warmer sub-Antarctic water in a sharp frontal zone, is of great significance in the lives of some plankton animals and plants which make vertical migrations between cold and warm waters. Otto Pettersson had predicted just such a system in 1905 from his studies in the Arctic; its existence in the south was revealed independently by two research ships working in the South Atlantic during the same years, *Discovery* and the *Meteor*, carrying the German Atlantic Expedition. The Antarctic Convergence had in fact been deduced earlier by Wilhelm Meinardus from the results of the German South Polar Expedition of 1901-03, and was sometimes referred to as the Meinardus Line.

SOUTH GEORGIA, FEBRUARY TO APRIL 1926

South Georgia, where Sir Ernest Shackleton had been buried only four years earlier, after his death on board *Quest*, was sighted from *Discovery* on 20 February 1926. It had not been explored until surveyed by Captain Cook in 1775, when he landed and took formal possession for the British Crown. Almost due east of Cape Horn, and to the southwest of the Cape of Good Hope, the island is over 100 miles long and 20 miles wide. Its spine of high mountains is covered in perpetual snow and intersected by glaciers. The coast is deeply indented, many of the bays being bordered by ice cliffs from which large pieces break off and float out to sea. The biggest glacier is the Nordenskjöld, 2 miles wide with a snout some 70ft high, at the head of East Cumberland Bay. Thousands of Elephant seals haul out on the beaches in summer to bear and bring up their young, and later to wallow and moult in the glorious mud between clumps of tussock grass. Four species of penguin, as well as albatrosses, petrels, cormorants, sheath-bills, gulls, terns and skuas nest there. The Fur seals, very scarce in 1926 through near-extermination in the nineteenth century, have now partly recovered their former numbers. Imported reindeer flourish on a diet of tussock grass.

South Georgia was well in view from *Discovery* by 7.30am on 20 February 1926. The mountains were most impressive, and many small whalers could be seen. The sea appeared increasingly greener as they drew nearer to land, with masses of feathers floating on its surface, this being the moulting season. As they entered Cumberland Bay, members of the shore sta-

tion came out in motorboats and circled *Discovery*. She dropped anchor in King Edward Cove, East Cumberland Bay, where a great reunion took place with colleagues of the Marine Station who had sailed from England in the autumn of 1924, as an integral part of the *Discovery* Expedition. The prefabricated single-storey wooden building had been completed in February 1925, and had withstood the fiercest gales. Its clean, polished and draught-free laboratory, which, above all, did not roll, and its comfortable quarters with a conservatory filled with geraniums and nasturtiums were the envy of the ship's party.

The shore staff's task was to investigate the whales towed to the station of the Compania Argentina de Pesca, a short boat ride away at the head of the cove at Grytviken. Here, on the flensing platform, the biologists examined the gigantic corpses that had been hauled up for dismemberment before

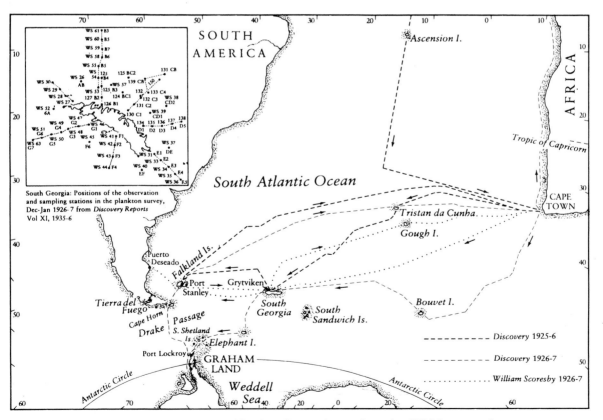

Map of The South Atlantic and Southern Oceans, showing the tracks of RRS *Discovery* and RSS *William Scoresby*, 1925-26 and 1926-27.

being rendered down into oil and meal. By April 1926 Messrs Mackintosh, Wheeler and, for a short time, Hamilton, working surrounded by blood, stench and slime, had made detailed measurements of 738 whales. Analysis revealed their breeding times, the period of gestation, the calves' rate of growth and their age at maturity. Important investigations of their food and a study of the Elephant seals and birds were made by Mr Harrison Matthews, while the hydrologist, Mr Clowes, analysed the chemical composition of the water samples landed from the ships. The shore party also worked, between South Georgia seasons, at the South African whaling station of Saldanha Bay, where complementary infor-

mation proved invaluable in connection with the migration and stocks of whales.

The morning after her arrival, *Discovery* reberthed alongside the wooden wharf at the whaling station to obtain fresh water and coal. The ship rode in the diluted blood of the slaughtered whales, and once again a watercolour by Hardy in *Great Waters* vividly depicts the scene, which he also described. The carcases of any Fin and Blue whales, filled with compressed air to keep them afloat, were floating in blood-red water, while small figures with long knives worked upon others being dismembered, as steel cables pulled the massive remains about the flensing platform from time to time. Clouds of steam

ejected from the factory itself, and sheer above it rose a mountain peak of dark rock splashed with brilliant sunlit snow, towering against the clear blue of the sky. The blue of the sky mixed with the blood-red water gave it a curious lilac tint, while at the quay-side row upon row of oil drums awaited shipment. At least ten thousand birds clamoured and fought for scraps of floating offal.

Cadet Bentley found the permeating smell frightful, but when the whale meat was properly cooked it tasted like beef. The new cook taken on in Cape Town had served in whalers and knew all the tricks of the trade. Bentley was saddened to see so many unborn youngsters taken from the bellies of females.

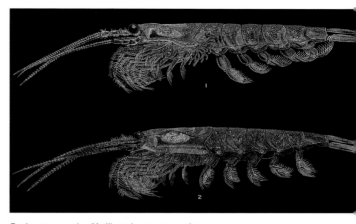

*Euphausia superba (*Krill), male specimen above, female below. Drawn by Helene Bargmann.
(AUTHOR'S COLLECTION)

ABOVE: A busy day at the whaling station at Grytviken, South Georgia, sketched from the deck of the *Discovery*, anchored in diluted blood. Painted by Sir Alister Hardy.
(NATIONAL MARITIME MUSEUM, GREENWICH)

LEFT: Mount Paget, South Georgia, lit by a low full moon, with King Edward Cove in shade, 14 February 1927. A passing whale catcher is seen on the right. Watercolour by E R Gunther.
(COURTESY E R GUNTHER TRUSTEES)

The pre-1914 regulations laid down by the Falkland Islands Government had forbidden the shooting of whale calves and cows accompanied by calves, but failed to protect pregnant cows, which cannot be recognised at sea. In practice it is still the same today. However, the extensive studies of all aspects of whaling begun by the *Discovery* Expedition have enabled many effective safeguards to be put in place.

The whales were about 80ft long. A warp would be shackled round the tail flukes and the whale hauled out of the gory water and up the gently sloping planks. Once the whale's head emerged from the water, the size of its jaws could be appreciated – some 6ft long and fringed with a sieve of hairs along the edge of the whalebone. Wooden-soled boots were essential, and spiked ones for those working on the whale itself. After the cuts were made, the blubber was stripped off by the winch, the warp being attached near the animal's mouth. The operation appeared no more difficult than peeling a banana. The strip of blubber would then be dragged up the platform like a long thick carpet, to be cut into small pieces and fed into the slicing machine. From there it was conveyed in a continuous line of buckets into the plant, where the blubber would be rendered down into oil. Flensing of the next whale began while the previous one was further processed, the entrails being removed, the meat separated and the bones converted into fertiliser. The shore biologists, each equipped with knife and tape measure, looked out especially for parasites in the gut and measured the genitalia, occasionally taking sections of these.

The workers at Grytviken were all Norwegian. At first they were highly suspicious of the shore biologists, fearing they would try to stop the whaling. They made no attempt to disguise their resentment, and sabotaged the scientists' efforts constantly by hiding interesting organs which had been extricated with difficulty and tripping up the biologists while they stepped warily across a slimy mass of flesh or strip of blubber. Later, the Norwegians overcame their suspicions and went out of their way to help. One of the station managers, Hansen, of Leith, was particularly helpful in shipping whale skeletons, and was prepared to take on any job, however formidable. Specimens of flippers and tails were also carried, pickled in salt, in one of the holds of the transport vessel, all destined for the British Museum (Natural History), now the Natural History Museum, in London.

Away from Grytviken whaling station, young Gunther found South Georgia a beautiful island, with the high snow-bound ridge of the Allardyce Range

The *Discovery* at Simonstown, South Africa.
(SOUTHAMPTON OCEANOGRAPHY CENTRE).

Whale catcher.
(SOUTHAMPTON OCEANOGRAPHY CENTRE.)

Research Steam Ship (later RRS) *William Scoresby*.
(AUTHOR'S COLLECTION)

dominated by Mount Paget, in strong contrast to the needle-sharp peaks of the other mountains. The colours of the landscape, with its abundance of grasses and flowering plants on the lower ground, and the warm, calm bays with steep slopes of scree, were breathtaking. Hardy's diary entry of the same time describes his harsh and sobering experiences in a whale catcher; the pursuit and killing of a whale, with its companion or mate swimming bravely and pathetically alongside, and the 'clouds of Cape pigeons' circling round, 'settling and rising again over the bloody water'. 'This barbarous business,' he writes, '… would never be allowed if it took place on land.' Hardy pointed out the paradox of the kind-heartedness of the whaling folk to their fellows, and their role as blind, unfeeling carnivorous hunters. Gunther also wrote an account of his trip in a whale catcher, finding the whales 'too beautiful for words'.

Discovery remained two months at South Georgia, during which time she carried out the first provisional biological and hydrographical survey of the whaling grounds. The Shore Station biologists, Mackintosh and Wheeler, examined more than 500 Blue and Fin whales, and found that the great majority had been feeding on what the Norwegian whalers called krill (*Euphausia superba*), small shrimp-like crustaceans. The biologists at sea were particularly concerned with the swarms of live krill and the whole 'pelagic community of which it forms a part'. By studying the plankton of the whaling grounds, they hoped to learn why the whales came to South Georgia in such numbers.

The delayed departure from England, the slow passage to Cape Town and the call at Tristan da Cunha, scheduled by the Colonial Office and favoured by the King, curtailed the amount of work that the scientists could accomplish during their first visit to the South Georgia whaling grounds. They missed most of the good weather and carried out only a fraction of their scientific programme. The biologists were nevertheless kept very busy examining the dredging hauls from Cumberland Bay and the station material taken at sea. Everything had to be sorted, labelled and preserved for later identification. Hardy and Gunther painted some specimens, particularly the fish, before their colours faded. Gunther's aggrieved letter home told of constant overworking, with only two trips ashore during the whole of March, and described Kemp as a 'craftsman to his fingertips, content to work for hours without exercise' without realising that others were unable to do likewise. Gunther also commented that while they added considerably to the fauna list of South Georgia and had gained an insight into whale food, they had contributed nothing of value to the problems they came to solve. There was a great deal of extra work aboard the ship. Cadet Bentley found the weekly cruises at this time 'interesting but very tiring for the crew, constantly setting and hauling nets'.

By March the southern winter was approaching, and on several occasions *Discovery* had to steer through light pack ice. She hit the wharf hard in King Edward Cove during a fierce gale on 5 April, but did not suffer any serious damage. The limitations of *Discovery* as an oceanographic research vessel became particularly apparent during these attempts to work nets and water bottles in howling northwesterly gales and to examine plankton samples at sea. Her rolling and tendency to be blown off course, owing to the windage and the engine's limited auxiliary power, were the main disadvantages.

TO THE FALKLANDS AND BACK TO CAPE TOWN

Discovery sailed from South Georgia on 17 April 1926. The Shore Station was closed for the winter and its inhabitants, apart from Hamilton and Matthews, went to work in South Africa. A line of stations was made *en route* for the Falkland Islands, off which trawling, dredging and additional stations were to be undertaken. The wind strengthened as she neared the coast, and at 9 knots, 'with all her canvas bellied to starboard', she seemed to skim the water more swiftly than ever before. The low, flat windswept moorland landscape of the Falklands contrasted strikingly with the ice-bound mountains of South Georgia, creating a feeling of wildness and freedom. Stanley, with a population of 800, reminded Gunther of a Cornish village. Among the old hulks at Port Stanley was Brunel's colossal *Great Britain*, then being used as a wool store, but now returned to Bristol.

The Governor and his wife, Sir John and Lady Middleton, made an official visit to the ship, and members of the *Discovery* Expedition much enjoyed various parties and dances in Stanley. A small group rode over to Fitzroy, 30 miles away, for a weekend, fording rivers and crossing large ditches on stubborn unshod ponies. The houses they found there were unpretentious and similar to those in suburban England.

Discovery sailed for Cape Town on 20 May 1926. For the next five weeks and five days she made a winter passage of the South Atlantic. Sometimes she suffered the turmoil of headwinds and heavy seas; at other times she was almost becalmed, or would run before the westerlies under a full stretch of canvas. During this long traverse nine full stations were worked, while the large plankton nets were towed during the intervals between. Of the creatures brought up from the ocean depths, ten proved to be new species. The weather made a great difference to the joys or sorrows of a station, but with practice the operators worked more surely and with greater speed. Gunther found working a station during a rough swell 'unspeakably nasty', especially after a sleepless night being tossed about in his bunk. Directly after clambering over the gunwhale of the rolling ship to take his place on the outboard platform in charge of the nets, his seaboots would fill with icy water as the waves swept by. However, a good catch, especially one containing undamaged specimens, compensated for the discomfort.

When the wind blew strongly on the beam, life on board *Discovery* became quite topsy-turvy. Green seas came cascading over the side, hitting the deck with tremendous force. Pots and jars would be hurled out of fiddles, crashing to pieces on the floor. Water would get into the biology laboratory, creating a damp and soggy atmosphere that worsened when a dish of formalin was upset or soup or gravy spilled. Anyone below at such times, in a stuffy wardroom or cabin, would wonder how much more the ship could stand. This state of confusion generally lasted no more than twelve hours, for the wind would either lessen or veer, so that more canvas could be spread.

After five weeks at sea the immensity of the Atlantic Ocean was impressed upon the scientists. Midway through the voyage Chief O'Connor demonstrated an old sailor's trick by catching a Wandering albatross with bait of salt pork towed on a line. The bird, with its 10ft wing span, did not enjoy standing on the rolling deck. When placed on the poop rail it took off easily and continued to circle *Discovery*. Nearing the African coast, the radio operator made contact with Walvis Bay. *Discovery* entered Table Bay on 29 June 1926, her officers in spruce uniforms and the scientists still in shirtsleeves, finishing the laboratory work. Apprehensive as they approached Cape Town with its noise and bustle, they soon adapted to life in port, and played football against the *Windsor Castle*.

18

SECOND SEASON IN THE ANTARCTIC, 1926 – 27

DISCOVERY spent three months in dry dock at the naval base of Simonstown while anti-rolling 'sister' (bilge) keels were fitted to the hull and the upper topgallant yards were struck down, to lessen her rolling and wind resistance. The first annual report summarised the scientific work done in South Africa meanwhile, including detailed studies of krill and analysis of *Discovery*'s water samples, the fat content of blubber, and the composition of the South Georgia plankton. Twenty-one whales were measured at the Union Company's whaling station at Durban. Some very early embryos were obtained, the smallest, a Sei whale, stated to be only 2-3mm long.

The oceanographic gear was overhauled, and plans laid for the next season's cruise. At that time Simonstown was a Royal Dockyard of the British Navy, and while *Discovery* was there her men were well entertained on board the naval ships of the fleet (South African Station) and by the whole of the South African Navy, which then consisted of two armed trawlers. Mr O'Connor left *Discovery* at the Cape, and Lieutenant-Commander Chaplin was promoted Chief Officer in his place. Chaplin had been lent by the Admiralty and was in charge of hydrographic surveying during the expedition.

During the stay in South Africa the event that caused the most stir was the arrival of the Research Steam Ship (later RRS) *William Scoresby* in Simonstown on 1 August 1926. Built for the *Discovery* Committee in 1925 at a cost of £33,000, to complement the work of *Discovery*, *William Scoresby* was designed for speed on the lines of a whale catcher. She had a displacement of about 370 tons and was 125ft long at the waterline. Her master was Lieutenant-Commander G Mercer, DSC, RD, RNR, who had come from the great liner *Mauretania*, and she carried two scien-

Parhelion effect (mock suns), seen off Graham Land, March 1927. Watercolour by Sir Alister Hardy. Reproduced in *Great Waters*. (NATIONAL MARITIME MUSEUM, GREENWICH.).

tific officers, both zoologists. Her remaining complement consisted of two deck officers, two engineer officers, six petty officers, five seamen and three stokers. Hardy described her as a 'compromise to satisfy three distinct purposes: whale hunter, trawler and research ship'. She had the whaler's lookout barrel at the masthead, a built-up bow for firing marking darts instead of harpoons, and a good turn of speed at 12 knots. Hardy was well pleased with what he saw.

Discovery made two short cruises north from the Cape, one of a fortnight over the whaling grounds off Saldanha Bay, and the other for a few days to take a series of hauls with large nets. The scientists found that the bilge keels greatly reduced the rolling of the ship, prolonging each movement and eliminating the lurch at the end of the roll, thus allowing them to work in quite rough weather. The removal of the donkey boiler, weighing five or six tons, from the starboard side of the forecastle, had lowered her centre of gravity and stiffened her.

FROM THE CAPE TO SOUTH GEORGIA, OCTOBER TO DECEMBER 1926

Discovery sailed from Simonstown for South Georgia to a good send-off by the navy on 27 October 1926, taking a more southerly route than before to avoid westerly winds, while *William Scoresby*, with greater power, took a direct one. The roaring forties lived up to their name, but nets were towed and stations worked whenever possible. Each day, one duty scientific officer saw that the nets and other apparatus were in order and ready to hand before a station took place. As they drew away from the shores of Africa it grew colder, and on went layers of winter clothing again. No heaters were allowed, to conserve coal. Working in the laboratory, the biologists felt the full blast of the untamed ocean winds each time the door was opened. A furious gale on 10 November put a stop to all scientific work, when huge waves engulfed *Discovery*, which plunged, rolled, slid and slithered among the grey mountains.

Armistice Day on 11 November was observed with two minutes' silence. Gunther's diary entry of the following day reveals that 'HB' – Hardy's Baby, the

Continuous Plankton Recorder — had worked particularly well as it was towed astern the ship, browsing its way through green pastures of diatoms. Samples from the nets revealed that the small plants and animals of the plankton lived in different layers of the sea by day and by night, which Gunther thought might well have a bearing on the habits of whales.

Pack ice appeared on 14 November in lat. 53°S, after a number of icebergs had been sighted during the previous two days. Gales, followed by fog and poor visibility, prevented sights being taken, and when the sun appeared at last the ship had been driven 90 miles southeast of Bouvet Island (now Bouvetøya), amid thick pack ice. The small supply of coal and the possibility of heavier ice made it too risky to continue farther south; the ship altered course to the northwest and emerged from the pack near Bouvet, a tiny ice-capped island with difficult access. *Discovery* came perilously close to hitting a rolling iceberg on 17 November and only just managed to break through the constraining pack ice at speed to escape by yards.

The scientists found it a bitterly cold and wretched experience to work a station on icy decks in an incessant snowstorm off Bouvet Island, and to handle the nets, on which the seawater froze soon after they came up. Gunther observed that the doctor's toaster, converted from medical apparatus, became a great feature of tea in the wardroom at this time. Buttered toast and magazines such as the *Illustrated London News* made life worth living. Growing anxieties about contrary winds and a shortage of coal forced the oceanographic work to be cut to a minimum, using only towed nets. Doctor Kemp's official report shows that the ship was within an ace of returning to Cape Town. From Bouvet onwards; over a stretch of ocean of the greatest interest to their research, they could do nothing. Their average speed was only 3.26 knots and, after three ocean crossings, Kemp concluded that *Discovery* was quite unsuitable for the work, and that their attempts to carry out a scientific programme had failed.

Despite the unpleasantness he knew would follow, Kemp felt obliged to tell the Committee that a new ship was crucial to the wide-ranging programme of whale research. Fortunately, in the end, strong and fair winds blew for four days while they neared South Georgia, whose approaches were guarded by countless icebergs of every shape and size. *Discovery* was met by *William Scoresby* and entered Cumberland Bay on 15 December 1926, with enough coal in hand for two days' steaming. She had just avoided the ignominy of being towed, and secured at the buoy in Grytviken harbour to bunker. Meanwhile, the scientists worked on the collections gathered by both ships, particularly the plankton, in preparation for a chart to illustrate their results.

SECOND SEASON AT SOUTH GEORGIA, DECEMBER 1926 TO FEBRUARY 1927

During the previous season at South Georgia Lieutenant-Commander John Chaplin, RN, had camped for six days at Undine Harbour, the northwest point of the island. This second season his party of three were able to complete the survey of the harbour, and subsequently worked at Larsen Harbour, at the extreme southwest, where the Elephant seals took exception to a tide gauge erected in their favourite wallow, pushing it over night after night. Having established the

latitudes and longitudes of South Georgia's geographical extremities, Chaplin charted Leith Harbour and Stromness Bay. He was able to fix Cape Buller and Cape Saunders. All the whalers needed to use the harbours in course of their business, and their captains were handicapped by inaccurate charts, in many instances as much as 15 miles out. Chaplin's aim, set out by the Hydrographer of the Navy, was to get as many good geographical positions as he could.

As soon as *Discovery* arrived in South Georgia, preparations began for the important oceanographic survey of the whaling grounds by both vessels. Five extremely hectic days were spent completing this, apart from the western side, which was left until later. With the island at their centre, the seven main lines of completed observations and sampling stations stretched out over the sea like the spokes of a cartwheel. This period of intensive work, with *Discovery* and *William Scoresby* in friendly rivalry, was a major achievement. Writing 35 years after the completion of this plankton and hydrological programme, Sir Alister Hardy doubted if it had ever been equalled. In five-and-a-half days more than half the

Bouvet Island seen from the *Discovery*, ten miles off shore on 17 November 1926. Watercolour by E R Gunther.
(COURTESY E R GUNTHER TRUSTEES)

programme of the whole expedition was achieved. Twenty-nine stations were worked over some 10,000 square miles of sea, yielding 370 water samples and 307 plankton net hauls. Every man in each ship did his utmost to make it a great success, in spite of solid, never-ending drudgery and a shortage of sleep. Kemp declared it to be a 'very decent piece of work', and recorded his pride in the scientists' achievement.

Christmas came two days after the end of the survey. A punchbowl party was held at the Marine Station and the whole expedition of sailors and scientists spent Christmas Eve in songs, games, high jinks and general jollification. On Christmas morning, after a special treat of bacon and eggs for breakfast, a simple service aboard *Discovery* was held with the old Christmas hymns. It was followed by Christmas dinner of tinned turkey and all the trimmings, and Christmas pudding with flaming rum and brandy butter, amid all the decorations, and with presents all round. The magistrate, Mr Binnie, brought a fine rose and some sweet peas from his greenhouse as a centrepiece for the table. After the two main toasts to 'The King' and 'Sweethearts and Wives', John Bentley, as youngest cadet, was obliged to propose the health of the expedition. At midnight on New Year's Eve Bentley also had to strike sixteen bells on *Discovery*'s forecastle bell, eight for the old year and eight for the new. After this the ships gave a searchlight display.

January 1927 was spent completing the plankton survey of the waters surrounding South Georgia. *William Scoresby* worked largely off the rugged and little-known west coast and *Discovery* to the east, where she ran aground on gravel off Sappho Point, East Bay, but escaped without damage. The limits of the continental shelf were ascertained, the patchiness of krill, which swarmed like underwater bees, was observed, currents were measured and plankton analysed. Gales were followed by fine weather, which enabled the scientists on board the *Scoresby* to complete thirteen stations in just over three days, working without rest from Friday 7 to Sunday 9 January. Perhaps because they were overtired, the first vertical net on the Monday

Iceberg in Discovery Sound, which was visited by *Discovery* in March 1927. In the background is Anvers Island, part of the Palmer Archipelago.
(SOUTHAMPTON OCEANOGRAPHY CENTRE.)

was lowered too soon and fouled the propeller. Fortunately, the captain and one of the hands, working in a dangerous position, eventually cleared it.

William Scoresby found herself in an even more potentially dangerous situation when the first trial was made of the 90ft otter trawl to the west of the island. One of the thick steel warps from the trawl wrapped itself round the propeller, bringing the main engine abruptly to a halt. Steam was shut off and the stokers, bathed in sweat, worked like supermen to turn the shaft by hand. After two hours' effort in vain, with the ship drifting out of control off a rocky lee shore, a whale catcher came to the rescue. Still towing four whales as well as the *Scoresby*, she brought the ship into safe anchorage in Undine Harbour, where a diver eventually managed to free the propeller. Meanwhile, Hardy, Gunther and Wheeler took the opportunity to go ashore to see the Wandering albatrosses, enthroned on their nests and temporarily earthbound.

On the eastern side, Dr Kemp had been trawling and dredging in Cumberland Bay, after being prevented by bad weather from working farther out to sea. Kemp, the enthusiastic collector, searched for every burrowing form of life in rock fragments, coral and kelp roots, and his wilting colleagues, covered in mud and looking like pirates, were compelled by his example to keep on. If they stopped to rest or relax, Kemp persisted in working, sometimes through the night. Towards the end of this second southern season Kemp described the krill as 'abominable organisms living in small patches of great density at almost any level'. A series of surface nets, towed continuously over 25 miles, had gathered 10,000 in one haul and only 50 in the next.

After many years of work by the later Discovery Investigations in the Southern Ocean, it was concluded that the density of krill depends upon surface, shallow and deep-water currents. In *Great Waters* Hardy summarised and discussed the results of the South Georgia survey of 1926-27 and paid tribute to the work and devotion of all officers and ratings, which yielded a detailed picture of the whole living community of the whaling grounds.

THE SOUTH ORKNEYS AND SOUTH SHETLANDS

At the beginning of February the ships went their separate ways, *Discovery* to the South Orkneys and South Shetlands and *William Scoresby* to the Falkland Islands, where until the end of April she marked whales and carried out an extensive trawling survey. The application of a marking system to whales was not easy. A marker, similar to a large drawing pin and shot from a shoulder gun, was devised for the *Discovery* Expedition, and a great many of these were fired from *William Scoresby*, which had the speed to approach Blue and Fin whales. Initially the work was aborted when it was found that the whales could rid themselves of the 2½in markers, but, after a pencil shaped one was designed, results were obtained. One of the most significant of these involved a Fin whale calf, marked in the Southern Ocean, which was killed two years later off the coast of South Africa. This definite link between the South African and Antarctic whale stocks proved that the same stocks were being depleted in the Antarctic and in warmer waters.

Discovery left Grytviken on 4 February 1927, sailing north of South Georgia and making a station in only 177m between Shag Rocks and Bird Island, proving the existence of a connecting ridge. The dredge brought up some fine soft corals which Hardy described so beautifully in his book, *Great Waters*. Strong winds on the morning of 9 February made the ship fly along at 8½ knots, an achievement for the *Discovery*. By the afternoon the sky darkened and the wind increased with startling suddenness to a full gale. Hardy wrote of the glory of the old ship and the skills of her square-rig sailing crew as the sails were taken in. 'Up aloft go the sailors, as calmly as if the ship had been in port.' he wrote, 'and out upon the swaying yards which are describing great arcs through the roaring air.'

The mountainous South Orkney Islands, some 500 miles south of South Georgia and therefore colder and more desolate, were reached on 16 February. *Discovery* secured alongside the whale factory ship *Orwell*, whose captain and officers proved most hospitable. *Orwell* was the type of factory ship common at this time, before the stern slipway was generally adopted.

The whales were flensed in the sea from a raft, not on deck, as later. *Discovery* coaled again here, and Chaplin took advantage of a sunny day to 'move' Coronation Island some 15 miles east. As they proceeded towards Bransfield Strait a huge tabular iceberg, some 30 miles long, was encountered. *Discovery* sailed past Clarence Island and then Elephant Island, both of which were black, white, bleak and forbidding. Rich and intriguing dredges continued to be made, their contents being carefully sorted, labelled and stored. Chaplin corrected the position of Clarence Island and others of the group by many miles.

The next call, from 26 February to 2 March, was at Deception Island in the South Shetland group, just off the Antarctic Peninsula, the long tail of the continent, separated from the tip of South America by Drake Passage. This was named after Sir Francis Drake, who was blown to the south of Cape Horn in the *Golden Hind* during his famous voyage around the world. Deception Island is a dormant volcano whose central crater has been invaded by the sea to form a sheltered harbour, entered through a narrow channel between high overhanging cliffs, which dwarfed the masts of *Discovery*. The central lagoon, known as Port Foster, is some four miles across and 100 fathoms deep. *Discovery* was greeted by the extraordinary sight of eight former 'crack ocean liners' lying in a small desolate bay. They had been refitted as factory ships, and each was serviced by its own whale catchers operating in Bransfield Strait.

Discovery anchored between two factory ships, but in a near-hurricane needed the help of two whale catchers to secure to cables ashore. That evening the expedition was royally entertained by Norwegians on board *Falk*, representing all the ships in the bay. The scientists explored the island while the barque took on coal from a warm beach with steam rising from the water's edge, while on the upper slopes lay ice and snow. The water temperature measured in Port Foster was found to fall steadily with depth to 39.3°F at the bottom. One of the whaling captains vividly recounted the earthquake and underwater eruption earlier in the 1920s, a terrifying experience, when they found themselves 'powerless to

The *Discovery* at Port Lockroy, Wiencke Island
(Palmer Archipelago), March 1927.
(SOUTHAMPTON OCEANOGRAPHY CENTRE)

move…anchored in a cauldron of boiling water'.

The ship departed Deception Island on 2 March to sail south along the western shore of the Antarctic Peninsula, anchoring in Melchior Harbour a week later. At that time the region was poorly charted, and one of *Discovery*'s tasks was to check and correct the reported position of the Kendall Rocks and the Austin Rocks. The locations of Hoseason, Snow and Smith Islands were also corrected, and a running survey was completed of Schollaert Channel, Gerlache Strait and Neumayer Channel, as well as a rough plan of Discovery Sound. A new island was named after the ship. Fog and blizzards delayed progress southwards, but the hauls made with dredge, trawl and tow-net were most rewarding. A purple octopus, new to science, was an especially valuable prize. The more interesting specimens were often painted or photographed. As they sailed south through the 'fairyland channel' from Melchior Harbour to Port Lockroy, the surgeon, Lieutenant-Colonel E H Marshall, doubted if there were a more beautiful place in the whole world in fine weather. Herdman, the hydrologist, found things less peaceful, with the glaciers breaking off all the time with a tremendous noise, plus the raucous sound of the Cape Pigeons fighting day and night over the 'graks' – refuse from the whaling station.

Discovery sheltered from rough weather on 21 and 22 March. On the 24th the ship steamed through the Peltier Channel to take a full station and put down a dredge off Cape Renard on the mainland. That same afternoon mock suns were seen, a well-known Antarctic phenomenon. Hardy's diary recorded the glorious gradations of colour, the contrasts and perpetual change of translucent light, with the water in the channel reflecting every detail from above. He wrote: 'It was as if we were steaming in a giant kaleidoscope'.

With autumn approaching, Discovery turned north through Gerlache Strait to King George Island, working two stations on the way. The doctor recorded that the need for fresh meat and vegetables was beginning to be felt, some not wanting to touch the seal meat he had procured. A further station near Deception Island proved particularly rewarding when a quantity of young krill was collected, each of which had only a single light-organ developed. Even so, there were enough of them to make the end of the tow-net glow a brilliant blue-green as it came to the surface.

Lines of stations were worked across the krill nursey in Bransfield Strait during cold frosty weather before the ship re-entered Port Foster, Deception Island, where she sheltered and coaled for the next leg of the voyage. A series of stations was planned across Drake Passage from the South Shetlands to Cape Horn, where the Atlantic and Pacific meet, and just to the west of the whaling area being studied by the Discovery Expedition.

The first station was at 5am on 15 April 1927 in good weather, between Snow and Smith Islands. The complete series resulted in a whole section of the ocean traverse showing the Antarctic current system and the varying temperature and salinity of the sea. Hardy's invention, the plankton recorder, not unlike a horizontal vacuum cleaner, came into its own. Any plankton in the water was sieved and retained on a continuous silk roll that wound on to a storage roller immersed in a preserving fluid, thus providing a complete record.

The sixth and last station was completed some miles off Cape Horn, in huge seas. The ship anchored afterwards in St Martin's Cove on the east coast of Hermite Island, earlier known as Wigwam Bay after the tents of the natives of Tierra del Fuego. Both Dr Marshall and Hardy recorded their joy at seeing trees again after seven months of nothing but sea, snow and ice.

With the plankton and water samples packed away, a course was set for the Falkland Islands by way of the difficult shallow waters of Le Maire Strait, which separates Staten Island from the tip of Tierra del Fuego. Discovery's passage through the strait, where there is a strong tide of four knots or more, was a constant battle against the changing elements. The old ship pitched as never before, putting her head down and then lifting it as if coming up for air. Then, suddenly, the wind changed from direct ahead to off the port bow. The cry 'All hands on deck!' brought everyone to the ropes, and in a very short time the upper and lower topsails were set on both the fore and main, and then fore and main courses, with staysails and spankers. The ship looked magnificent against the jagged mountains of Staten Island, and with sails filled and engines at full blast she pushed into the heavy sea at nine or ten knots and, before long, was through the strait.

Six stations were worked with difficulty during the voyage to Port Stanley in the Falkland Islands, where the ship anchored on 6 May 1927. The two scientists, Herdman and Fraser, standing on the outboard platforms, were often up to their waists in seawater as waves swept by, and had to be secured with lifelines. William Scoresby was already in harbour, back from her trawling survey between the Falklands and South America. The two ships separated again at the Falklands, and each made lines of tow-net stations across the Southern Ocean to Cape Town.

From the Cape, Scoresby returned direct to England for alterations while Discovery travelled up the west coast of Africa into the Gulf of Guinea to investigate the whales' breeding grounds and pick up pertinent information from the different coastal whaling stations. She berthed in Falmouth on 29 September 1927, ending what Sir Sydney Harmer called 'the largest and most important scientific expedition that has left our shores since the time of the Challenger'.

ORIGINS OF THE BANZARE AND THE FIRST VOYAGE, 1929-30

THE SIGHT OF *Discovery* preparing in London for her next voyage in the summer of 1929 so excited K N MacKenzie, Second Mate of the *City of Valencia*, that he called on *Discovery*'s master, Captain John King Davis, the very next day. Only five days later, despite his lack of experience in sail, MacKenzie received a letter confirming his appointment as Chief Officer of *Discovery* on her first British, Australian and New Zealand Antarctic Research Expedition (BANZARE) voyage. He was soon deep in her bowels, preparing her for the voyage, choosing the crew, and ordering and stowing two years' supplies and equipment in separate lots, so that everything could be located promptly at sea or in the ice. All this despite a constant flow of visitors, sightseers and reporters, for whom he had very little time.

Antarctica, from an Australian point of view, is hardly remote. The Australasian Antarctic Expedition of 1911-14, the first to be led by Sir Douglas Mawson, made a very considerable contribution towards the exploration of the great arc of Antarctic coastline that faces Australia across the Southern Ocean. Mawson had already ventured to delineate the hypothetical typography of Antarctica in two maps of the south polar region, published in 1911. After the First World War, calls were made for the work of the Australasian Antarctic Expedition to continue. Mawson outlined the geographical and scientific tasks still to be accomplished, observing that 'more than half the circumference of the globe' remained to be charted in high southern latitudes. This would be the principal geographical objective of the BANZARE. The important political side of the expedition was the subject of extensive negotiations between the Commonwealth Government in Canberra and the British Government in London.

As we have seen, the Antarctic whaling industry had expanded rapidly in the early decades of the twentieth century. In 1923 a British Order in Council established the Ross Dependency between longs. 160°E and 159°W, after which a number of regulations were published affecting the Norwegians, who began whaling in the Ross Sea that year. Decrees protecting French interests came a year later.

British imperial policy considered it desirable to establish sovereignty over the whole continent for several reasons: the conservation of the whales and whaling industry; the strategic significance of both the Antarctic coasts and waters; and of Antarctica in the southern hemisphere's weather system. By January 1920 the British Government apparently favoured a policy of discreet and gradual extension of imperial control over the whole of the continent.

At the Imperial Conference of 1926 it was pointed out that at that time only two areas in the Antarctic were formally part of the British Empire, the Falkland Islands Dependencies (1908), and the Ross Dependency (1923), administered by New Zealand.

The committee recommended that formal title should be asserted to seven other areas to which British titles already existed by virtue of discovery. These were listed as: 1, The outlying parts of Coats Land; 2, Enderby Land; 3, Kemp Land; 4, Queen Mary Land; 5, The area which lies to the west of Adélie Land, which on its discovery by the Australasian Antarctic Expedition in 1912 was denominated Wilkes Land; 6, King George V Land; and 7, Oates Land. The first of these should become part of the Falkland Islands Dependencies, and the other six would be placed under Australian control with the agreement of the Commonwealth Government. It was recognised that the French had a valid title to some territory in Adélie Land. Gradual and cautious progress was urged by the committee, to bring the Antarctic regions under British sovereignty and 'practically complete British domination'.

It was suggested that control need not be continuous to be effective, and that the best way was to send ships to the Antarctic, whose officers would be authorised to act in the government's name. Discovery and exploration could also be pursued.

The Antarctic Committee's report of November 1926 was moved by the Prime Minister, Mr Stanley Baldwin. It was circulated to the Dominions the following year. On 25 July 1927 the Australian National Research Council recommended establishing claims to the regions lying within the Australian sector by means of an expedition sent from Australia, to be controlled, financed and equipped by the Commonwealth Government in Canberra. The committee also recommended obtaining the loan of Discovery, 'the only existing vessel suitably constructed for this purpose', for a period of two years.

Sir Douglas Mawson aboard Discovery.
(MACKENZIE COLLECTION)

The Australian Prime Minister, Mr S M Bruce (later Viscount Bruce), proposed to the British Government on 26 July 1928 that a joint expedition should be sent to the Antarctic to take formal possession of the seven areas in the recommendation, suggesting that scientific investigations into whaling and sealing could also be made. Bruce suggested that Sir Douglas Mawson should lead the expedition in Discovery, and that in addition to £7,500 each from Australia and Great Britain, and £2,500 from New Zealand, a public appeal should provide the balance of funds.

The need for the expedition was now acute, given the increasing activity of foreign powers, particularly Norway and the Unites States of America.

The second meeting, on 16 August, reported on the meeting of the Discovery Committee. The matter had been considered on a purely scientific basis, and not from any political point of view. Discovery was not to be used by them during the 1928-29 season, and certain alterations were to be made to her before she resumed the Committee's work the following season. If she were to be released to the Commonwealth Government for an expedition, the Discovery Committee would require a new ship for 1929-30 and, in any event, they did not wish to part with Discovery for good. Further consultations revealed that their obligations precluded them from lending the vessel free of charge, but that she could be provided at 'the exceptionally low rate of £8,000 per annum'. The Australian Commonwealth Government's offer to finance a 1929-30 expedition was on condition that the ship should be loaned free of charge or offered to them for sale at no more than £10,000.

Finding that the ship was nominally the property of the Falkland Islands and Dependencies, negotiations were accelerated eventually by the concern that the activity of foreign powers was threatening the British position in the Antarctic.

Norway raised the flag on Bouvet Island from the Norvegia. The island, to which Great Britain also had a claim, was formally annexed by Norway on 1 December 1927. A Norwegian expedition was planned for the 1929-30 Antarctic season which might establish a base on the mainland, and Commander Byrd's expedition had aroused interest in the United States which might result in further American activity. The French and Germans too might step in, and the whaling industry would always attract foreign vessels.

Any diplomatic measures taken would require Imperial co-operation. Many members of the Interdepartmental Committee thought that the Australian offer to finance the proposed expedition was generous and should be accepted, as a chance to consolidate the work of previous explorers. In addition, whaling grounds might be discovered and valuable scientific work undertaken, although the expedition would be 'primarily territorial in object'. The Dominions Office requested the sanction of the Treasury contribution of £16,000 in two instalments.

BANZARE CONFIRMED

Sir Douglas Mawson put considerable personal effort into the inception and financing of the BANZARE. In Hobart he was reported to have made a forceful statement on the need for British annexation of the Antarctic, and later that year he visited London in connection with the expedition. On 30 January 1929 he received news from the office of the High Commissioner for Australia that all was well, that the British Government had decided to lend *Discovery* without charge for the next two Antarctic seasons, and that the offer had been accepted by the Commonwealth Government. A new ship would be designed for the *Discovery* Committee. Arrangements could be put in hand, but there was to be no publicity for obvious reasons.

Getting possession of *Discovery* was no easy task for Mawson, who had requisitioned for J K Davis to come to England in June to organise the ship. He anticipated sailing from London towards the end of August. As a spur to Mawson's efforts, on 2 February 1929 Captain Nils Larsen of *Norvegia* landed and took possession of Peter I Island in the Antarctic. Sir Douglas Mawson was officially appointed leader of the BANZARE on 4 February 1929. He found that although *Discovery* was being lent free of charge, the insurance would cost almost £15,000, a heavy expense. Sir Douglas was to do much of the fund-raising himself, despite the expedition's official origins.

Meanwhile, in Australia, an Antarctic Committee had been formed. In the light of subsequent events it is interesting to read Captain Davis's remarks in the minutes. He thought it preferable, from the point of view of navigation, not to begin in Cape Town as Mawson had suggested, but in Australia and then work from east to west, starting with King George V Land and finishing at Enderby Land by the end of the season. Advantage could then be taken of prevailing easterly winds, and more work could be done. Despite the pressing need to plant the British flag on Enderby

Land, the Committee agreed with Davis. They felt it would be more appropriate for a predominantly Australian expedition to set off from Australia.

Davis believed that the deck crew had to have sailing experience, and this effectively ruled out volunteers from the Royal Australian Navy. He doubted *Discovery*'s capacity to carry an aeroplane, and stressed that the amount of coal the vessel could bunker would be the deciding factor as to the length of the voyage; 85 days maximum.

Mawson's Instructions authorised him to take possession of such lands as he should discover, and of those others listed in the document by reason of earlier British discovery. In an article in *The Times* of 12 October 1929, he likened the ship's destination to a southern Eldorado with scientific treasures instead of gold.

Sir Douglas touched on the potential mineral wealth and the prospects for future exploitation. The roles of the various governments and the generosity of many private benefactors were also set out. He summarised the route that *Discovery* would take from Cape Town, the work to be undertaken and the intention to survey and study islands and the Antarctic coast, predicting that the ship would arrive back in Australia in April 1930 unless she became stuck fast in the ice for the winter, for which eventuality they would be well prepared.

The ship's company comprised the 'navigating captain', John King Davis, second-in-command of the expedition, and a crew of twenty-five officers and men whom Captain Davis described in his diary as 'an excellent ship's company and a credit to the Merchant Service'.

THE VOYAGE TO THE CAPE

Discovery departed the East India Dock on 1 August 1929, a day of gusty winds and pouring rain. Flags and ensigns dipped ashore and afloat, and many *Bon Voyage* signals were run up. *The Times* reported her as flying the Union Jack at her forepeak, the white Antarctic flag at the foremast and the Australian flag at the stern. At a reception before her departure, some 300 guests had been received on board by Captain

Davis and his officers. A Gipsy Moth aeroplane was secured with wire ropes on deck. Reports in the press commented on the small trim sailing ship, nosing her way eagerly into the Thames Basin.

When asked if he was pleased with the ship, Davis declared her to be unsinkable and expressed pride in his men, none said to be over 30 years old. All on board was spic and span, with everything put away in its proper place. On passage from London to Cardiff Davis took with him Captain Hamilton Blair, a veteran of Antarctic seas, as his right-hand man, since none of his three officers had any deep-sea sail experience. Blair had served under Davis in *Aurora* during her voyage to relieve Mawson at Cape Denison in 1913-14.

Davis had been allowed leave from his post as Commonwealth Director of Navigation to command *Discovery*. He, Hurley and Marr had considerable past experience in Antarctic expeditions led by Shackleton and Mawson. J W S Marr, the first of the expedition's scientists to join the ship, had been in Shackleton's *Quest* in 1921-22, and was in charge of oceanography. The photographer, Captain Frank

Discovery at Cape Town, October 1929, flying the Australian ensign.
(FALLA COLLECTION, WELLINGTON HARBOUR BOARD MUSEUM.)

Hurley, had taken part in Mawson's earlier expedition and also in Shackleton's Trans-Antarctic Expedition of 1914-17, in *Endurance*. MacKenzie, the First Officer, described Marr as firm, helpful and unassuming, and Hurley as extraordinary and well worth knowing. Both kept everyone cheerful with their boyish pranks and buoyant spirits. If the other scientists were anything like so good, he observed, the expedition must succeed.

The master of *Discovery*, Captain John King Davis, and the leader of the BANZARE Expedition, Sir Douglas Mawson, who was to join the ship at Cape Town, were old shipmates from *Nimrod* days, when Davis was Chief Officer and Mawson a young geologist during Shackleton's British Antarctic Expedition of 1907-09.

On 10 August 1929 *Discovery* sailed down the Bristol Channel. The ship was searched for stowaways that day, and a boy of 14 was found by Hurley in port boat No 2. He was taken ashore in tears by the pilot.

Once the great Welsh coal terminal at Cardiff and the Bristol Channel were cleared, topsails were hoisted and fore- and mainsails set. *Discovery* coaled again at St Vincent, Cape Verde Islands, then laid a course for Cape Town, where Mawson and the remaining scientific staff were to be embarked. Many of the party wrote of their eager anticipation at seeing and setting foot on new land.

After many hot days in the doldrums and even longer nights, the breeze came at last, and on 5 September the barque crossed the Equator in long. 27°W and followed the windjammer track down the South American coast, passing only 200 miles off its easterly point. When strong winds and rough seas caused *Discovery* to sail close-hauled (for her, 7 to 8 points into the wind), Davis and the ship often fell out, and the officers took the brunt of his annoyance. First mate MacKenzie wrote in his diary: 'Damn sailing ships. We've pulled and hauled – cursed and groaned, and still J K has a grouse because the wind has changed.' But the captain's diary told the other side of the story, with none of the three officers having any experience in sail and needing constant guidance.

The westerlies came eventually, and by 1 October, in a strong gale and high full sea, the ship was

ABOVE: First Mate K N MacKenzie catting the anchor from the bows of the *Discovery*.
(MACKENZIE COLLECTION)

RIGHT: *Discovery* under sail, *c*1930.
(FALLA COLLECTION, WELLINGTON HARBOUR BOARD MUSEUM)

carrying all sail and flying along at speeds of up to ten knots, fast indeed for *Discovery*. On 5 October 1929 they dropped anchor in Table Bay at 1am, after a passage of fifty-five days, three less than on her maiden voyage under Captain Scott.

Sir Douglas Mawson, the two airmen and the scientists from Australia and New Zealand came aboard in Cape Town. A fortnight of feverish activity followed, when the ship was invaded, through the goodwill of the South African Government, by carpenters, shipwrights, steelworkers, blacksmiths, painters, caulkers, riggers, gold-braided firemen, port officers and officials. A new motor boat was shipped and a whaler landed in place on a specially constructed platform. All the main yards were sent down and landed without mishap, while the 40ft fore topgallant yards were lashed on deck. The main yards were left in charge of the Port Authority. Davis's

intention in striking the yards off the mainmast was to make the vessel easier to handle with a small crew, especially in the higher latitudes, and to reduce wind resistance aloft when under steam.

The vast amount of gear the scientists brought aboard caused consternation among the officers. Twenty-six cases were brought by the meteorologist, Ritchie Simmers, alone. Delighted to be 'on the old bus at last', he observed tea laid on a table-cloth, and wondered how long that would last. When Mawson joined the ship, Simmers wrote: 'He'll do me as leader, and, from wardroom remarks, he'll do the rest. In a few minutes of his arrival he had control, or to me, seemed to have control.'

FIRST SEASON IN THE ANTARCTIC, 1929-30
Discovery was given an enthusiastic send-off at Cape Town when she left Table Bay on Saturday 19 Octo-

ber 1929. His Majesty King George V sent a message to Mawson, wishing the expedition success and a safe journey. The Mayor of Cape Town bade farewell with a large basket of oranges, an addition to the fruit already embarked.

A Reuters report headlined the rivalry between a Norwegian expedition already in the south and the British expedition in their efforts to discover new lands and mineral resources, both being equipped with aeroplanes for reconnaissance. The memory of the Anglo-Norwegian rivalry personified in Scott and Amundsen would still have been vivid in 1929.

A course was set for the Iles Crozet, a group of volcanic sub-Antarctic islands. The fifteen sheep (and many men) found the going tough aboard ship in gale-force winds, with icy water awash everywhere. On 29 October 1929, ten days out of Cape Town, with Discovery 'belting along under fore and lower topsails only'. The following day proved wild and tempestuous, with the 'big drop in temperature and icy blasts' which caused them all to don warm clothing. MacKenzie observed a great contrast between the leader and captain, finding Mawson 'sociable and friendly' and Davis 'as much aloof and as distant as a master can be'. Davis was well aware he could be 'nasty' in bad weather, when he was worried and short of sleep. Nevertheless, Simmers made a perceptive judgement when he wrote in his diary: 'One sleeps better for his presence'. Simmers's pen-portrait of Mawson was similarly perceptive.

> Sir Douglas's conversation is always interesting...
> anything remotely connected with polar regions on and
> in land, sea or air has been studied or remembered...
> But he's not absolutely the best organiser – beforehand
> yes...but in carrying things out, oh no ...All the same I
> wouldn't rather have a different leader for any money as
> he is capable himself, looks after everyone, and is such a
> continual cheerful inspiration.

On 2 November Discovery anchored in American Bay, Possession Island, one of the Crozet group, and her crew were surprised to find the sealer SS Kilfinora of Cape Town at anchor inshore. The scientists landed and found themselves witnessing the slaughter of

the Sea Elephants. MacKenzie called it 'an absolute outrage'. In spite of newspaper talk about the danger of seal and whale extermination, they found that nothing had been done to control the 'murder of a whole beach', bulls, cows and pups.

During two days ashore they observed other rich wildlife, including penguins and various birds which were quite unafraid of man. Extensive collections were made, which were afterwards spread out, sorted and classified on the wardroom table, or preserved in the laboratory. Colbeck and Child struggled with their first survey; they knew the existing chart was wrong, and Davis agreed, but they found it difficult to prove.

Swept towards Kerguelen Islands under bare poles, Discovery steamed up Royal Sound on 12 November 1929. Scientific and survey work was carried out by motor launch along one of the longest fjords, the Bras de Bossière. Mawson contrasted the verdure of the small islands in these waterways with the bareness of the mainland, unfortunately devastated by rabbits. Wild dogs were a further menace there, having become like wolves, although many kinds of seabird still survived on the islets. Altogether, 213 tons of coal were loaded with the help of the scientists, including Mawson, and the crew of the whaler SS Kilfinora, which took away the expedition's mail.

Discovery departed Kerguelen on 24 November for Heard Island, further to the southeast and far more desolate due to its position within the Antarctic Convergence. Investigations into the marine life of the Southern Ocean were undertaken by A Howard, the hydrologist, and J W S Marr, seconded to the expedition by the Discovery Committee. They used three different instruments to measure the depth of the ocean and provide information on the contours and nature of the sea floor: a Kelvin sounding machine for use in shallow water, which was also particularly valuable for navigation when steaming close to land; a Lucas-type machine for deeper water; and a newly fitted echo-sounding installation capable of measuring depths of several thousand fathoms in a few seconds. The temperature, salinity, current movements and biology of the sea were studied too, and water was sampled. Dr Kemp had shown that abundant nitrogen and phosphorus in the waters off South Georgia fertilise plant life (just as they do on land) on which small crustaceans, the principal food of the southern whales, feed. Marr's contribution was vital. 'Without him there would have been little or no oceanography on the first voyage,' wrote Sir George Deacon. 'He rigged all the equipment, bought missing items with his own money in Cape Town, showed them how to use it, and worked all hours of the day and night.'

Heard Island was sighted at dawn on 26 November 1929. A shore party of nine, including Mawson, landed in Atlas Cove, where the motor launch was moored. They were able to sleep in a hexagonal sealers' hut, after first removing 3in of ice from the floor. Thousands of penguins were nesting, and Sea Elephants lay like logs along the beach, shedding their winter coats. After the long sea voyage in the ever-rolling Discovery, the shore party found life on Heard Island most entertaining.

A full scientific programme was carried out ashore each day in snow and rain, after which it was 'a relief to retire within the tiny Norwegian hut where sodden clothes are dried and a hot meal prepared'. The stove was 'kept roaring with an ample

Able Seaman James Holland Martin with the ship's cat which he attempted to rescue by jumping into the icy sea after it had fallen from the rigging.
(AUTHOR'S COLLECTION)

application of seal blubber'. Eight men slept in the bunks, while the ninth on the floor had anxious moments when Sea Elephants pushed their way into the hut on two occasions. The scientists enjoyed omelettes cooked with prion, skua and Dominican gull eggs. Wreckage on the south shore provided ample fuel.

On board Discovery, Davis and his officers watched anxiously as the barometer remained at just over 28in for several days. Anchored in Corinthian Bay, he semaphored the shore party to embark to allow the ship to leave. Delay at the island was eating into their meagre coal supply, and could jeopardise the main purpose of the expedition.

Discovery's engines were heavily taxed to prevent her from being driven out to sea but somehow, the motor launch and 'the stout little pram in tow, laden with all manner of birds' were hoisted, swung in and landed in place. Handling the anchor proved just as hazardous. Black squalls of snow and sleet swept round the headland, while the wind increased to a terrifying roar. Two hours passed before the two-ton topmasts were secured on deck. Davis thought they were fortunate to have got the whole party safely on board, and that it 'was sheer folly to allow inexperienced people to be fooling about in such places'.

They departed Heard Island on 4 December 1929, setting a course approximately east-south-east. Three days of continuous gales made Discovery roll and roll, straining the ship and making every rope and wire chafe.

Davis was evidently already feeling the strain of the voyage and needed rest, which was impossible in bad weather. He had not had his clothes off since leaving Cape Town. He liked to do things quietly, but Mawson's impulsive operations, even in fine spells, made him feel that he had to be always on watch, to protect the safety of the ship.

By 8 December icebergs of all shapes and sizes dotted a calm and sunlit sea all around. Steaming at full speed, they came through them in safety. They nosed slowly into the pack on 11 December, observing Blue whales, Crab-eater seals and snow-white Antarctic petrels. Emperor penguins stood on the floes. The King penguin embarked at Heard Island strutted the deck, making friends with all, even with Nigger, the ship's cat. After traversing the immense area of heavy and continuous pack ice to the south of Heard Island in fog and snow, Discovery edged up towards the Antarctic Circle.

Meanwhile, the bright yellow Gipsy Moth seaplane was unpacked and assembled for scouting operations. On Christmas Eve both Davis and Child saw what they believed to be an island. Christmas

Day, spent 'far within icefields', never before traversed, was given over to festivities. Wireless messages greeted them at the breakfast table, and an excellent dinner was full of fun, with presents and table decorations from Australia. An Emperor penguin was declared to be every bit as good as grouse.

On Boxing Day MacKenzie, on watch, saw 'hitherto unknown and unsighted land'. There was a wild rush for the rigging and a heavy demand for field glasses. Davis, 'delighted and in high spirits', thought the land to be 30 miles off, but next day in clear visibility this land could not be seen. It must have been a mirage induced by refraction, a phenomenon not uncommon in these latitudes. By the evening of 28 December they were in more open water, proceeding towards Enderby Land, the expedition's main goal.

Wind and cloud prevented the seaplane from taking off until 31 December, when the pilots taxied from an ice-free pool within the pack. From an altitude of 5,000ft they sighted what appeared to be low, hilly, ice-covered land about 50 miles to the south.

The *Norvegia* off the Antarctic coast of Enderby Land, 14 January 1930, seen from the *Discovery*.
(MACKENZIE COLLECTION)

More oceanographic work was done during this period, and on one occasion a 30ft trawl was brought to the surface with an amazingly rich catch, which caused the powerful derrick to crash to the deck, narrowly missing members of the staff.

A radio message, received on 2 January, reported the discovery by *Norvegia* of land between Coats Land and Enderby Land. Mawson did his best to cheer and humour the disenchanted Davis, but the latter remained pessimistic, unable to 'see anything in a cheerful light'.

On 4 January 1930 Kemp Land, discovered in 1833 by the British sealer Captain Peter Kemp, was confirmed. Piloted in the plane next day, Mawson examined the magnificent panorama of new land

spread out below, with a long, low coast and three high peaks. The great area of heavy pack through which *Discovery* had battled for weeks could also be seen from the air. While the ship was hove to for the flight, Simmers followed the drift of a meteorological balloon to a height of 40,000ft and the other scientists made oceanographical observations at a depth of 1,100 fathoms.

Within a few hours, however, this idyllic scene was transformed to chaos by a blizzard of extraordinary ferocity. The wind velocity averaged 50mph, gusting to 70mph. Great blocks of ice falling from the rigging punctured the aeroplane. Gaping tears began to appear all over it, and ten ribs were stove in, which took ten days to repair.

On 9 January more news came through about Norwegian activities in the Antarctic. Sir Douglas had gone to much trouble to inform Norway of the BANZARE plans, and was exasperated to learn of the claim to land between Kemp Land and Enderby Land. He declared it unhelpful to an organised programme of detailed scientific work, if it meant that such 'explorers' should 'rush to the most likely places to make landings and raise flags'. At the same time Mawson was hoping that a landing could be made and the flag raised on the new land discovered east of Kemp Land, to be called MacRobertson Land, to commemorate their benefactor.

Because of the heavy pack ice it proved impossible for the ship to approach the coast. Nor was it possible to fly. Mawson decided they could no longer wait, but must press on westward following the edge of heavy pack, and look for an opening to the land. The presence of the Norwegians somewhere nearby, trying to claim territory, was a crucial factor in this decision.

To the great excitement of all, Enderby Land was

sighted soon after midday on 12 January 1930 to the south and southwest of the ship by Child, the third mate. Davis estimated a distance of 25 miles, describing 'snow covered slopes with eight rocky tops which emerged from the snow slope, the highest I should estimate being 3,000ft'.

On 14 January the flag was raised on Proclamation Island, first spotted by Child. Diary entries once again reveal differences between captain and leader that day. Davis made it clear to Mawson that there was no suitable bottom for anchoring, and asked him to 'get ashore as quickly as possible, get the flag up and come off – we can't stop here'. Davis was consistently unwilling to allow anyone to land, which was naturally disappointing to the scientists and frustrating and infuriating for Mawson contemplating territorial claims. Weather conditions were ideal, and the glorious coast of Enderby Island was in full view. Davis watched the shore party climb to the summit and hoist the British flag. The proclamation in the name of King George V, dated 13 January 1930, signed by Sir Douglas Mawson and witnessed by Captain Davis, declared the territory for which full sovereignty was claimed to be Enderby Land, Kemp Land and Mac.Robertson Land, together with off-lying islands.

On the evening of 14 January there was a dramatic meeting of the two exploring ships, *Norvegia* and *Discovery*. Both vessels dipped flags. Mawson asked Davis to send a friendly message, so flags for 'Wish you a pleasant voyage' were run up. They replied 'Thank you' and asked, through the megaphone, if Captain Riiser-Larsen might come aboard. They lowered a boat and Davis received the distinguished Norwegian aviator and explorer at the gangway. He told them he had been warned from Norway not to do anything that Great Britain might resent. Each told the other of their plans for the following season. *Discovery* gave three cheers for *Norvegia* as the Norwegians left, then steamed west as the others departed in the opposite direction. Long. 45°E was subsequently made the boundary between

Maps showing the *Discovery's* tracks in the Southern Ocean, 1929-30 and 1930-31.

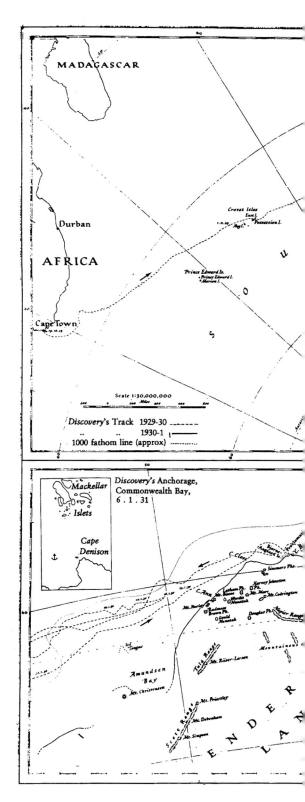

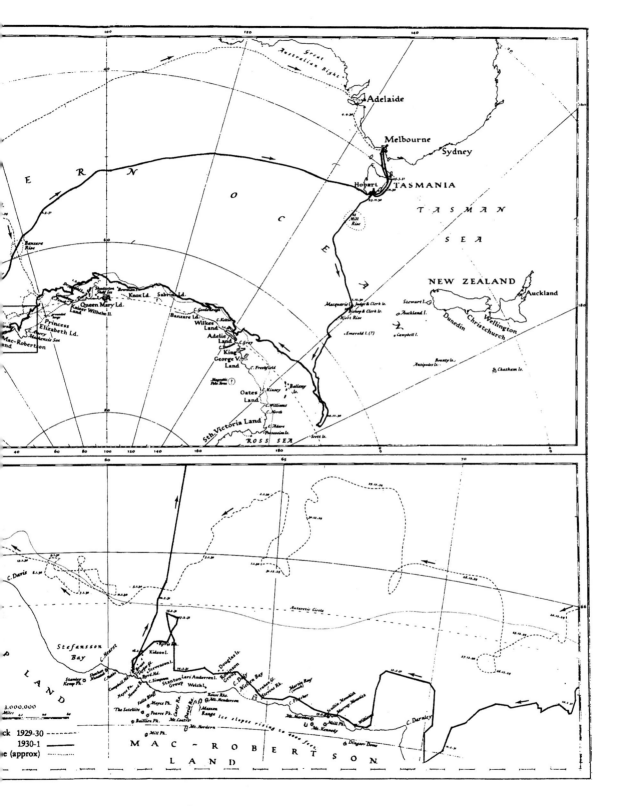

British and Norwegian claims in the Antarctic.

Riiser-Larsen recorded that he had hailed *Discovery* because he wanted to meet the two famous Antarctic explorers, and because he had heard of the unfavourable British press reports on his expedition.

Discovery was now forced to run for some 150 miles before a northeasterly gale to her furthest west. There were many anxious moments whenever she was thrown into a trough, but all praised the vessel as a marvel, riding out the storm splendidly. There was very little change in the weather and the deck hands were all miserable, Davis noted. The vessel was becoming unwieldy as the coal was consumed and she became lighter. The disagreement over coal was a constant and major contention between leader and captain. Mawson thought they would have no difficulty in reaching Kerguelen, while Davis thought to arrive there without coal was a 'foolish act', and hoped Mawson 'would stop biologising' until all risks had passed.

Steaming eastwards when wind and sea moderated, they discovered one of the 'world's finest mountain ranges…from 5,000ft upwards, and the number of peaks beyond our count' on their way to 'Point Biscoe', or Cape Ann. 'Never were mountains more wonderful,' wrote MacKenzie.

At this point of the voyage the two leaders were heard to be openly criticising each other. Mawson had delivered a schedule to Davis on 18 January, setting out the work that was still to be completed, including making a further proclamation on the mainland of Enderby Land. On 23 January preparations for the landing had been made when Davis declared: 'Launch the plane, we may, but go in there, we can't', and that was that. Unfortunately, the swell proved too great for the seaplane to be launched near the cape. Once again there was huge disappointment as they appeared to steam aimlessly along the coast.

Flights were made from open water in the vicinity of Proclamation Island on 25 January, during which Hurley shot both still and motion pictures. It was too risky for the aeroplane to come down on the open water near the shore, so Mawson dropped a flag on the ice sheet from about 3,000ft, some two miles inland, retaining the Proclamation. He remarked in his

In a cabin during the first BANZARE voyage: Frank Hurley on left, J W S Marr centre and (probably) Professor T Harvey Johnston to right. (ANTARCTIC DIVISION, DEPARTMENT OF SCIENCE AND TECHNOLOGY, TASMANIA)

diary that all members of staff were heartbroken that Davis would not steam two miles through loose pack ice to set foot upon the mainland of Enderby Land.

More flights to over 4,000ft were made the next day, 26 January 1930, from which height 73 nunataks (mountain peaks) were seen projecting above the ice sheet. *Discovery* remained outside the pack ice. Davis explained to Mawson the dangers of the rocks in uncharted waters between islands, and said he could not justify taking such a risk. Mawson recorded that 'the whole area is most attractive for land operations' and many other activities, including observations from test balloons and the gathering of marine collections from the continental shelf. Saturday 25 January was their last full day off the Antarctic coast. In his report to the Commonwealth Parliament, presented in May 1930, Mawson confirmed that: 'On the evening of 26 January Captain Davis informed me that having reached the limit of 120 tons of coal, he would carry on no further in Antarctic waters and was about to set course for Kergulen'.

Mawson's diary entry of 26 January expresses his regret at having to leave at Davis's wish, once coal stocks were down to 120 tons. Given another week, he thought they could have completed the aerial survey of Mac.Robertson Land and added detail of what he named the Scott Mountains, the nunataks of Enderby Land. But, despite being Commander, Mawson felt obliged to bow to Davis's advice, even though he himself would not have left until coal stocks were down to 80 tons. Press reports show that Mawson was prepared to winter in the pack if necessary. They were well supplied with equipment and food, and with enough coal left to manoeuvre in the ice, *Discovery* would have had a great advantage over the earlier navigators with sail alone. And if she were blown past Kerguelen, where the remainder of her coal depot was waiting, she could have sailed the Great Circle route to Australia, an option of which Davis, with his very considerable experience in clipper ships, must have been aware.

THE VOYAGE HOME

Discovery turned north on 26 January 1930, more than a month before the navigation season generally ends. Davis's resolve was stiffened by the chief engineer's announcement that the boilers could only continue for three more weeks without cleaning. Many of the members of the expedition wrote of the captain having 'coal fever'. Captain Williamson, who had sailed aboard *Discovery* in 1911 as a seaman, commented pertinently that, by striking down the square yards in Cape Town, Davis had converted a barque-rigged efficient sailing vessel with an auxiliary engine into a low-powered steamer with small bunker capacity and a few fore and aft sails. Thus the safety of the vessel depended on the amount of coal in the bunkers. (In fact Davis did retain the yards on the foremast)

Second Officer Captain W R Colbeck felt that Davis was concerned that his three officers did not have any deep-sea sail experience. Even so their wireless communication would have ensured their whereabouts would be known and they could have been picked up if necessary.

On 31 January Davis was noted as being 'far more cheerful now we are homeward bound', but on 3 February, with 79 tons of coal remaining, *Discovery* was hove to for an oceanographic station and once again he felt they should be pressing on for Kerguelen while the weather was fine. On 8 February, between Enderby Island and Kerguelen, Mawson

despatched two press reports summarising the work accomplished by the expedition in Antarctic waters.

The outstanding achievements were the charting or location of the edge of the Antarctic continent between 45°E and 73°E, the claim to all this land and offshore islands for the Crown, and the discovery of whales off Enderby Land.

Discovery arrived at Kerguelen and secured again to the old jetty of Port Jeanne d'Arc. She coaled 190 tons in ten days. Meanwhile, the engine-room staff chipped her boilers. More survey flights were made, while scientific specimens were collected from the launch. The manager's hut at the abandoned whaling station became the *Discovery* Club, making a cosy place for evening entertainment, with a fire and lamp, the gramophone and a sing-song. Davis, too, was glad to get ashore for some exercise. 'A passage perilous maketh a port pleasant,' he remarked in his diary.

The sudden onset of severe gales forced Mawson to abandon his plans for a flag-raising visit to Queen Mary Land or a cruise to Heard Island. A rather dull month followed, with what MacKenzie called 'everlasting trawling and dredging'. Mawson considered it wiser to proceed to Adelaide for the sake of the projected second Antarctic voyage. The Australian coast was sighted on 30 March 1930, and two days later *Discovery* berthed in Port Adelaide, where they were welcomed by Lord Stonehaven, the Governor-General, and the Antarctic Committee. Civic receptions were given in Adelaide and Melbourne in honour of the expedition. *Discovery* went into dock in Melbourne for an overhaul. Twelve English seamen were paid off and given free passage home, only a maintenance crew being retained.

Captain Davis returned to his post as Director of Commonwealth Navigation. His diary records his being 'released from a very thankless task'. Mawson's diary claimed to have had no troubles on the expedition, 'only Davis,' whose 'attitude has always been that he is the virtual leader'. However, the two men did not let these differences spoil their lifelong friendship. Mawson sought the help once again of Mr MacPherson-Robertson and the £6,000 that he promised assured a second BANZARE voyage.

CHAPTER 20

SECOND BANZARE VOYAGE, 1930-31

I N JUNE 1930 Sir Douglas Mawson wrote to H R Mill, outlining his difficulties in obtaining money for a second expedition in a time of economic recession. It was, however, sanctioned by the Australian Government, mainly because of the formidable Norwegian competition. The British Government made *Discovery* available without charge for a second year, and Mawson was reappointed leader. Many British and Australian firms helped the expedition materially, and the proceeds from press news and photographs also contributed funds.

Captain Davis, who had not supported Mawson in his attempts to secure another expedition, did not apply to command *Discovery* for a second season, nor did Mawson invite him to do so. But Davis strongly praised the abilities of K N MacKenzie, formerly first officer, and wrote to him warmly when he heard of his appointment as master. MacKenzie's diary of the BANZARE voyages manifests his great faith in God. Aged only 16 in 1914, he had volunteered for service and had been invalided from the trenches of the Somme two years later. He next qualified as a wireless operator in the Merchant Navy, and gained his Master's ticket in 1929. There were several changes of personnel, including J W S Marr, who returned home in ill health and was replaced by A L Kennedy.

The Sailing Orders issued to Mawson for the second BANZARE voyage, dated 30 October 1930, were succinct. When *Discovery* was in all respects ready for sea, she was to leave Hobart on 22 November 1930 and proceed to Macquarie Island on a course 'best calculated to provide new scientific information from observations made during the voyage'. A course was then to be set to the south, and oceanographic investigations were to be made in the neighbourhood of the Balleny Islands and to the north of

Captain K N MacKenzie, Mr MacPherson-Robertson and Captain J K Davis on the *Discovery*'s return from the second BANZARE voyage.
(MACKENZIE COLLECTION)

King George V Land. This work was to be carried out until approximately 25 December 1930, when the *Sir James Clark Ross* was to be located, from which vessel coal was to be taken on. *Discovery* would then work steadily westward around the Antarctic continent, making every effort to map its coastline, filling in details and collecting scientific information of every kind, as time might permit. A British flag was to be planted on such lands or islands within the area specified, a proclamation read and attached to the flagstaff, and a record kept of each act of annexation.

On a brilliantly fine day, watched by Lady Mawson and many hundreds of spectators, *Discovery* left Hobart on 22 November 1930, flying the white flag at her foremast. Well down in the water, with a large deck cargo of coal briquettes from Cardiff in addition to an abundance of stores, including twenty sheep penned on the roof of the main winch house and over 1,000lbs of meat, the ship was drawing 17ft forward and 19ft at the stern. Mawson, who confessed to being tired as they set off, had deeply appreciated the generous help and hospitality received in Tasmania, and called for a final 'hurrah' from the ship's company for the people of Hobart. Hurley filmed their departure as the 'historic little vessel', with short blasts from her siren and bedecked with streamers, responded to the crowd's farewell.

The expedition expected to return to Australia in April 1931, but sledges, skis, tents and special woollen clothing were taken in case the ship were forced to winter in the south. Mawson wrote that though their progress was 'gratifying,' the ship's motion was 'downright aggravating' in the Roaring Forties, where they were 'bucked from their bunks' in a 'sea-going Rodeo'.

On the evening of the 27 November, the ship sailed over a volcanic ridge only 14 miles wide and rising to more than 6,000ft above the generally uniform sea floor. The temperature of the seawater dropped suddenly next day, and the first iceberg was sighted in lat. 53° 23'S. More were sighted on 1 December, an unusual occurrence so far to the north. Macquarie Island, long, green and treeless, appeared close at hand through the fog. *Discovery* anchored in Buckles Bay.

The penguins, filmed by Hurley, Campbell and Douglas, were the noisy stars of the island. Ingram and Fletcher collected life from the island's inland lakes, and alpine plants. Specimens of rare birds were taken and magnetic observations made. The twelve men ashore slept in four tents, badly because of the gale and the noisy activities of the Sea Elephants.

The Bishop and Clerk Rocks to the south of Macquarie Island had been closely observed and soundings made on 5 December 1930, the day the expedition departed. With the vessel in 18 fathoms and in fitful fog and uncharted waters, MacKenzie's diary reveals that they were at one point obliged to go astern. Like Davis before him, he was feeling the strain of four days and nights without taking off his clothes, and needing to use all his experience to find a way through the icebergs and rocks. On 6 December all sails were taken in except staysails, 'for the topgallant masts were bending to a nasty angle, and all the stays singing like harp strings'. By 8 December the wind and sea had moderated enough for the scientists to continue skinning or pickling the specimens from Macquarie Island, and for the captain to undress for a night's sleep. On 13 December the remaining sheep were killed and hung in the rigging to freeze.

Mawson had arranged to bunker from a whaler when approaching the Antarctic, to make up for

The peaks of Enderby Land, Antarctica, seen from the *Discovery*, January 1930 during the first BANZARE voyage.
(MAWSON INSTITUTE, UNIVERSITY OF ADELAIDE).

LEFT: The hydrologist, A Howard, on one of the outboard platforms with the Nansen-Petersson water sampling bottle. (MAWSON INSTITUTE, UNIVERSITY OF ADELAIDE)

BELOW: Cooks in *Discovery's* galley during BANZARE. (MAWSON INSTITUTE, UNIVERSITY OF ADELAIDE)

RIGHT: Gypsy Moth seaplane seen from the *Discovery*. (MACKENZIE COLLECTION.)

Discovery's limited coal capacity, which had so curtailed the 1929-30 season. He was exasperated to find that *Sir James Clark Ross* was four days' steaming further east than their agreed rendezvous, having moved east with her catchers in search of whales. The ships eventually met on 15 December 1930, at a cost of 60 tons of coal and ten days' extra time. With a dead whale between them as a fender, it was truly a meeting of old and new, *Discovery* now effectively devoted to the conservation of the whale, while the great factory ship represented the latest development in whaling on the high seas. One hundred tons of coal were taken on board in 5 hours, and 25 tons of fresh water were pumped into the tanks. Some of the men worked from 4am to 8pm, 'thoroughly earning their double issue of whisky'. All hands were allowed to climb up the rope ladder afterwards to visit the giant alongside. The diary entries describe the scenes of carnage that greeted them, and the pervading stench of whale. The one-hour life of the whale on a factory ship was described in sickening detail. One of the scientists, Harold Fletcher, summarised the products of a Blue whale of about 27 m long as: 26 tonnes of blubber, which would yield about 13 tonnes of oil; 57 tonnes of meat and 22 tonnes of fertiliser.

The swell had steadily increased during the day, causing *Discovery* to snap free of her mooring wire and bump heavily against the side of *Sir James Clark Ross*. MacKenzie had ordered everyone back on board, and cast off at 7.30pm. Carpenter Williams, still shell-shocked by the war, was left in the factory ship to return home, and one of the airmen, Douglas, was accidentally left on board too. In a rising sea Child sculled the two miles over from where *Discovery* lay, only to find that he had departed in a whale catcher with Hurley, who had been detailed by Mawson to film operations on board the whale catcher, or 'chaser'. This unauthorised second trip delayed the expedition for 24 hours, and the culprits received a severe reprimand from Mawson.

The ship at last got under way, with topsail set and fore and aft hoisting. The ensign was dipped to bid farewell to the hardy Norsemen and a course set westward with a fair wind and sunshine, a 'crystal sea of bobbing ice' and a temperature on deck of

25°F, for Adélie Land. Mawson recorded that the cold promoted sleep, stimulated appetite and quickened beards to grow.

Mawson's press release of 22 December 1930 recorded that this was an abnormally heavy year for ice, the pack extending 'at least over a million square miles more than normally'. One hundred and eleven bergs had been counted from the foretop the day before. For several days navigation was made difficult by thick mist, snow and gales; nevertheless a good run of 142 miles was made.

The airmen began assembling the Moth seaplane on 21 December, but bad weather redirected them to making sledge harnesses under Hurley's instruction, for use after landing in Commonwealth Bay. Attempts to reach the Balleny Islands had to be abandoned owing to ice. Krill was taken in the nets and four Blue and three Fin whales were seen. Christmas Day 1930 was celebrated at Divine Service, conducted by the captain in the mess at 11am, when all crew except those on watch were present. The engineer's band excelled itself in the rendering of sacred and other music. Gifts were distributed and an excellent

dinner was enjoyed in festive surroundings. Radiograms, parcels and letters from family, friends, schoolchildren and the Royal Geographical Society of South Australia were opened with great pleasure. On Boxing Day the steering gear of Discovery was overhauled and the chains set taut, after which a resolute attempt was made to break through to the south. Next morning, in heavy floes and dense ice-fields, they could get no heading at all, and to make matters worse the compasses had become erratic and almost useless. A faint sun and wind were their only guides. By 28 December better progress towards the west was being made, but thick ice prevented the ship from getting much farther south than 64° 57' on the 145th meridian of longitude. That day several whales were observed, including a stinking carcass on which multitudes of birds were feeding, indicating the presence of whalers.

The wireless officer, A J Williams, located the whaler Kosmos of Sandefjord, described by Mawson as 'a gigantic motor whaling ship', with a total capacity of 22,000 tons, whose captain kindly offered the expedition 50 tons of loose coal. This was accepted, and *Discovery*'s yards were cockbilled nearing *Kosmos*.

MacKenzie and Mawson were given a good dinner by the captain and officers of the *Kosmos*, and coaling was completed by chute at 8pm. Captain MacKenzie remarked then that 'he wouldn't go alongside a 20,000 tonner again in such a swell for 50 tons of gold, let alone coal.'

MacKenzie recorded the events of a New Year's eve he would never forget. He was called by the Second Officer at 2am after the rising gale had caused a heavy swell in the close pack in which they lay, and the movements of the ice floes had become dangerous. They got out and made before the wind to the drifting ice, hoping to find more shelter. As the wind increased to force 11 they were blown broadside into storm-tossed pack, some pieces being as big as the ship and higher than the bridge. The swell caused *Discovery* to lift and roll over hard down on the ice. Everyone rushed on deck, fearing they would be crushed and smashed in minutes, and wondering for how long the rudder and propeller could last. It was by then 10am, and the captain had been on the bridge for eight hours. Each hour the situation grew more serious, and all prepared for whatever might happen. The timbers groaned and strained, but the ship was still afloat and slowly moving away from the fierce pack edge. The little vessel had withstood a test which must have sunk any other vessel when, suddenly, a great iceberg was seen to be closing down on them, berg smoke or snow drift flying from its top. MacKenzie called all hands and, even in the teeth of a blizzard, ordered them aloft to set sail; their only hope of escape. 'God, how they fought...the sheets manned and away the topsails blew...All hands kept handy'. They watched the 'monster draw closer' and their ship drive hard against the great ice floes. At 1pm they had passed through, only to be caught between an eddy and the pack, two oncoming streams which swept round the big berg, and in less than five seconds they were surrounded by great big sharp pieces which hurled themselves against the ship. Again sail was set and fresh courage taken. Somehow, with orders 'snapped out to everyone', God saw them through.

Whale factory ship, *Kosmos*, showing the stern slipway up which the whales' carcasses were hauled for processing on board.
(AUTHOR'S COLLECTION)

Discovery was able to anchor off Cape Denison, Mawson's old winter quarters in King George V Land, on 4 January 1931, after having real difficulty finding good holding ground in the force 9 to 10 gale. Despite the gale, Simmers managed a balloon flight, which revealed an almost flat calm at 500ft. It blew all night, while *Discovery* strained at her cable and, even with a hand at the wheel, 'shoved about in a nasty and dangerous manner'.

Mawson had left a message at Cape Denison in 1913, inviting anyone who followed to make full use of the hut, and nearly 20 years later the message was still there, as were the chocolate and tobacco greatly enjoyed by the BANZARE men. Because snow and ice were banked against the walls, entry had to be forced through a skylight into the sparkling ice bound spaces below. Kennedy made observations over 18 hours in the old magnetic hut, which showed that the south magnetic pole had moved steadily to the northwest and was now probably no more than 250 miles from Cape Denison.

At noon on 5 January a Proclamation was read by Sir Douglas Mawson. The flag was hoisted by MacKenzie with great pride as the National Anthem was sung. From that day, the whole area around

Commonwealth Bay was included in George V Land.

Discovery got under way on the early evening of 6 January, and proceeded westward along the coast of Adélie Land, discovered by the French explorer J S C Dumont d'Urville in 1840.

Flights were made on 15 and 16 January to 8,000ft, and on 18 January to 3,000ft in low cloud, when 'Banzare Land' (now Banzare Coast) was sighted about 100 miles from the ship and named after the expedition. The edge of the dense pack itself prevented Discovery attempting to reach the channel of ice-free water along the coast. The seaplane was badly shaken and its wing tips torn and bent while it was being hoisted on board in the pack, causing the captain considerable anxiety. Scientific work also continued, including pioneering studies of cosmic rays. Nothing can have equalled the excitement of finding Arctic terns in the Antarctic, proving that these small, delicate-looking birds migrate almost from Pole to Pole, covering immense distances on the wing.

Oceanographic work made progress, and many varieties of fish and multitudes of invertebrates were taken from the sea at about 500 fathoms. While one of the nets was being hauled in, a Blue whale became curious in the operation, but fortunately lost interest just in time. Several days of bad weather prevented the Moth being flown to confirm land to the south, much to everyone's disappointment. In better weather no land was found in the positions of 'Budd Land' and 'Knox Land' as charted by the US Exploring Expedition of 1838-42.

As Discovery again headed westward, towards the Shackleton Ice Shelf, a domed and ice-covered offshore island was discovered on 28 January 1931, which they named Bowman Island after the director of the American Geographical Society, who had secured £8,500 from the American Press for the expedition. In this region Discovery was traversing completely unknown seas in lat. 64° 50'S, and MacKenzie's diary once again reveals his great anxieties in a gale of 'demon-like force'. He experienced an extraordinary sense of some new danger ahead, and without hesitation altered course, to the surprise of the Second Officer. Thirty large bergs were just cleared as a result, for which he thanked their great Protector.

MacKenzie continued to navigate Discovery, at times almost by intuition alone, in fearsome conditions, concerned too also not to collide with the factory ship Nielsen Alonso, which had promised to provide them with coal. They released gallons of oil to reduce the swell and help them turn, eventually reaching open sea.

Ceremony of taking possession, King George V Land, during the BANZARE Expedition 1929-31.
(MACKENZIE COLLECTION)

The Antarctic was no longer a lonely place. With 40 factory ships and 240 chasers operating during the 1930-31 season it seemed to seaman Martin as busy as the English Channel.

The seaplane was miraculously repaired, and flights revealed solid irregular pack to the west and the appearance of land some 90 miles to the southwest. On 11 February 1931, the 'Day of Great Discoveries' in MacKenzie's words, after negotiating a 'great array of massive grounded bergs', the bare white slopes of the continent lay before them, rising from 2,000 to 3,000ft. To their astonishment, clear, ice-free water stretched away to the south as far as the eye could see. They continued nearly parallel to and only 10 miles off the coast all day in great excitement, and that night celebrated further sightings by the seaplane with champagne for the wardroom and port for the crew. The aeroplane dropped the flag over the land, which after discussion was named Princess Elizabeth Land, with the permission of her grandfather, HM King George V.

Three days later a massive black rock came into view, rising straight from the sea to over 1,000ft, which was later named the Murray Monolith after Sir George Murray of Adelaide. A landing proved impracticable, so the proclamation and flag were thrown ashore as the boat touched bottom. A rich catch resulted from dredging in shallow waters offshore, and a party was able to land from the launch in an adjacent rocky bay formed by the lower slopes of a crescent-shaped nunatak, nearly 2,000ft high, named Scullin Monolith after the Australian prime minister. The flag was raised and the proclamation read during this first landing on Mac.Robertson Land. The ship had to negotiate many hidden rocks, shoals and other dangerous hazards . When the Second Officer called that they were in only 5 fathoms MacKenzie ordered 'full astern', and within ten minutes *Discovery* was heading into 100 fathoms, going northwards towards safety. 'My life is nothing and I care less for yours,' declared the captain to Mawson, 'but my ship is everything and she must be saved.'

By 18 February the coal was officially down to 100 tons, the amount that both leader and captain agreed was the minimum for *Discovery*'s 4,000-mile return voyage to Australia. Mawson was anxious to return to Queen Mary Land, on which he had been instructed to raise the flag, but the captain refused to consider it.

Murray Monolith, Antarctic Coast, 13 February 1931.
(MAWSON INSTITUTE, UNIVERSITY OF ADELAIDE)

Frank Hurley filming 'Southward Ho',
watched by Sir Douglas Mawson.
(MACKENZIE COLLECTION)

The last day off the Antarctic coast proved notable for a further landing on Mac.Robertson Land at Cape Bruce, where Colbeck located an excellent boat harbour, and for some valuable scientific investigations. A cairn was erected, the proclamation made, and the flag hoisted; a document relating to their discoveries was deposited and they gave three rousing cheers for the King. Greatly annoyed at the landing party's late return, MacKenzie ruefully recounted that 'darkness among icebergs, islands and breakers is no concern of theirs (the scientists) and none of them appreciate the dangers …From now on they will, as passengers, be a damn nuisance.'

The 'Antarctic turned on a good show' as they left, when one of the green-and-white-striped icebergs 'turned turtle', slowly rolling completely over and continuing to roll for at least another 20 minutes.

THE VOYAGE HOME

On 19 February 1931, preparations began for the long homeward voyage to Australia. In the lee of a large tabular iceberg, the topgallant yards were sent up and crossed on the foremast of *Discovery*. All movable gear was stowed below, as near the keel as possible, and sacks of ashes from the boiler, damped with seawater, were used as ballast to replace the coal consumed.

The call of 'homeward bound' ran through the ship, and MacKenzie felt a big burden lifted from his shoulders. He knew that he would never again come south to undertake such responsibility, the worry of it 'having been enough to last a lifetime', but his diary still tells of 'hellish nights' and the worst gale the ship had ever come through. Frank Hurley must have considered rough weather an excellent opportunity to shoot some exciting film. No doubt anxious about his antics aloft, MacKenzie made him sign a disclaimer.

At the height of the gale, without steam and with only foresail and lower topsail, the ship did 183 miles, at a rate of 8.5 knots. One of the scientists, Harold Fletcher, wrote of the colossal size of the seas, wave crests almost 400m apart being separated by great valleys. The masts, 34m high, were well below the height of the waves, while the wire sheets 'sang like harp strings'. MacKenzie concluded the day's diary with an affectionate tribute to 'My wonderful little ship'.

Fine weather followed, with good steady westerlies, enabling the vessel to make excellent runs under sail alone. After much washing of persons and shearing of beards, the expedition arrived in Hobart on 19 March 1931. They had been away for 117 days, and *Discovery* had covered 10,557 miles.

Reflecting in a news report upon the voyage while homeward bound, Mawson considered its most outstanding feature to be the feverish activity of the many whaling vessels observed in the south, and he forecast the decline of the whale. He summarised the achievements of the 1930-31 expedition as, not only resulting in the discovery of much new land, but also proving the existence of a continental coastline from Cape Adare to Enderby Land. It was R A Falla's overall impression of the second

BANZARE voyage, from the scientist's point of view, written in a personal letter to James Marr, that the scientific programme had been 'too extensive to make a first-class show in any department'.

Finance was still a problem for Mawson on his return. It had been hoped that Hurley's 'talkie' film, *Southward-Ho! with Mawson*, would provide funds to help with the publication of the scientific results, but it was released in the end as the Commonwealth Government's official record of the expedition. The scientific results were eventually published in a series of volumes between 1937 and 1975. It was not until 1962 that the *Geographical Record* appeared, edited from Mawson's papers by Sir Archibald Grenfell Price as *The winning of Australian Antarctica*.

As to the political results of the expedition, a British Order in Council of 7 February 1933 eventually affirmed the sovereign rights of the Crown over the Antarctic lands (other than the French Terre Adélie) south of lat. 60°S and between longs. 45°E and 160°E; about one-third of the coastline of the continent. The territory was placed under the authority of the Commonwealth of Australia. Such claims have been 'frozen' under the Antarctic Treaty of 1959, allowing other nations beside the postwar Australian National Antarctic Research Expeditions (ANARE) to establish scientific stations there.

THE RETURN TO LONDON

Sir Douglas Mawson and the scientists left ship in Australia, all bar Simmers, who continued to take meteorological observations for some 1,500 miles across the Tasman Sea. Lieutenant C Reid joined the

Albatrosses in the wake of *Discovery* in the days before their decimation by 'long lining' from fishing vessels.
(AUTHOR'S COLLECTION)

ship as fourth officer in Melbourne and kept an informative log of the homeward voyage. *Discovery* made some good days' runs towards Cape Horn, which was rounded on 1 June 1931, making *Discovery* one of the last British square-riggers to do so.

Discovery arrived in Montevideo on 10 June, where the British Vice-Consul, ship agents and reporters came aboard.

In contrast to the many albatrosses and cormorants seen in Le Maire Strait, the number of birds in company quickly diminished as the ship proceeded through the tropics, where flying fish and porpoises were seen for the first time. The ship made good speed under all canvas in the southeast Trade Winds, and painting and cleaning began. On 30 July, a beautiful summer's day, *Discovery* made up the English Channel, taking a pilot on board at Dungeness and the river pilot at Gravesend. As she proceeded up the Thames several vessels dipped their Ensign in salute, and the ship made fast in the East India Dock during the late afternoon of 1 August 1931, just two years to the day from her departure.

Discovery's arrival and achievements during the BANZARE voyages were reported in the London papers. From Melbourne she had come 14,449 miles in 105 days at an average speed of 5¾ knots. Mawson wrote to H R Mill from Adelaide at the end of July, commending Captain MacKenzie and reporting that the second voyage had been exceedingly happy and harmonious. As Sir Douglas Mawson was full of praise for him, so Captain MacKenzie was for his little ship. He had brought her back safely at last to Old Father Thames.

21

BERTHED IN LONDON
1932-86

ANOTHER ANTARCTIC EXPEDITION was mooted but never sailed. The Discovery Committee generously offered to charter *Discovery* to H G Watkins, a young Englishman who made a reputation for himself as a leader of small private expeditions to the Arctic in the late 1920s, at a nominal charge, the expedition paying only the £12,000 annual running costs and insurance. Later the Committee offered the vessel free of charter. Watkins would have gladly accepted, had he been able, but decided to charter a small sealer, the *Quest*. Despite the support of an eminent expedition committee, no substantial sums of money were forthcoming at the time of the Depression, so Watkins abandoned the scheme and organised an expedition to Greenland, during which he died.

In the years immediately after the BANZARE, from 1932 to 1936, *Discovery* was laid up in the London Docks but regularly inspected and

Lady Houston, who came to the rescue of *Discovery* in the 1930s.
(AUTHOR'S COLLECTION)

maintained. However, it had become obvious that the vessel had outlived her usefulness. The Discovery Committee was well served in the prosecution of Discovery Investigations by the steel-hulled, custom-built *Discovery II* and by *William Scoresby*. Two members of the Committee's staff heard that *Discovery* might be sold by the Crown Agents, and began to raise funds to secure her for the new National Maritime Museum at Greenwich and pay for her upkeep. As the 'finest in existence for use in ice' and a 'national asset', she should be preserved for the nation.

HEADQUARTERS OF THE SEA SCOUTS, 1937-54, AND A MEMORIAL TO SCOTT AND SHACKLETON

Discovery was eventually offered in October 1936 to the Boy Scouts Association as a training ship for Sea Scouts and as a memorial to Captain Scott and his comrades. The acceptance was mainly contingent on the need to raise sufficient money to ensure her proper upkeep, and the consent of the Port of London Authority to allot her moorings easily accessible to the boys who were to use her. The offer delighted Lord Baden-Powell, the Chief Scout, who wrote to Lady Houston, the sponsor of the British entry to the Schneider Trophy seaplane race, sending her a sketch of the barque and playing on her love for horses by adding the comment: 'She's going to the knacker's yard unless you care to save her'. The result was a £30,000 trust fund for expenses. The agreement drawn up between Lady Houston and the Boy Scouts Association specified that *Discovery* would serve as a living memorial to Scott, Oates, Shackleton and other heroes of Antarctic exploration, as Sea Scout Heaquarters, a training centre for Sea Scouts and their officers, including poor and unemployed Scouts, a rendezvous for Deep Sea Scouts and a hostel for Sea Scouts from overseas.

A committee chaired by the Chief Sea Scout was to administer the fund and implement the agreement. Sadly, Lady Houston died before the handing-over ceremony on board ship on 9 October 1937.

Discovery by then lay at her moorings in King's Reach, alongside the Thames Embankment above

Blackfriars Bridge, the berth she was to occupy for the next 40 years. During that time she became one of the landmarks of London. The Pilgrim Trust supplied funds to build the pier connecting the ship with the shore, and a small museum was set up on board. The Governor of the Falkland Islands handed over *Discovery* to the Duke of Kent, Commodore of Sea Scouts, at an official ceremony. She was used by Sea Scouts from 1937 to 1954, serving as a training ship and hostel. She had a small full-time crew, and a Rover Service Crew to run the courses and do much of the work in the ship. The last member of the crew was a Husky dog, who expected to be cooled down in hot weather when decks were scrubbed.

Discovery was re-rigged as a barque, with the yards crossed on fore- and mainmasts and the mizzen fore and aft rigged. The 25ft carvel-built whalers remained unused in their chocks either side of the bridge, as they were reputed to be rotten. The vessel still had her two boilers and triple-expansion engine, which one pre-war Deep Sea Scout described as unusual, with each cylinder a separate 'pot', lagged with teak staves over asbestos.

A timber jetty had been built to provide access from the embankment, with two levels and steps between. A short gangway had to be constantly

Sea Scout at the wheel, aboard the *Discovery* in the Thames, c1950.
(COURTESY M R C PARR)

adjusted every hour with the tide. Downstream of the jetty were three sets of buoyed moorings on which were kept two 27ft Montague whalers that were in constant use.

Only two years after *Discovery* had assumed her new role as a training ship, the Second World War broke out. She survived the Blitz in spite of being in the heart of London, but it was at that time that her yards and engine were removed. It is said that the trailing cable of a wandering barrage balloon collided with one of the yards, which were found to be rotten. All were therefore struck down and she lost much of her beauty, remaining a de-rigged barque for several decades. The fine triple-expansion engine and boilers were cut into pieces and sent, like many railings from London town houses, for scrap.

During the early years of the war *Discovery* became the headquarters of the River Emergency Service, an ambulance service with twenty-two stations between Chelsea and the Nore. It is recorded that, despite the air raids, no Sea Scout failed to report at his station for his eight-hour watch. The operation was taken over by the navy in 1941. For the rest of the war the ship was a Parachute Mine Station. Sea Scouts kept a round-the-clock watch for falling parachute mines and, upon sighting them, immediately telephoned a compass bearing through to RN headquarters. Pre-Naval Entry courses held on board during this period were attended by some 2,500 Sea Scouts, and one in four gained a commission.

When the war ended, in 1945, *Discovery* returned to her peacetime role as Sea Scout training ship, and the first Queen's Scout presentations were organised from the ship. During 1948 all activities ceased while she underwent a major refit, when much of the deterioration of the war years was arrested and repaired.

A DRILL SHIP FOR THE RNVR, 1954-79
By the early 1950s the cost of the *Discovery*'s upkeep had proved too much for the Boy Scouts Association. In June 1953 she was offered unconditionally to the Admiralty by the Chief Scout. She was to be accepted, subject to survey, as an additional drill ship for the Royal Naval Volunteer Reserve, with reasonable access

for the public to be ensured by the Board of Admiralty. The Board also undertook to leave the original wardroom and cabins as they were, and to endeavour to allow facilities for Sea Scouts' weekend training and the mooring of their boats. On hearing of the negotiations, Peter Scott intervened to protest in September 1954. He was anxious to save her from being gutted, to preserve public access and to keep her for youth training. A *Discovery* Trust was formed, but after its first meeting Peter Scott (later Sir Peter) withdrew the Committee's claim and stated that he felt the preservation of *Discovery* as a memorial to his father would be 'best served by accepting the proposals outlined'.

The First Lord of the Admiralty wrote to the Chief Scout on 4 June 1954, accepting *Discovery* and confirming that the Sea Scouts could continue to keep their boats alongside and use facilities on board, and that the public would also be permitted to visit the ship. Between 1955 and 1979 most of the vessel's surviving Vosper internal fittings and the echo-sounding gear were removed. Many other alterations were made and, despite the agreement, two cabins were done away with and the chart room table was taken away.

Discovery without her yards, moored beside the Thames probably in the 1970s.
(AUTHOR'S COLLECTION)

After a year undergoing repairs and alterations in the graving dock at Blackwall she was commissioned as HMS *Discovery* on 20 July 1955, wearing the flag of the Admiral Commanding Reserves. She was used mainly for training those about to begin their National Service until its abolition in 1960, after which her role was reduced, but she continued to fly the flag of the Admiral Commanding Reserves until late 1976, just before that post was abolished. The ship also served for some years as a naval recruiting centre in London.

In March 1978 the Press announced that a new owner was being sought for *Discovery*, owing to reductions in the Reserves, reduced votes for defence expenditure and the need for an extensive refit. It was at that time that the Maritime Trust (London) and the National Maritime Museum assumed an active interest in her preservation.

WITH THE MARITIME TRUST

On 2 April 1979 HMS *Discovery* was handed over to the Maritime Trust during a ceremony on board ship at her mooring in the Thames near Waterloo Bridge. On that day she became once again a Royal Research Ship. Her new owner was to take charge of her structure, while the National Maritime Museum would mount displays and provide warding staff. The Maritime Trust had been established in 1969, in the words of HRH Prince Philip, Duke of Edinburgh, 'to do for historic ships what the National Trust does for buildings'.

Discovery was first towed to Sheerness, where a major docking enabled essential repairs to be made to the seams, which needed to be recaulked and repayed. The Vosper propeller of 1925 was taken off, the shingle ballast was removed and the masts were stepped. She returned to a berth in the picturesque St Katharine's Dock, near the Tower of London, entering the dock on the high spring tide to lie near the Trust's outstanding collection of historic ships. It was decided that she should not return to the Embankment because of access and parking difficulties, and the lack of other facilities for visitors there. It was considered essential for her preservation to keep her wooden hull afloat.

During her seven years in St Katharine's Dock the vessel's port side from waterline to bulwark capping was restored, as were the forward hold and galley. Ten yards and a mizzen spanker boom were made from New Forest trees, vastly improving her looks. Essential maintenance was carried out on the ship's fabric to reduce the ingress of rainwater and to treat and contain the wet and dry rot then prevalent throughout. More than half a million pounds were raised and spent on *Discovery* by the Trust, half of it from the Greater London Council, which matched other donations. At an early stage the decision was taken to restore her only to her 1925 condition. At least a hundred Vosper drawings of her refit and a thousand photographs of her in 1925 existed, and that had been the time when she was most active at sea, during the *Discovery* (Oceanographic) Expedition of 1925-27 and the oceanographic voyages of 1929-31. To reproduce her original form in Scott's day she would have had to be partly rebuilt.

Various stages of the vessel's restoration were filmed, and temporary displays were mounted for the public. Plans for permanent displays covering all her voyages were made but, in the end, once her move to Scotland was known, only those showing her construction and the National Antarctic Expedition were actually placed in the hold. *Discovery*'s history was researched, which resulted in the fuller version of this book, and two symposia were held at Greenwich, attended by old 'Discoverers' and interested individuals and organisations.

It was never intended that she should remain in St Katharine's Dock, as she warranted star treatment. Various other berths in London were considered, particularly in Docklands, but either the berth was unsuitable or the funding to complete restoration was uncertain. Then came an offer from Scotland, where there was no nationally significant ship on show, whereas London already had two. Thus it was that *Discovery* returned to Dundee, where she had been built 85 years before.

The *Discovery* in St Katharine's Dock, 1985.
(THE MARITIME TRUST)

22

HOME TO DUNDEE

'HOME TO DUNDEE' proclaimed the banners as *Discovery* headed away from her berth in St Katharine's Dock on 27 March 1986. She was nudged and towed gently through the narrow lock and into the Thames at the height of an equinoctial tide of 25ft, the only one that year. Detailed planning had begun after the signing, on 29 November 1985, of the Charter agreement between the Maritime Trust and the main financial backers for her return to Scotland, the Dundee Heritage Trust and the Scottish Development Agency. The Greater London Council and others who wished to keep *Discovery* in London were finally won over by the promised salt-water dock and financial backing in Dundee.

The *Discovery*, cradled aboard the *Happy Mariner*, entering the River Tay at the end of her voyage from London to Dundee in the spring of 1986.
(FOTOPRESS, DUNDEE)

The barque's displacement and stabilty had first been checked, showing that, as in Scott's day, she was 'stiff but stable'. To reduce the strain on the lower masts and lessen the top weight for towing, the yards had to be sent down, together with the topgallant masts. Work was carried out to ensure that she was watertight, pumps being installed and safety equipment embarked. The dock had to be dredged and a clear passage provided. A team of volunteers, the *Discovery* Service Crew, manned ropes and warps. *Discovery* made the 500-mile voyage north as dry cargo in the floating dock ship *Happy Mariner*, after docking safely into the mother vessel above Tower Bridge on Easter Sunday, 30 March 1986.

Crowds lined the estuary to cheer her on her arrival two days later in Dundee, and a Royal Air Force flypast by an Avro Shackleton maritime reconnaissance aircraft from Lossiemouth and three Phantom jet fighters welcomed *Discovery* home. She had returned to Dundee not to be laid up and forgotten, but to take on a new role as the symbol of regeneration for the city that built her. By the summer of 1991 the city had contributed more than half a million pounds towards the ship's restoration. *Discovery*'s final berthing was dramatic. She became jammed in the hold of the *Happy Mariner*, and finally reached the Victoria Dock on the midnight tide of 3rd/4th April. By this time the crowds had gone, apart from a 'few romantics left to see her safely back to where her lifetime's voyaging began', as one newspaper reported. The lock swung open to allow her access into the inner Victoria Dock, where an RNR piper aboard the old wooden fighting ship *Unicorn* saluted her new neighbour. *Discovery* 'slipped home to her final haven to the sound of Scotland's music across the water of the dock. The wind sent her flags and pennants snapping as she rocked against the harbour wall. ...The tugs cast off their lines and sounded their sirens. ...*Discovery* was home at last.'

Appendix: Restoration and Display

THE RETURN OF *Discovery* to her home port of Dundee in 1986 was an historic occasion, witnessed by thousands of spectators who lined the shores of the River Tay to watch her arrival aboard the floating dock, the *Happy Mariner*. *Discovery* was to be the focal point of a major new waterfront development which would include other leisure and tourist facilities such as a multi-screen cinema and restaurants. Unfortunately, however, the full scheme never came to fruition but the enhanced facilities for the ship at its purpose-built dock on the waterfront have proved a resounding success. The Discovery Point building was designed by the Michael Laird Partnership of Edinburgh and the combination of its prime location and unusual design has made it a prominent local landmark.

Discovery returned to Dundee on a charter agreement with her then owners, The Maritime Trust who had taken the decision to restore *Discovery* to the layout which followed her extensive refit in 1924. Like many vessels, *Discovery* was adapted and altered throughout her life for her changing roles, and to restore her to the 1901 arrangement would not only have been impractical but would have destroyed many of the elements relating to her important later history. Dundee Heritage Trust are honouring this decision and are following the same policy. Historic ships are particularly vulnerable objects and the conservation challenges are immense.

Although *Discovery* is to stay afloat she will not be 'putting to sea' again so does not require to be in sea-going condition; for this reason, and for the need to preserve as much of the original ship as possible, timber preservation, sterilisation and conservation techniques are always considered before replacement. Historic shipbuilding techniques and tradi-

tional materials are also used wherever practical. A full-time team dedicated to the care of *Discovery* consists of a ship's manager, a shipwright, a rigger and a painter who carry out a year-round programme of maintenance which aims to reduce the need for major repairs.

On her arrival *Discovery* was berthed in Victoria Dock, and Dundee Heritage Trust undertook an immediate visual inspection of the ship to help formulate the initial restoration work required which then began almost immediately. She was also made ready for visitors. Guides took groups of twenty-five people round the ship at fifteen-minute intervals. Her return created enormous interest and queues of more than a hundred people waiting for a tour were not unusual. These visitors gave the Trust a welcome source of revenue.

While *Discovery* was in Dundee her custom-built dock at Discovery Point was being completed. By 1992 her home was ready and the ship was prepared for the move by being stripped of all movable upperworks to negotiate the Tay road bridge. Due to tidal restrictions the move was a complicated and dangerous exercise spread over two days, the final act being the entry of the vessel into her new dock early enough on the tide to allow the caisson gate to be floated into position after her.

Discovery was now in her own custom-built dock with the facility to dry-dock her as and when required, allowing assessment and repairs to be carried out without having to move the ship, always a potentially risky manoeuvre. She is also still able to accept visitors while restoration work takes place. Having access to the excellent dry-docking facility, major hull restoration could now start in earnest.

In 1995 Dundee Heritage Trust purchased Discovery from the Maritime Trust for the nominal sum of £1, securing the future of the ship for the people of Dundee and for the Nation. During 1998 Dundee Heritage Trust commissioned an extensive conservation plan to assess the current state of *Discovery* and to draw up strategies for her future care. The document included a full structural ship's survey which recorded any decay and defects, giving the Trust a definitive understanding of what restoration would be required. The survey recommended treatments and solutions to be applied, and set out the future measures which would be needed to help ensure the long-term survival of *Discovery*.

Since her arrival in Dundee the Trust has been responsible for major phases of hull and rig restoration as well as replacing and restoring many of the interior compartments and furnishings. Between 1986 and 2000, Dundee Heritage Trust have raised and spent over two million pounds on extensive conservation work.

Listed below is the major work which has been undertaken.

In 2000 *Discovery* was officially designated as one of the most important historic ships in the United Kingdom. She was named as one of the forty-six vessels in the National Historic Ships Committee's Core Collection which is for vessels of 'pre-eminent national significance in terms of maritime heritage,

• Three thousand feet of underwater hull seams were re-caulked and payed. Nine feet of false keel was replaced aft, the underwater hull cleaned off and anti-fouled, and the propeller burnished. An assessment of the condition of the hull was undertaken and dimensions for a hull expansion plan lifted off.

• Informal endiscope observations into salt boxes were made.

• Steel repairs to the engine-room deck-house base have been carried out, and to the steel bulkhead base.

• Dundee Heritage Trust shipwrights started repairs around the port quarter. Ballast pigs from the engine-room and boiler-room were removed, bilges cleaned and the ballast cleaned off and coated with Crocell Plastic. Repairs were made to the many decayed bulwark stanchions.

• Three trees for new lower masts bought and laid down to season. Work was continued around both aft quarters by the ship's own staff. Restoration to port side quarter between frames 62 and 72. Restoration to starboard quarter between frames 66 and 78 by Mackays Boatbuilders. A galley exhibition was set up. Major asbestos removal was carried out. The mizzenmast was unstepped for work at the mizzen chainplates.

• Continued stern restoration work. Wardroom cabins were rebuilt after asbestos removal. All other areas were re-lined after asbestos removal. The mizzenmast was restepped after repair to lower mast top.

• The complete rig was removed and the funnel lowered in preparation for the move to Discovery Point. She was then dry-docked in the new purpose-built dock, the underwater hull cleaned, seams hardened up and repayed, new anodes fitted, two coats of Arcinol and one coat of Interclene anti-fouling were applied. Standing and running rigging was overhauled. The ship was re-wired, a heating and ventilation system introduced to help dry the ship out, and a bilge pumping system fitted to cope with any emergencies

• New lower masts were stepped, a new mizzen boom fitted, and all spars heat sterilised and soaked in Protim Preservative. The bridge deck-house partitions were replaced and engine-room and boiler-room steel fitted. With the installation of the ventilation system the ship began to dry out and work on the interior was started with the restoration of the wardroom and its cabins the first priority. On board exhibits were set up.

• Decay at both ends of the ship was evident and the ship was dry-docked for bow and stern restoration. A new rudderpost was fitted, and a new sternpost above the stern tube. The propeller well was restored, and new deck beams and associated carlings fitted aft of the engine-room casing. New decking and a part of the beam shelf were also fitted. The chartroom was fitted out. The bow was opened up for assessment of decay. The port coal bunker was fitted out as a lecture/education room.

• The bow area was steam sterilised from the upper deck down to the keel and from the forward bulkhead to the stem. The area was treated and sterilised with Polybor. Major bow repairs were carried out including new deadwood and frames. Major decayed timbers from the bow 'fortifications' were removed and the bow planking replaced.

• Work on stem and bow was continued and a bad leak in the repaired bow area had to be investigated. The ship's staff pumped white lead mixture between sheathing and planking in the repaired area, and the ship was refloated. The bridge deck after beam and deck were repaired, and then Mackays Boatbuilders embarked on the starboard side restoration. Foremast yards and foremast were scraped back and re-coated.

• The ship was dry-docked in order to continue starboard side restoration. Mainmast yards, mainmast and mizzen spars were scraped back and re-coated. A comprehensive conservation plan and structural survey of ship was carried out.

• Restoration of the ship's navigation bridge to the 1924 configuration was carried out, offering full access for the public for the first time. It was refurbished with a chart table, steering equipment, flag locker etc. Replica whalers were fitted to the bridge boat decks. The lifting of 800ft of teak decking and relaying with African opepe timber was undertaken in the continuing quest to keep the decks tight. A quayside film booth was provided which shows a 'virtual tour' of the ship above and below decks for visitors with disabilities.

LEFT: RRS *Discovery* alongside Discovery Point with the spectacular backdrop of the River Tay, Fife and the Tay rail bridge. Photograph by Alex Coupar.
(DUNDEE HERITAGE TRUST)

BELOW: New, less-invasive technologies are utilised such as steam treatment of infected timber. This was a first in the world of ship restoration and the project attracted international attention.
(DUNDEE HERITAGE TRUST)

historical association or innovation of technology'.

Discovery Point was designed to house an interpretative account of the history of the ship, focusing on the British National Antarctic Expedition of 1901-1904 led by Captain Robert Falcon Scott. It was opened on 1st July 1993 by His Royal Highness Prince Philip, the Duke of Edinburgh, and received both critical and public acclaim for the quality and dramatic impact of its displays.

However, by 1997, Dundee Heritage Trust felt the time had come for some changes and improvements to be made. Since the centre had opened there had been a general increase in the use of interactive exhibits throughout the museum world, including both hands-on mechanical displays and multimedia computers, but this kind of display was somewhat lacking at Discovery Point.

In addition, a number of important and popular themes were not covered in the initial displays, particularly the heroic aspect of the sea journey from Dundee to Antarctica and the social background of the expedition. Who were the men of *Discovery* and what were their day-to-day lives like, their diet, health and clothing? How did they spend their spare time while in Antarctica?

When Discovery Point opened the collections of Dundee Heritage Trust relating to *Discovery* and the

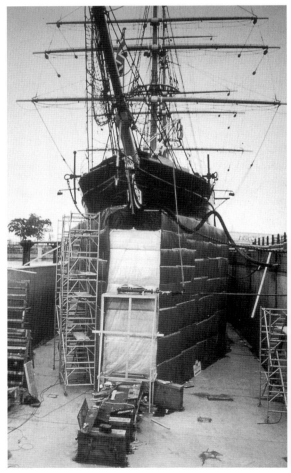

expedition were minimal. Since then, however, the collections of The Maritime Trust have been transferred to them (included in the purchase of the ship in 1995) and further additions have been made through donations, purchases and loans. The Trust now possesses such wonderful objects as Captain Scott's pipe, wooden snow goggles and rifle; Skelton's sledging flag and wooden skis; man and dog harnesses; The South Polar Times; and scientific items such as a flensing knife, microscope and an Emperor penguin egg. These are very special objects with emotional and heroic associations.

To compensate for some of the omissions the Dundee Heritage Trust embarked on a phased programme of gallery improvements, beginning in 1999 with the opening of Polarama, an interactive gallery all about Antarctic geography and science. The first major phase of the re-developments was completed in July 2000 after work to six galleries was finished and improvements made to the exterior of the building; a new interpretation aboard the ship was introduced. The second phase of re-development was completed in March 2001, timed to coincide with the centenary of Discovery's launch.

The emphasis has been on interactive interpretation, the widening of the narrative of the ship's career and the events with which she was associated, and the display of more historic objects and photographs.

At Discovery Point a concerted effort has been made to ensure that our displays are accessible to all, taking into account the needs of family groups, schoolchildren, people of different ages or learning abilities and those with disabilities. The exhibitions use a wide variety of displays – audio, visual and tactile – intended to stimulate all the senses so that all of our visitors can enjoy a memorable experience.

A visit to Discovery Point and Discovery involves guides, showcases of historic objects, graphic panels, audio-visual shows, models and dioramas, audio tracks, lighting and sound effects, interactive computer programmes and mechanical exhibits. The museum has received considerable critical acclaim, and won Scottish Museum of the Year in 1994 and a Scottish Tourism Oscar in 1993 for the Best Visitor Attraction created within the past ten years. Perhaps most satisfying have been the positive reactions and comments of our visitors, both local people and tourists. Over ten thousand children are enthusiastic visitors every year.

Dundee Heritage Trust, and its operating company Dundee Industrial Heritage Ltd, are both registered charities. As such they are dependant on fundraising initiatives and the trading revenue generated by the museum and ship. Development capital for Discovery Point and Discovery has been secured, with great success, but like many museums across the country the challenge of meeting operating and day-to-day maintenance costs is often the greatest challenge of all.

Since her return to Dundee in 1986 Discovery has acted as an icon for the regeneration of the city. As the old industries, like shipbuilding, have withered a new breed of hi-tech businesses have sprung up. In 1996 Dundee branded itself 'Dundee, City of Discovery' and the highly successful campaign has seen the image of Dundee improved and a new pride return to the city. The rebirth of the city has resulted in new investment coming into the area and Dundee is now at the forefront of biotechnological research with ground-breaking discoveries into a cure for cancer being carried out almost in sight of the ship. The people of Dundee can be very proud of the ship that was launched in their city at the beginning of the twentieth century and Dundee Heritage Trust will continue to strive to ensure that Discovery is preserved as an inspiration for future generations as she was for those of the past.

CONTRIBUTIONS:
Gill Poulter, *Heritage and Exhibitions Manager*
Hugh Scott, *Ship's Manager*
Alan Rankin, *Chief Executive*

INDEX

Page numbers in italics refer to illustrations